MW00622345

How Tyrants Fall

How Tyrants Fall

And How Nations Survive

MARCEL DIRSUS

JOHN MURRAY

First published in Great Britain in 2024 by John Murray (Publishers)

1

Copyright © Marcel Dirsus 2024

A CIP catalogue record for this title is available from the British Library

Hardback ISBN 9781399809481
Trade Paperback ISBN 9781399809498
ebook ISBN 9781399809511

Typeset in Bembo by Hewer Text UK Ltd, Edinburgh
Printed and bound in Great Britain by Clays Ltd, Elcograf S.p.A.

John Murray policy is to use papers that are natural, renewable and
recyclable products and made from wood grown in sustainable forests.
The logging and manufacturing processes are expected to conform
to the environmental regulations of the country of origin.

Carmelite House
50 Victoria Embankment
London EC4Y 0DZ

www.johnmurraypress.co.uk

John Murray Press, part of Hodder & Stoughton Limited
An Hachette UK company

For Anneliese

Contents

Introduction: The Golden Gun

I don't deny I'm lonely. Deeply so. A king, when he doesn't have to account to anyone for what he says and does, is inevitably very much alone.[1]

Mohamed Reza Pahlavi, shah of Iran

The most powerful tyrants on earth are condemned to live their life in fear. They can make their enemies disappear with a snap of their fingers. They, their families and their acolytes may control entire countries from the luxury of their palace, but they also have to spend their every waking hour plagued by the fear of losing everything. No matter how powerful they become, they cannot pay for or order that fear to disappear. If such tyrants make one wrong move, they will fall. And when tyrants fall, they often land up in exile, in a jail cell, or under the ground.

On a cold winter day in late 2007, the patrolling Amazonian Guards in their green camouflage gave the all clear. A moment later, Colonel Muammar Gaddafi emerged from the Hôtel de Marigny in central Paris. After descending the steps, he walked along a red carpet draped over the pristine grass. At the end of the carpet lay a giant tent. The Hôtel de Marigny, the building used by the French government to accommodate state guests, was used to catering to the whims of powerful rulers, but never before had a Bedouin tent been constructed in the garden so that a visiting dictator could meet guests in the 'desert tradition'.[2]

Inside, the tent was adorned with images of camels and palm trees. It was furnished with huge leather chairs in which an attentive audience could sit and listen. In the evening, visitors were greeted by the flames of a large fire.

Beyond his tent, which was a workplace, Gaddafi made Paris his personal playground. Originally invited to France for just three days, he decided he would stay for five. He had arrived in Paris with his infamous all-female bodyguards and an entourage so large it required a hundred vehicles to snake through the city. He was received by President Nicolas Sarkozy with full military honours. When Gaddafi decided that he would like to see the Palace of Versailles because he was fascinated by Louis XIV, he brought with him a 'delegation' of a hundred people. He was whisked from his tent in an extra-long white limousine that caused traffic jams wherever it went. When he wanted to take a boat down the Seine, the bridges along the river had to be closed to the public.[3] Gaddafi even went on a pheasant shoot, a highly unusual outing for a twenty-first-century visiting head of state.[4] But for Gaddafi, it was normality. His high-handed approach to the rest of the world had been exemplified by his response to an incident in 2008 when his son was arrested in Geneva for assaulting two domestic employees in a luxury hotel. The following year the dictator asked Italy, Germany and France to 'abolish' Switzerland.[5] When that didn't happen, Gaddafi called on Muslims around the world to wage a holy war against the country. And at the United Nations General Assembly, where leaders usually get fifteen minutes to speak, Gaddafi spoke for ninety-three. During the speech, he called the Security Council the 'terror council', promoted his own website, complained about being jet-lagged and discussed the assassination of John F. Kennedy.[6]

Eccentricities aside, Gaddafi, who had controlled Libya since the late 1960s, was a murderous dictator. If he wanted this life to continue, he needed to stay in power. And to stay in power, he relied on striking fear into everyone he ruled. On the streets of Tripoli, ordinary people, if they ever spoke out against the regime, faced immediate danger of imprisonment or even death. On a single day in the summer of 1996, his security forces massacred more than twelve hundred people in one of the regime's torture prisons.[7] Even anti-regime thoughts were deemed dangerous. As one Libyan put it: 'Not only would we not dare express any criticism, we wouldn't even dare *thinking* anything critical in our heads.'[8]

Yet even at the height of his power, with many of his enemies rotting underground or in prisons, Gaddafi saw threats all around. The walls around his main compound were four metres high and one metre thick. Underneath the compound, Gaddafi had his men construct a network of tunnels so vast that a golf cart was used to move around within it.[9] The tunnels served as a means of escape and also contained an underground television station to allow the dictator to address his people while under siege.[10] Another Gaddafi compound in Tripoli contained an operating theatre behind heavy blast doors, so the dictator's life could be saved, even during a bloody revolution. The underground labyrinth there was so extensive that one journalist referred to it as a 'maze'.[11]

A man who thinks his future will be bright doesn't need multiple compounds with kilometres of underground tunnels. But Gaddafi knew his future wasn't secure. For dictators, there is a very real need to construct such defences. The threats are huge and constant.

On 15 February 2011, protests broke out in Benghazi, Libya's second most populous city, after the regime arrested a lawyer who represented victims of the 1996 prison massacre. In Gaddafi's Libya, where opposition wasn't tolerated, it was a rare sign of dissent.[12] With the regime's armour cracked, the situation rapidly escalated as opposition intensified and spread to other cities. In response, Gaddafi gave a speech on national television in which he vowed to 'cleanse Libya house by house'.[13] 'I will not leave the country,' Gaddafi said, before adding that he would 'die as a martyr'.[14]

But at this stage, Gaddafi was still confident that he wouldn't have to die. And although the rebels came to control entire cities, the regime retained the ability to go on the offensive. By 16 March, Gaddafi's forces were closing in on rebel-held Benghazi when one of his sons gave an interview in which he boasted that 'everything will be over in 48 hours.'[15]

With Gaddafi having referred to his enemies as rats, there was now the real possibility that a campaign of mass killing would unfold in front of the world's eyes.[16] Faced with that prospect, the United Nations Security Council voted 10-0 in favour of taking 'all necessary measures' to protect civilians.[17] The end was a long time coming, but this was its beginning. Two days later, French fighter jets took to the air to attack the regime while warships of the United States Navy launched cruise missiles to neutralise Libyan air defence systems. Speaking from Brazil, President Barack Obama said: 'We cannot stand idly by when a tyrant tells his people there will be no mercy.'[18]

In October, with the regime severely diminished and bombs still falling from above, Gaddafi knew the moment he had long feared had arrived. There were no more compounds, no more tunnels, no more walls that could protect the dictator. Instead, Gaddafi and his men moved from house to house in Sirte, the coastal town near which the dictator had been born. Supplies were limited and his bodyguards were forced to scrounge around to find pasta and rice to feed the group. Gaddafi himself was clearly confused. 'Why is there no water? Why is there no electricity?' he would ask the head of his guard. Trying to flee was risky, but with the rebels so close and the shelling constant, staying in Sirte was not an option. Eventually, a reluctant Gaddafi agreed to escape. Originally scheduled to leave at 3 a.m., under the cover of darkness, his convoy of around forty cars didn't leave until five hours later. By that time, the sun was up. Half an hour after the convoy left, it was struck by missiles. One of the explosions was so close that the airbag deployed in the Toyota Land Cruiser in which Gaddafi was travelling.[19] The leader and a few of his men decided to flee on foot. After making their way across a farm, they had no option other than to hide in a foul-smelling drain.[20]

When rebels grabbed him, he was unable to compute what was happening. He was Colonel Muammar Gaddafi, the Godfather of Libya, King of Kings of Africa. And, as he once described himself: the Leader Who Lived in All Libyans' Hearts. 'What's this? What's this, my sons? What are you doing?' Gaddafi asked.[21] His 'sons' proceeded to brutalise him. Beaten by the mob and sodomised with a bayonet, the last footage of Gaddafi shows him on top of a car, his head blood-ied, asking for mercy.[22]

With the dictator finally under their control, the rebels celebrated. In one of the defining images of the conflict, a young rebel was seen being carried on his comrades' shoul-ders, holding a golden gun decorated with intricate engrav-ings. That gun belonged to Gaddafi himself, supposedly given to him by one of his sons.[23] This is what I call the Golden Gun paradox: tyrants can have all the trappings of power, even a gun made of gold, but at the point where they need to use their power to save themselves, it is already too late. A dictator can never save himself with a golden gun. For Gaddafi, holding the gun only imbued power as long as people believed it did. The moment they stopped, the gun was useless.

By the end of that day, 20 October 2011, the gun was gone and the dictator was dead. As a final indignity, Gaddafi wasn't afforded the quick burial that is customary in Islam. Instead, his topless corpse was displayed in the meat locker of a local shopping mall for all to see.[24] When a journalist talked to a local man about it, he responded that Gaddafi had chosen his own destiny. 'If he had been a good man, we would have buried him,' he said.[25]

And indeed, if Gaddafi had been a good man, or even just a democratic leader instead of a dictator, chances are he would have had a very different end.

Tyranny is hazardous.

According to a recent study that examined the way 2,790 national rulers lost power, 1,925 (69 per cent) were just fine after leaving office. 'Only' about 23 per cent of them were exiled, imprisoned or killed.[26] But that was across all countries and political systems. Zoom in on the personalist dictators – the leaders with most power concentrated in their hands – and the numbers are reversed: 69 per cent of those tyrants are thrown into jail, forced to live their life abroad or killed.[27] The odds for a tranquil retirement are worse than the flip of a coin.

I've studied dictators and the way they stay in power or lose it for more than a decade. As a postgraduate at Oxford, I examined the lives of the Politburo of the Communist Party of the Soviet Union. Who were these people? How did they rise to the top in a system that could be so hostile? And what did they care about?

After I left Oxford, I thought I was done with worrying about tyranny (and sitting in dusty libraries). Eager to see the world, I decided to work for a brewery in the Democratic

Republic of Congo. But the most memorable lessons I learned there weren't about hops or barley, but about how authoritarian regimes work – and how many tyrants are constantly living on a knife edge.

While I was in Lubumbashi on 30 December 2013, armed attackers stormed the studios of the national broadcaster in Kinshasa. Gunmen took control of the airwaves and delivered a message against the president, Joseph Kabila. They told him he was finished, his time was up. While they spoke, their accomplices attacked the country's main airport. A military base was hit.[28]

On the other side of the country in Lubumbashi, reliable information was hard to come by: 'Have you heard what's happening in Kinshasa?' curious people asked at the brewery. During lunch, I tried to find out what exactly was going on. Nobody knew. With the violence seemingly far away, I started to make my way back to the office which, like my bungalow, was within the same compound. On a normal Monday, this walk would have been one of the best parts of the day. Lubumbashi itself is not exactly a green city, but the vegetation within the compound was lush. While walking, I'd marvel at the size of the palm trees or watch strange-looking birds flying overhead. It seemed like an oasis.

That day was different. On my way back to work, the stillness of the air was broken with a crack. It was a gunshot. Then, another one and another one, a rat-a-tat of gunfire coming from three directions. Then I heard something bigger, an explosion. A million thoughts were running through my mind. Behind the walls of the compound, a stray bullet was unlikely to become a problem. But what if that explosion was a mortar? Another one of those could do serious damage even if I wasn't the intended target. I was more than 1,500 kilometres from the German Embassy. The airports were closed, so flying wasn't an option if things got worse. If we had to evacuate, it would have to be to the south, via land, across the border to Zambia. Now in a slight panic, I turned round to talk to colleagues. 'What are we going to do?' The answer was: 'Nothing.' Yes, they had heard the shots, but they had heard them before and nothing very serious ever affected them, so why should it now?

And that was that. As a visiting European behind a concrete wall, there was a layer of insulation between the danger and me. Out in the city, others weren't so lucky.

I turned around again and went back to work.

The coup attempt in Kinshasa had been launched by a religious leader – Paul-Joseph Mukungubila – and the military was attacking his church in Lubumbashi.[29] When it became evident to the self-declared prophet that he wasn't going to be successful, he fled the country with five of his eighteen wives and twelve of his nineteen children.[30] Joseph Kabila, who had ruled the country since his father was assassinated, stayed in power.

I remember thinking that the calm reactions were strange. Shouldn't *something* be done? But then again, when it comes to a struggle like Mukungubila's with Kabila, what can you do? Nothing. All you can do is wait and see if the tyrant will fall, paving the way for another tyrant to take his place.

A few months later, I returned to Europe, but I could never get that day out of my head. How can it be that some countries experience severe instability with such regularity that their people have grown so inured to it? Why did Kabila manage to hold onto power for five more years? When do leaders like him lose power? And, when they do, what happens next?

I decided to research how tyrants fall. During my doctorate I focused on irregular leadership changes like the one

Mukungubila attempted in the Democratic Republic of Congo. Since then, I have worked on these issues not just at university but also with multinational companies, foundations and international organisations such as NATO and the OECD, always drawn to the question of how tyrants fall.

In October 1938, when Nazi Germany had already annexed Austria and taken over the Sudetenland, Winston Churchill gave a speech to the people of the United States. It was a call to arms:

> You see these dictators on their pedestals, surrounded by the bayonets of their soldiers and the truncheons of their police. On all sides they are guarded by masses of armed men, cannons, aeroplanes, fortifications, and the like – they boast and vaunt themselves before the world, yet in their hearts there is unspoken fear.[31]

When most people think of tyrants, they conjure images of a man (and it is almost always a man) who wields absolute power. That is a myth. No political leader has ever had absolute power. Even the most powerful dictators need others in order to stay in power. To remain on their pedestal, they need to manage those closest to them. If they don't, they are at immediate risk.

The central problem that tyrants face is that eliminating the many immediate threats to their position can be costly and creates a never-ending cycle of new problems. Eventually, the tyrant may fall off his pedestal. And when that happens, it's not just the tyrant who is at risk, because entire countries can crumble under the weight of a falling dictator.

Before we go further, a word of caution: no two dictatorships are alike. North Korea isn't Turkmenistan and Cuba isn't Russia. Similarly, tyrants are different from one another.

Nowadays, leaders are usually described as tyrants when they act in a way that is cruel and oppressive. That leads to an incredibly broad array of leaders. Since most of them are men, I will usually refer to the tyrant as he. The tyrant could be a king, a personalist dictator or the head of a military junta. Or perhaps the tyrant is general secretary of the party in a one-party state or at the top of a theocracy – deriving its legitimacy from God's supposed will. The nation he leads can be rich or poor, mountainous or flat.

This diversity also applies to the tyrants themselves. Some, such as Saddam Hussein, have had terrible childhoods in which they were regularly beaten and abused.[32] Others, such as Mao, were coddled when they were young.[33] Adolf Hitler was such a choleric that he could barely stop himself from shouting once he became agitated. Pol Pot rarely showed any emotion. There are also massive differences between the way these tyrants have attained power. Some have climbed the pedestal by being good at organising and outmanoeuvring their competitors. Others, such as Idi Amin, were simply more brutal than everyone else. The most 'successful' tyrants, for example Stalin, were good at both.

As a result of this diversity, every sweeping statement will have an exception. But there are patterns and common traits. By looking at the forest, we can better understand most of the trees. Unfortunately, we can't always inspect them close up. Unlike democracies, which are comparatively transparent and open, dictatorships are dens of secrets. People who talk out of turn can disappear. Government documents are laced with lies. Journalists who report the truth may not last long.

Trying to understand tyranny is not easy. Perhaps the deputy prime minister is a mere puppet, or perhaps he really is the second most important political figure in the country. Or perhaps the institutions of the state don't matter much because they are controlled by a revolutionary political party. Or, maybe neither state nor party matters anymore because power is so personalised. It is quite possible that the tyrant's bodyguard is more powerful than cabinet members or party elites because he has the dictator's ear and proximity is more important than formal power. It's hard to tell. Dictatorships run on whispers, clandestine deals and cover-ups.

The other difficulty of studying the fall of tyrants is that, however severe the political instability, however frequent the rebellions, it's not every day that a tyrant actually falls.[34] In a functioning democracy with meaningful elections, you get plenty of chances to observe how leaders lose office. Dictators, on the other hand, can remain in office for many decades. When they do go, they might fall in an instant, taken out by a single gunshot, or toppled within hours during a coup. And it can be difficult to determine how exactly they did fall – partly because it happens so rarely, but partly because the fall of tyrants often involves a tipping point, at which leaders become so unstable that their supporters desert them en masse – only later to pretend that they had been opposed to them all along.[35]

You also can't understand tyrants just by looking at the person. They operate within a system – and they need that system to stay in power. We'll therefore be exploring how authoritarian regimes work. One way to think of a regime, as opposed to the leader, is to think of it as the rules by which new leaders are chosen.[36] So when the generals that make up a military dictatorship replace the top general with a new general, it's a different leader but still the same regime. But if protestors sweep away the entire military junta to create a democracy or a communist dictatorship in its stead, that's a new regime. It's not just the person, but the system itself, that has changed.

When I started working on this book, I spoke to diplomats, journalists, dissidents, human rights activists and (former) spies. Since the subject of the book is so broad, I also consulted experts on economic sanctions, nuclear weapons, military history, quantitative forecasting and many other topics. Not everyone can be quoted, but all of them were fascinating.

There were also some more unusual encounters. Early on, I spoke to a professor of Roman history who was kind enough to discuss Emperor Caligula's reign with me at great length. Next, I met an American-Gambian who went to prison for plotting to liberate his homeland from a tyrant who had pledged to rule for a billion years. At one point, I was in a WhatsApp call with a Central African politician accused of war crimes, wondering whether I genuinely thought it was 'nice to meet him'.

The book also allowed me to discover more of my own country. To me, born in western Germany just after the end of the Cold War, the German Democratic Republic (GDR) always felt distant. The GDR existed neither long ago nor far away, but it might as well have been in a different universe because it was almost impossible to imagine it existing so close by. The journey of writing this book changed that. To speak to Siegbert Schefke, who was instrumental in bringing down the regime beyond the wall, I drove to Leipzig. Hearing him talk about 9 October 1989 – the day that 'fear changed sides' – made all the things that had seemed so abstract feel real and essential for me and for all of us to understand.[37]

This is a book about the trade-offs faced by dictators and the people around them. They all want multiple things and they can't have them all, so there are tough choices to be made. In the next chapter, 'The Dictator's Treadmill', I am going to lay out why tyrants usually try to stay in power once they have attained it. For starters, tyranny can be an attractive position. But more importantly, stepping down voluntarily is incredibly dangerous. Most aren't willing to take the risk, so they attempt to stay in power. To have any chance of staying in power, they have to focus on palace elites and soldiers. But, as I demonstrate in the chapters 'The Enemy Within' and 'Weakening the Warriors', doing so is difficult. Also, focusing time and money on neutralising threats from armed men and powerful elites creates plenty of problems down the line. As resources are taken from the masses and given to a narrow group near the top, the population may rise up against the regime. As members of the elite are purged from the capital, they may return from the hinterland as rebel leaders. And as the military is paralysed, soldiers have a more difficult time dealing with rebels or foreign invaders. Lastly, some things simply exist outside the tyrant's control. A dictator can do everything to maximise his chances of staying in power, but still be assassinated. The risk might even be higher as a result of doing everything 'right'. In the end, whether through natural death or violent removal, every tyrant does fall. But what happens next? The fall of tyrants often leads to chaos and conflict. In the chapter 'Be Careful What You Wish For', I explore under what circumstances that can be prevented. Now that we know how tyrants fall and what happens when they do, other questions come into focus. Can outsiders accelerate the fall? If so, how? And should they?

Tyrants cannot be ignored. We must pay attention to them – and understand them better. Losing power can easily mean not just a loss of privilege but a loss of freedom or even life. And to a large extent, this peril explains why tyrants act the way they do while they are in power. We've all read outlandish stories about dictators who seem unhinged. The Turkmen dictator Saparmurat Niyazov built a twelve-metre-high gold statue of himself on top of a monument in Ashgabat that rotated to follow the sun.[38] The North Korean leader, Kim Jong-un, had an education ministry official executed with an anti-aircraft gun — supposedly for falling asleep in a meeting.[39] Part of Idi Amin's self-bestowed title was 'Lord of All The Beasts of the Earth and Fishes of the Seas and Conqueror of the British Empire in Africa in General and Uganda in Particular'.[40]

At first glance, these rulers seem insane. And evidently, these aren't normal people. They're often narcissists; sometimes psychopathic; and almost always ruthless. But the surprising truth is that most of them are also *rational*. They haven't lost their minds. Instead, given the system in which they operate and the information they have, strategies to torture, kill and let the masses starve while they collect riches in the presidential palace are rational. It's a way to survive.

And it has been that way for thousands of years. Democracy as we now understand it is young, dictatorship is old. Most humans, throughout recorded history, have suffered under the rule of tyrants. In 1800, nobody on earth was living in a genuine democracy. Cruel and oppressive governments weren't an exception but the norm. Whether the tyrant was a chief, duke, king, emperor, bishop, sultan or colonial governor, that's how societies were organised. People were subjects and tyranny felt inevitable. Political change largely determined who was the tyrant, not whether there was one.

Even in comparatively recent history, tyrants reigned supreme. At the end of the Second World War, more than 90 per cent of countries were not democracies.[41] This was also a time when vast swathes of the world didn't rule themselves at all. Instead, they were colonies ruled from afar. Following this, during the Cold War, both sides supported tyrants if they judged it to be in their interest. London had a hand in overthrowing a democratically elected leader in Iran in favour of

Shah Pahlavi. Beijing kept Pol Pot's regime alive while it kept killing. Worried about falling dominoes, the United States fought wars in defence of vile dictatorships in Korea and Vietnam. The French government paid for the coronation of Jean-Bédel Bokassa, the Central African dictator who crowned himself emperor, while his people starved. Bokassa might have been a despot, but he was their despot. That was in 1977.

But the Cold War was also a time of national liberation – with many people who had once been colonised taking back control. Originally, the United Nations had just fifty-one members. By the middle of the 1970s, it had reached 144. Now it's 193.[42] Unfortunately, that hasn't always led to freedom or democracy. In fact, studies show that the number of dictatorships grew between 1946 and the 1970s.[43] For many, independence meant trading in a foreign power for a local tyrant. And those foreign powers were apt to back a loyal despot in order to retain influence. A friendly tyrant, they frequently figured, was more useful to them than an elected adversary.

After the end of the Cold War, democracy blossomed. By 2012, less than 12 per cent of countries remained closed autocracies – the type of system in which citizens don't get any choice at all.[44] For a while, it even looked as if the model of liberal democracies had triumphed to become the new normal. Western societies waited for what Francis Fukuyama called the 'End of History', the ultimate triumph of democracy.[45]

But of course, tyranny had never truly gone away – it was just easier to ignore. In the twenty-first century, that became impossible. The world couldn't ignore Kim Jong-un, who had access to a nuclear arsenal capable of wiping out entire cities in a single attack, when he fired missiles over Japan. Vladimir Putin destabilised an entire continent, committing war crimes along the way. Saudi tyrants sent a death squad to dismember a journalist working for the *Washington Post*. Rwanda's regime has repeatedly hunted down opponents to murder them.[46] After securing his position at the top of the Chinese Communist Party for life, Xi Jinping told his generals that they should 'dare to fight'.[47]

Those, of course, are only the autocracies that already exist. In Europe, for example, multiple democracies are at imminent risk. In 2014 Viktor Orbán declared he would make Hungary an 'illiberal democracy' – in reality, a form of authoritarianism. In Turkey, Recep Tayyip Erdoğan and his allies have restricted the political space to such an extent that it has become increasingly difficult for the opposition to win elections.

And while totalitarian leaders have become rarer, the world's remaining dictators continue to persecute their own people and opponents. Whether it be via wars of conquest or the attempted destruction of entire cultures, the threat of tyranny remains acute. If we don't understand how tyrants operate, we can't constrain them at home or limit their threat abroad.

Over the last decade, there have been countless newspaper articles, tweets and books about the defence of liberal democracies. None of them will be sufficient. Whether it happens suddenly by means of a *coup d'état* or gradually through the dismantling of core institutions, some democracies will die. When that happens, all of us should know what comes next and how it can be reversed.

That is the primary purpose of this book: to provide a guide to despots' limitations, their regimes' weaknesses and the ways they collapse. But understanding them isn't enough. This book will also explore how to bring them down.

That can seem idealistic. Tyranny often looks remarkably stable, after all. Some of the world's most famous dictators support this view: Muammar Gaddafi, for example, ruled Libya for over four decades, more than twice as long as Angela Merkel was chancellor of Germany. And on top of that, the data show that autocratic regimes can be even more durable than individual leaders.[48] To give just one example, North Korea has been ruled by three men for more than half a century, father, son and grandson.

Look closer, though, and you soon realise that authoritarian stability tends to be a mirage. Most non-democracies aren't like Gaddafi's Libya. Instead, they are often more like Kabila's Democratic Republic of Congo, with a lack of central government control and constant conflict, sometimes civil war. And even Gaddafi's type of tyranny only looks to be stable – but isn't. Unlike democracies, these are political systems which are designed to revolve around a single individual or a small group of elites. That might work for them, for a time, but systems such as those are not resilient. When a shock comes and the system is challenged, the consequences can be devastating, leading to conflict, starvation or war. In the case of Libya, the war against Gaddafi was followed by war amongst the militias that wanted to replace him. More than a decade after his golden gun failed to save him, the shooting still hadn't stopped.

The amateurish coup attempt that happened while I was in the Democratic Republic of Congo wasn't an anomaly. Most attempts to take out a tyrant fail because strongmen are prepared. But inevitably, they do fall. The question, then, is how.

I

The Dictator's Treadmill

I will never be known as the former President of Zaire.[1]
Mobutu Sese Seko, president of Zaire

Being a dictator is like being stuck on a treadmill that one can never get off.[2] Tyrants can run and run, but the best they'll ever do is stay upright. If they get distracted for even an instant, their legs may shoot out from under them, and they'll get hurt. Many dictators who fall off never get on again. And they can't step off safely either. In the world of tyrants, trying to stay in power may end badly, but voluntarily relinquishing it can be even more dangerous.

But if it's so difficult to get off the treadmill, why would anyone get on in the first place?

It's not necessarily a bad place to be, at least for a while. Politicians everywhere tend to be comparatively wealthy. For example, the median wealth of a member of the United States Senate stood at $1.76 million in 2018.[3] In democracies, some former leaders can make millions from speaking events and book deals. Boris Johnson (or Alexander Boris de Pfeffel Johnson to be more accurate), for example, was paid almost £250,000 for giving a single speech in Singapore after he left Downing Street.[4]

But democracies have rules that prevent politicians from dipping their hands into the coffers of the state. As much as democratic political leaders might want to, there's a good chance they'll be found out if they engage in corruption, as they face investigative journalists, independent policemen and a vibrant civil society. If they do get found out, there are likely to be serious consequences because judges can rarely be swayed (or paid) to look the other way. Once an infraction comes to light, opposition politicians are going to do their best to make leaders' lives as miserable as possible in order to win the next election. It's not a perfect system, but it usually stops the worst abuses.

Tyrants, by contrast, operate in an environment that more closely resembles the Wild West. There may be rules, but they aren't enforced, or are enforced selectively. Autocracies are enrichment machines. Unencumbered by the restrictions that hold back democratic leaders, the opportunities for stealing are almost endless.

The capital needs a new airport? Tyrants can give the contract to their daughter-in-law to make sure things stay in the family. A foreign firm no longer wants trouble with the tax authorities? Get them to pay a 'fee' to make the case go away. Does it really matter if all of the ammunition that was ordered makes its way to the army? Perhaps some can be lost in transit after a certain foreign bank account is credited with the value of the balance. A company owned by the state is about to be privatised? Why not sell it to a loyalist for 10 per cent of its actual value? I scratch your back, you scratch mine and the money never stops flowing.

When done effectively, everyone at the top makes money. But the tyrant himself? He can get rich beyond belief.

Turkmenistan is one of the most secretive societies on earth. As one of the least visited countries on the planet, its people used to be incredibly poor. In 1998, more than four out of ten Turkmen lived in extreme poverty – having access to less than

$2.15 per day.[5] But that's not to say that Turkmenistan, the country, is poor. Far from it. According to the World Bank, 'Turkmenistan's gas reserves are estimated to be the world's fourth largest, representing about 10 per cent of global reserves.' 'In addition to cotton and natural gas,' the Bank's analysts say, 'the country is rich in petroleum, sulphur, iodine, salt, bentonite clays, limestone, gypsum, and cement – all potential inputs to chemical and construction industries.'[6]

Turkmenistan's problem wasn't so much that there was no money, but that the money wasn't distributed to the people who needed it. But at least one Turkmen is always rich: the man at the top. At the turn of the millennium, that man was Saparmurat Niyazov, a dictator best-known for the absurd cult of personality he created after coming to power in 1985. Among other things, Niyazov banned smoking in public after heart surgery meant he had to give up cigarettes, gave himself the title of 'Turkmenbashi' (father of the nation), banned men from listening to car radios and renamed months of the year after himself and his mother.[7]

Niyazov also wrote a book called *Ruhnama*. A combination of biography, poetry and self-help, the book was essentially treated like a religious text. Every single Turkmen student had to read it. Civil servants had compulsory study sessions on it every week. (The Ministry of Foreign Affairs, for example, met for theirs at 5.30 p.m. on Wednesdays.) The glorification was so extreme that Niyazov himself once noted drily: 'Various people say it's a personality cult.'[8] It was.

When Niyazov wasn't busy coming up with arbitrary rules for the Turkmen people, he stole from them. In 2001, Turkmenistan and Ukraine signed a gas deal. According to a later investigation by the German magazine *Der Spiegel*, the deal was set to generate around $1.7 billion in the following year alone. But since Turkmenistan was (and continues to be) a dictatorship, much of the money didn't go into the government budget but into foreign bank accounts under direct control of Saparmurat Niyazov. The exact details are unknown, but even if the reports are somewhat inaccurate and Niyazov skimmed off 'only' 10 per cent, that's $170 million on a single deal in a single year. And of course, that wasn't the only instance of corruption. When a London-based non-governmental organisation (NGO) looked into the dictator's finances, it concluded: 'A significant portion of revenue never finds its way into state coffers.' 'A horrifying 75% of the state's spending', they continued, 'appears to take place off [the government's] budget.'⁹ Given such opportunities, it's little wonder that dictators are often the richest men in their country.

That's a pretty big incentive to ascend the treadmill. But the treadmill is relentless.

On 5 January 2022, fifty-seven-year-old Asel stood on Almaty's main square. The ruling regime in Kazakhstan, Turkmenistan's biggest neighbour, had been cutting subsidies on liquefied petroleum gas. Protests quickly began in the west of the country, where the gas was especially important for people to get around. By the time Asel stepped into Republic Square in front of what used to be the presidential residence, the country was gripped by protestors.

On that day in Kazakhstan's biggest city, the situation got out of control. While Asel protested peacefully, a group of young men arrived. Their faces hidden by masks, they smashed windows and destroyed cars on their way to the government building just off the square. Bullets started flying and people started to panic. Asel lost consciousness. When she came to, her leg was bleeding heavily. She'd been hit and if she couldn't get medical treatment, she wouldn't have long to live. More bullets whizzed through the air, narrowly missing her.

Dragged towards a truck by two men, she was driven to hospital. The pain was now so severe that she couldn't help but moan in anguish. Some others on the crowded vehicle were much worse off. 'Several people were on top of my wounded leg. Some of them were not breathing,' Asel later told the BBC. At the hospital, Asel's nightmare didn't stop. Armed men went from ward to ward, looking for people who had dared to protest against the regime. 'If you go out to protest again, we will kill you,' one of them shouted. The only reason why Asel wasn't taken away by them that day is because the bullet to her leg made it impossible for her to walk.[10]

From the outside looking in, it seemed to be the classic story of a tyrannical regime fighting against its own people: the people rose up, the regime did its best to put them back down. But on the inside, the Kazakh unrest was much more than that. It was the struggle of one tyrant, who had formally stepped down, against another, who was trying to step out of his boss's shadow.

Nursultan Nazarbayev stepped onto the treadmill in 1984, at the young age of forty-three, when he became first secretary of the Communist Party of Kazakhstan. At the time, the country was still part of the Soviet Union. After the USSR dissolved, he became Kazakhstan's dictator. Then, in 2019, he tried to step down.

Nazarbayev had succeeded in amassing incredible personal power over the years. On the day of his resignation from the presidency, he said: 'I have taken a decision, which was not easy for me, to resign as president . . . I am staying with you. Caring for the country and its people will remain my concern.'[11]

Initially, things seemed to be going well for the former president. Astana, the country's capital, was named 'Nur-Sultan' in his honour. If you visited it from abroad, chances are you were going to fly into Nur-Sultan International Airport, also named after Nazarbayev. In the city itself, you might also come across Nazarbayev University or Nazarbayev Avenue.[12] The man himself was no longer president, but he retained the title of 'Elbasy' – or 'Father of the Nation' in Kazakh. The Elbasy title, which was given to him in 2010, meant that he continued to have special privileges – like immunity from prosecution. Nazarbayev was untouchable; or at least that's how it seemed. But then he ran into a problem that many have faced before him: it's difficult to protect oneself after giving up the levers of government. That's because it's impossible to be a dictator without breaking laws and making enemies. Dictators have stolen, tortured, maybe killed. So if they ever want to step down, they need to make sure that none of that catches up with them. To do that, they need someone at the top who will look after them. Finding that someone is incredibly challenging.

Nazarbayev's hand-picked successor, the career diplomat Kassym-Jomart Tokayev, was seen as so toothless that he was once described as Nazarbayev's 'furniture'.[13] In fact, Nazarbayev's control initially remained so tight that the new president had to get the old president's formal approval to choose most new ministers. President Tokayev wasn't even able to choose the head of his own secret service without Nazarbayev's approval.[14] That Nazarbayev could fence Tokayev in like this was always part of the reason why he was chosen. In addition, since Tokayev had spent much of his working life abroad representing the regime in places such as Singapore and China, Nazarbayev thought Tokayev lacked the networks and alliances at home to challenge him.[15] The plan was simple: Nazarbayev would formally step down but continue to exercise power through Tokayev and others to ensure that he would remain safe.

It's not an unusual story. Dictators step onto the treadmill thinking that they can become rich or enjoy the power such a position brings. And for a while, it works out for them. But eventually, due to old age or fatigue, they want to step down. So they make a plan: give a little here, give a little there, step off the machine.

In reality, giving an inch doesn't work: they give a little, they risk it all. Before long, this also became clear to Nazarbayev. His luck started to run out as the protests spread. 'Shal, ket' ('Old man, go!') the protestors shouted.[16] With much of the anger directed at the system the old man had created, Tokayev seized the opportunity to expand his power.

On 5 January 2022, the day Asel was shot in Almaty, Nazarbayev lost his chairmanship of the Security Council. Tokayev also took on the leadership of Nur Otan, the presidential political party that has since been renamed Amanat.[17] The public holiday celebrating the country's former president? Cancelled.[18] The capital city of Nur-Sultan? It became Astana again.[19] Perhaps more worrying for the former president, the handpicked successor also began to remove some of Nazarbayev's men from the power structures of the regime. The head of the KNB, the country's powerful domestic intelligence agency, was not just replaced in his role but arrested for treason.[20] Then, on the morning of 6 January, came the final blow for Nazarbayev as three thousand Russian paratroopers, at the request of Tokayev, landed in Kazakhstan to defend the regime. With the might of the Russian military seemingly on his side, Tokayev was now unquestionably the country's strongest man.

None of the laws, fancy titles or council posts mean anything once tyrants have left power. The only thing that matters is whether the people that come after the tyrant are powerful enough to start chipping away at their predecessor's power in order to expand theirs. If they are, they usually will – and that started to happen in Nur-Sultan Astana. Events were out of Nazarbayev's control. He risked losing his money, his freedom or even his life. His family was at risk, too. There's a central trade-off here that cannot be resolved. On the one hand, tyrants looking to step down have to find someone powerful and competent enough to protect them once they are no longer in power. On the other hand, somebody who is competent and powerful enough to protect them can also destroy them. And often, their successors do destroy the outgoing tyrant, because it is rare for a self-respecting tyrant to allow themselves to play second fiddle.

Dictators who try to pass the torch often get burned. So, if that doesn't work, what alternatives are there once they set foot on the treadmill? One option would be to turn the country into a democracy instead of passing on power to the next tyrant. It sounds attractive, not least because harsh punishments for former leaders are less likely in democracies than they are in autocracies. As the political scientists Barbara Geddes, Joseph Wright and Erica Frantz have found, democratisation more than doubles the chance of a 'good' outcome for leaders once they leave office.[21]

There are all kinds of different models of democracy. German democracy involves a parliamentary system in which multiple parties come together to form coalitions. In the United Kingdom, the voting system is different so coalitions are more unusual – but no longer unheard of. In the United States, the president is also the commander-in-chief and, if need be, he or she can order military action. The Swiss have organised their democracy in a way that is a lot more direct. From time to time, when enough signatures are collected, everybody involved can vote not just for politicians to represent them, but for or against individual policies. In September 2022, for example, Swiss voters got a direct vote on 'factory farming' – they could have banned it but chose not to.[22]

Most tyrants would rather hinder than help democracy. Democracies vary hugely but what they all have in common is that voters are in charge. There might be intermediaries (in the form of politicians) and not everybody's vote will carry the same importance, but the people can change their government if they are unhappy with it.

For tyrants, being an average president or prime minister in a democracy is not a substitute for commanding the entire state from the confines of the presidential palace. All of a sudden they're supposed to allow investigative journalism? The Glorious Father of the Revolution is to be constrained by parliamentarians? And it's no longer possible to turn mining concessions into millions? No, thank you.

Perhaps more importantly, there's no guarantee that an attempt to democratise would allow tyrants to stay in power. They may end up still losing office or worse; or be held accountable by empowered parliamentarians or independent judges. Such scenarios are especially threatening to personalist dictators. According to a study on the breakdown of autocratic regimes, their chance of a 'good' outcome only stands at 36 per cent even if democratisation works out. Other sorts of dictator have more of an incentive to democratise. For authoritarian leaders who derive their power from being at the top of a political party, the party can act as a shield, protecting the former tyrant from the masses.[23] But a personalist dictator, the type with the most personal power, has no such thing. So even if a transition to democracy happens, there's every chance he will be in trouble.

And even if turning off the treadmill were desirable, it's not an option all tyrants have. They can try pulling the plug, but it doesn't mean that they will actually reach a point at which their country turns into a democracy. The primary reasons for this are the concerns of the elites around them.

For this is not just a decision for leaders but also one for courtiers and power brokers around the palace, who will also have a stake in the survival of the regime. Just like the tyrant, many of these people will have broken their fair share of laws. Perhaps they were the ones to make the leader's enemies disappear. Maybe they were the loyalists who received a newly privatised company at 10 per cent of its real value.

All these factors can complicate a move towards democracy, but it can become even more challenging when the military is opposed to democratisation. Imagine the following scenario: an autocrat decides that the time for democratisation has come because it's the least bad way forward for him personally.[24] Military officers don't agree. Perhaps they currently have a lot of opportunities for enrichment and they'd rather be rich and serve a dictator than be poor and serve a democratic leader.

But for soldiers, it's about more than money. The nightmare scenario for the officers is an attempted democratisation that leads not just to a new system of government but also a new leader. When that happens, there's a dual threat: the existence of democracy itself makes it more likely that the soldiers, who have previously served the dictatorship, will be held accountable. But not just that: the new leader has a huge incentive to make a move against the military because he is likely to be concerned that the military, fearing for their former privileges, may move against him. The military officers, on the other hand, have a strong incentive to make the first move because many new democratic leaders start their time in office by reforming the security sector. For understandable reasons, they don't trust the old guard that has protected the dictatorship.

This scenario isn't purely hypothetical, it has been repeatedly played out and it's one of the reasons why turning off the treadmill can be so risky for tyrants. Leaders might want to turn it off, but the people around them simply won't let that happen. So instead, they are effectively forced to keep running even if they are sick and tired of doing so.

When dictators do make way for democracy, it's usually not by choice. They are either forced into it or they simply blunder. Power is taken, not given. As Daniel Treisman at the University of California has argued after examining the history of democratisations since the year 1800, democracy often happens by mistake.[25]

In spring 1982, the Argentinian dictatorship of Leopoldo Galtieri was facing tens of thousands of people out on the streets. 'Elections now', they demanded. Unwilling to give the protestors what they wanted, Galtieri made a massive gamble: he went to war. Days later, Argentinian forces attacked the Falkland Islands, a British-controlled archipelago lying some 480 kilometres east of Argentina in the southern Atlantic Ocean. Initially, Galtieri's plan worked: the crowds cheered and Galtieri basked in his newfound popularity.[26] There was just one problem: the whole plan rested on the assumption that the British wouldn't be willing to use force to take back the islands. And indeed, this is what the dictator believed. A response would be 'absolutely improbable,' he said.[27]

Margaret Thatcher, prime minister at the time, was pushed by many of her closest advisors to make a deal with Buenos Aires. But after her predecessor gave her the advice to exclude the chancellor from her War Cabinet 'so that money would not be an issue in making military decisions', the Iron Lady went to war.[28] A British fleet comprising 127 warships, submarines and repurposed merchant ships set sail within days.[29] It didn't take long for it to become clear that Galtieri had miscalculated. Instead of a glorious victory that would allow him to stay in power, his forces were beaten by the Brits and he no longer had any cards to play.

On 14 June, Buenos Aires' Plaza de Mayo was again filled with angry crowds because the government had surrendered to the British. Three days later, Galtieri was forced to resign and Argentina was on its path to democracy.[30] In Argentina, democratisation wasn't a choice: it's what happened when the tyrant desperately tried to stay in place, to remain on the treadmill.

For most dictators, kings and theocrats, stepping down is not a real option and they know it. Even if it were possible, doing it would be dangerous because it doesn't guarantee that the tyrant won't be held accountable. This leaves two options: keep running or look around and see what other countries have to offer. If retirement isn't possible at home, perhaps it's possible elsewhere? The magic word is exile. But as we're about to learn, that's an option fraught with difficulty and uncertainty as well.

Exile is common – or rather has been common. When Abel Escribà-Folch and Daniel Krcmaric looked at the data in 2017, they found that around one in five dictators who lost power after the end of the Second World War fled abroad.[31]

The Ugandan dictator Idi Amin went from Libya to Iraq to Saudi Arabia after losing a war against Tanzania; Tunisia's Ben Ali, to Saudi Arabia. The self-declared Congolese 'Messiah' Mobuto settled in Morocco despite saying that he would never be known as the former president of Zaire. But it's not just shady regimes that offer exile to these cruel leaders who have created so much suffering for their own people. Plenty of unsavoury characters have found refuge in liberal democracies. France has taken in a host of deposed African dictators during and after the Cold War. Alberto Fujimori, the former Peruvian tyrant, fled to Japan after losing power.[32]

Exile is an option that is usually taken not because it's attract-ive but because there's no alternative – apart from death or a life in prison, obviously. Autocrats rarely just pack up and leave because they are no longer interested in having political power. In the vast majority of cases, dictators are pushed out. According to the 2017 study mentioned above, around 84 per cent of exiled dictators who went abroad 'did so in the midst of a coup, revolt, or civil war and were thus at risk of retribution'.[33]

There are multiple reasons why exile isn't an attractive option. The first is, obviously, that it leads to a loss of power. Having worked tirelessly to put themselves into a palace, to be someone, exiled dictators are suddenly reduced to being a has-been. But more importantly, it is extremely difficult to find the right spot to hide away. And if tyrants mess up their exile strategy, they've merely delayed death by a day or a month instead of sailing towards retirement.

Since these decisions tend to be made at a moment of crisis, it is difficult to say how rational leaders are when they make them, but there are quite a few things they should consider when they think about their future 'retirement' destination. That can be difficult, because time is of the essence when a regime-threatening (or at least leader-threatening) moment arrives and thinking is hard to do under those circumstances.[34]

On 21 December 1989, after being general secretary of the Romanian Communist Party for more than twenty-four years, Nicolae Ceaușescu stood on the balcony of the party's headquarters. Dressed in a black coat and matching hat to brave the eastern European winter, he was about to give the most important speech of his life. Tens of thousands of people were in front of him on Bucharest's Palace Square. Days earlier, the dictator had ordered his security forces to shoot protestors in Timișoara in the west of the country. Now Romania was in chaos and, shown on television, the great leader's speech was meant to do its part in restoring order. It was going to be difficult, no doubt, but the self-declared Genius of the Carpathians saw himself as up to the task.

But as the genius spoke, the expression on his face slowly changed when he could feel himself losing the crowd. Instead of cheering him, they heckled and booed. Ceaușescu had a flustered look on his face. How dare they? And how was this possible? In a political system built on perceptions of invulnerability and strength, it was an embarrassing moment for the regime and the television transmission was cut quickly.[35]

The general secretary had struggled before, but this crisis was different. Later that night, Nicolae and Elena, his wife of forty-three years, made their way to the roof of the building. A helicopter of the Romanian military, having taken off from the capital's airport, picked them up. The plan was for the helicopter to go to a town nearby, where other helicopters were supposed to meet them. When it became clear that the other helicopters were not going to arrive, the pilot took off again towards a military airfield.[36]

Now in the air for what must have felt like an eternity, a voice came through the helicopter's radio. The government had been toppled, it said. With the military no longer supporting the dictatorship, Ceaușescu (and everyone else on the aircraft) was now in acute danger. When the pilot told

Ceauşescu what he had just learned, he was in disbelief. They had to land, and they had to do so quickly.

'No. Those are only horrible lies. Are you not serving the cause?' he asked. But after being told that they could be blown up at any moment if they didn't land, he finally relented. Upon leaving the aircraft, Ceauşescu asked the pilot again: 'Are you serving the cause?' 'Which cause should I serve?' the pilot replied.

With the military having switched sides and the dictator and his wife now on land, it was too late to escape and the Ceauşescus were found shortly afterwards. After a show trial that was more show than trial, both were sentenced to death. Being led out of the court room, Ceauşescu sang the *Internationale*, a communist fighting song, while his wife Elena screamed 'fuck you' at a soldier who mocked them.[37] Knowing that death was now certain, they had one final request: they wanted to be executed together. The executioner granted them their wish. He lined them up against a wall and fired on them with his Kalashnikov.[38] They both died instantly.

'Any revolution demands blood,' the executioner would later say about that day. He had been forced to swear an oath of loyalty to Ceauşescu just four days before he pulled the trigger – an oath that he would support and protect the dictator.[39]

The big mistake that the Romanian dictator had made (aside from choosing an exceedingly dangerous profession) was that he didn't make proper plans for the day he might fall before the day actually arrived. He was way, way too confident. By the time that it finally dawned on him that this might be his last day in power, he could no longer escape.

But is that really surprising? We're dealing with people here who have led impossible lives and done impossible things.[40] The young Ceauşescu went to prison for communist activities at the age of eighteen; his country then went through the Second World War and Soviet rule. Born into a family of peasants, Nicolae carved out a life in which he could build himself one of the largest palaces the world had ever seen.

He's not alone in having lived a life so unreal that it would seem unconvincing if you saw it in a film. Ben Ali went from fighting French colonial forces in the deserts of Tunisia to becoming his country's dictator, only to be toppled by mass protest against his regime. Colonel Gaddafi or Idi Amin or Mobutu: all these people had countless brushes with death. Why should the occasion that actually brought about their end feel any different? Having done the impossible before, they undoubtedly believed that they could do it again. Perhaps they even had to believe it in order to continue in power for as long as they did.

Because when it's all over, time is so important: it's essential to be able to flee to a place within reach – if only en route to a final destination.[41] For many, that's already an insurmountable obstacle because plenty of dictatorships aren't exactly surrounded by friends. But that's not the only problem. Even if a neighbourhood leader is friendly and does offer a former tyrant a chance for a comparatively tranquil retirement, the tyrant's many enemies will use everything at their disposal to change that leader's mind. To survive in relative freedom, tyrants need to find a country that will not yield to pressure and kick them out. That's much easier said than done, especially for the world's most cruel leaders.

For Charles Taylor, a notoriously brutal West African war criminal, this became a very concrete concern. When he stepped down from power in 2003, he did it on the condition that he would be able to live out the rest of his days in Nigerian exile.[42] Initially, things seemed to be going well – as if Taylor's previous life wouldn't come catching up with him. Nigeria's then president explicitly promised that he would not deport him to face justice.[43] 'We will endeavour to be good hosts while he is in Nigeria,' President Obasanjo said when Taylor arrived in Abuja. His new living arrangements weren't too shabby, either: three hilltop villas guarded by a corps of Nigerian policemen. Even the president of the United States said that it was up to Nigerians how they dealt with him.[44]

But Taylor's comfortable life on the seafront didn't last long. Under massive pressure from human rights organisations and liberal democracies, the Nigerian government initially said that it was 'bound to honour its agreement to give him sanctuary'.[45] But ultimately, promises aren't worth much in a business that's all about power and money. Just three years after saying that this exact thing wouldn't happen on his watch, the Nigerian president stopped protecting Taylor. Without his protector, Taylor was done for. After being sentenced to fifty years in prison, Charles 'Butcher of Monrovia' Taylor is now spending the rest of his life in a British jail cell in County Durham.[46] He took a gamble by going abroad and it didn't work out.

To avoid a similar fate, dictators forced into exile have to find a country that won't give them up. But how? Tyrants have the best chance of reducing the possibility of being handed over if they find a host country that is non-democratic and powerful.[47] Democracies have in the past been willing to host former dictators, but their governments are much more vulnerable to popular pressure. Understandably, many voters are not going to be ecstatic when their government says that they will open the country's doors to a dictator who is primarily known for a string of war crimes. At Charles Taylor's trial, the presiding judge said: 'The accused has been found responsible for aiding and abetting as well as planning some of the most heinous and brutal crimes in recorded history.'[48] Which voter would want someone like that in their country? I don't. You probably don't.

Democratic leaders can withstand electoral pressure for a considerable time if they judge it to be in the country's national interest, but there comes a moment at which they will very probably crack. And even if that particular government manages to sit it out, the next government may not. Under those conditions, there's no genuine safety for tyrants. They're on a countdown.

Fellow autocratic regimes are preferable for two reasons: because they are more insulated from the demands of citizens and there's a serious chance that the regime will not change policy drastically over an extended period of time. But that only works if the host regime is stable and able to withstand foreign pressure.[49]

If tyrants are really unlucky, they flee to a non-democratic dictatorship only to find that it one day becomes a democracy. This happened to Chad's dictator Hissène Habré, who fled to Senegal.[50] As the political system there changed from authoritarian to democratic, so did Habré's chances for a relaxed retirement in the Senegalese sun. In 2013, after Senegalese democratisation, he was indicted for crimes against humanity, torture and a whole host of war crimes.[51]

There is also, of course, a more direct security concern: exile might reduce the immediate threat to a dictator because his enemies no longer stand in front of the palace, pitchforks in hand. But that doesn't mean that these enemies have vanished into thin air the moment a tyrant leaves the doors of the palace. The enemies are still around, potentially lurking behind every corner, waiting to pounce on their victim now that he is no longer on a pedestal, surrounded by soldiers armed with bayonets. Leaving power is going to release some pressure from the cooker, but it doesn't mean it can no longer explode. It always can. Resilience against pressure is not enough; resilience needs to be combined with strength, and that's a combination that few exile destinations can offer.

From the tyrant's perspective, the type of country to aim for is a place like Saudi Arabia. Governed by the same dynasty since it was unified by the House of Saud in 1932 and without civil wars ever since, it's remarkably stable – especially for a country ruled by an absolute monarch. It is also a huge oil producer with an estimated annual military expenditure in excess of $55 billion.[52] There's no freedom of speech, no free media and no real civil society in opposition to the government. While that doesn't make Riyadh invulnerable, it is certainly difficult to put pressure on from the outside. It has also demonstrated its suitability by 'successfully' hosting multiple deposed dictators in the past. And because its leaders change while the regime stays the same, drastic changes in policy are unlikely to happen quickly. If the father agrees to host a former dictator now, his son is probably not going to kick him out when it's his turn on the golden throne.

A central difficulty in all this is that tyrants have to persuade someone to take them in. And why would they be prepared to do that? Independent of regime type, there can be a number of reasons to provide exile to an ousted autocrat. The first is the use a government might derive from having said autocrat in their country – or, more generally, from keeping him alive. Perhaps said autocrat is well-connected in the country and the host government believes it can use that influence to its advantage. Or perhaps there's a chance that the tyrant will be able to stage a comeback, owing the host country a debt of gratitude once he's in power again. An example of despots returning to power after a period in exile is the Taliban, who actually had an office (at one point complete with flag) in Qatar.[53]

If a tyrant cannot play this card because a return to power looks highly unlikely, he has another card to play. Institutions and people have limited resources and attention. Every hour that they are busy thinking about a real or imagined bogeyman sitting in a place they can't control, they are distracted. That can be an advantage to another government, and it's potentially a way for the tyrant to make himself valuable.

Another strategy is to appeal to loyalty. When western troops hastily left Afghanistan in the summer of 2021, a great number of Afghans who had directly helped them – as translators, for example – were simply left behind. Without the protection of the Americans, Brits, Germans and so forth, they were now at the mercy of the very people they had sought to keep away from power. On a grand scale, and in public, this sent the message that western governments couldn't be trusted.

Providing exile for struggling national leaders who cooperated with other countries when they were in power can be all about sending the signal that such leaders will not be forgotten, even if the going gets tough. Loyalty aside, there's also a straightforward desire to avoid bloodshed. When dictators are in a situation in which they feel they have no other choice but to shoot to stay in power, they can appeal to outside powers to provide them with a 'Golden Parachute'. In the case of the Philippines, both of these elements came together. It was about loyalty to a cooperative leader who was now in trouble, but it was also about avoiding carnage.

On 30 June 2022, Ferdinand 'Bongbong' Marcos Jr got up onto the stage at the National Museum of Fine Arts in Manila. Newly sworn in as president of the Philippines, he told his people that he was not there to talk about the past. 'I am here to tell you about our future,' he said.[54] That was no coincidence. Thirty-six years earlier, his father Ferdinand Marcos had to make perhaps the most difficult decision of his long dictatorship. With masses of Filipinos in the streets and key figures of his regime defecting under popular pressure, he went on the phone to the American senator Paul Laxalt, a confidant of President Reagan.

It was the middle of the night and Marcos was scared. He couldn't sleep. 'Cut and cut cleanly. The time has come,' Laxalt told him. This was followed by a long pause. Eventually, the pause became so long that Laxalt asked Marcos whether he was still there. He was. 'I am so very, very disappointed,' Marcos said before hanging up.[55]

At 9.05 p.m., two American helicopters lifted off from near the Philippines presidential palace with Marcos and his entourage on board.[56] Direction: Clark Air Base, some sixty-four kilometres from Manila. From there, the dictator flew, via Guam, to Hawaii in a cold and noisy C141 transport aircraft.[57] Another aircraft flew the same route.

Aboard was more than his entourage – quite a lot more. We know exactly what he brought because it had to be recorded for customs. Given that Marcos officially earned no more than $13,500 a year, the twenty-three-page customs record surpasses belief. Among other things, the planes carried 140 jewel-studded cufflinks, two-dozen gold bricks and an ivory Jesus with a necklace made of diamonds; also, 27 million pesos, the Philippine's national currency. But even these ridiculous planes full of jewellery and gold only represent a tiny fraction of all the money Marcos stole from his people. According to a later estimate by the Supreme Court of the Philippines, Marcos may have stolen as much as 10 billion.[58] And that's American dollars, not Philippine pesos.

To democracies such as the United States, the question of

Golden Parachutes – granting exile to dictators – is a difficult one. On the one hand, exile for tyrants such as Marcos can significantly reduce the chance of bloodshed, thereby saving many innocent lives. On the other hand, the United States effectively helped Marcos steal yet more money from his nation after it had already contributed to keeping him in power for years. And was that really what Marcos deserved? Surely not. After all those years in power, stealing and mistreating his own people, the dictator should have been in front of a judge, not in a Hawaiian villa. But there's a trade-off here, as there always is: if outsiders don't help in that situation, a tired, scared and dangerous dictator has no way out that doesn't involve the killing of entirely innocent civilians. Chances are many more Filipinos would have died if those helicopters hadn't airlifted Marcos the elder to safety.

Over the last couple of decades, finding a safe place of exile has become even more difficult for tyrants. The reason for this is the International Criminal Court (ICC) and related advances in international justice. Situated in The Hague and operational since 2002, the idea behind the ICC is unquestionably a good one. In instances in which bad actors cannot be held accountable for their crimes by national courts, the international court may jump in and contribute some semblance of justice. The model has had some success. In 2012, for example, the court sentenced a Congolese warlord named Lubanga to fourteen years in jail for kidnapping children and then forcing them to fight. At the time of the trial, a prominent human rights NGO commented: 'Lubanga's sentence is important not only for the victims who want justice done, but also as a warning to those who use child soldiers around the world.'[59] It is a warning, and few would disagree that this is a good thing. If even one rebel commander or army general can be persuaded not to force a twelve-year-old to pick up a Kalashnikov because of the existence of the ICC, that's a victory.

But that victory doesn't come free. To the people who have used child soldiers or committed war crimes, the mere existence of the court and the threat of prosecution means that there is yet another reason to stay in power as long as possible – with all the bloody consequences that entails. Because even if tyrants manage not to 'disappear' or get killed by the person succeeding them, they might well disappear to the Netherlands (or County Durham, like Charles Taylor) where they will spend the rest of their life behind bars.

According to a study published in 2018, exile has drastically changed. It used to be that leaders who had presided over atrocities, and leaders who hadn't, went into exile at roughly the same rate. Now, with all the advances in international justice and states' reluctance to provide a Golden Parachute to the worst of the worst, the latter are 'about six times less likely to take the exile option'.[60]

That finding was published in an academic journal run by the Midwest Political Science Association so it might not have made its way to the world's presidential palaces, but dictators have undoubtedly taken note of the fact that things have changed. When Colonel Muammar Gaddafi of Libya found out that the Nigerian government had decided to hand over Taylor, he said: 'This means that every head of state could meet a similar fate. It sets a serious precedent.'[61] Robert Mugabe, the former dictator of Zimbabwe, was friends with Taylor. After seeing what had happened to him, he said there was only one way he would leave Zimbabwe: in a coffin.[62]

It was never easy to find a good exile destination to begin with, because of the constant threat of being killed or extradited. But now that the world has become smaller and the chances of being kicked out are higher, it's even more challenging. As a result, the only rational choice that some tyrants can make is to stay in power until they absolutely can stay no longer. If that means more killings and more thievery, that is what they will do.

Leaving the treadmill is technically possible, then, but the stakes are high and few are willing to take the gamble. Faced with the choice between running, reaching to pull the plug or trying to jump, most tyrants will choose to keep running. But as they're on that treadmill, the moving surface isn't all they have to worry about. As they move, they constantly have to watch their backs because the people closest to them usually pose the greatest danger.

2

The Enemy Within

You should also know that these enemies are here. They
are not to be found abroad. They are close to us and even
within our ranks.[1]

Hissène Habré, president of Chad

On the night of 28 June 1762, Catherine was asleep at
Monplaisir, a summer villa at Peterhof Palace. Sitting just
metres above the waters of the Gulf of Finland, it was a tranquil
retreat outside the hustle and bustle of imperial St Petersburg.[2]

Suddenly, a man stormed into Catherine's bedroom. 'The
time has come! You must get up and come with me!' the
soldier said. Not yet fully awake, a confused Catherine replied:
'What do you mean?' 'Passek is arrested,' he said.[3]

Catherine was now playing against time. Captain Passek
was in on her plot to overthrow her husband, Tsar Peter III
of Russia. If Passek were tortured, her involvement wouldn't
remain secret for long. And if she were to be found out, her
journey to the scaffold would follow swiftly.[4]

The last couple of years had been difficult for Catherine.
The tsar had long alienated his wife, and Catherine eventually
became convinced that he wanted to remove her and marry
his mistress Elizaveta. Peter insulted and humiliated his wife
in public.[5] He made drunken threats. He lied, deceived and
plotted. Catherine's life was in acute danger.

Months into his reign, Peter had antagonised just about every faction around the court that mattered. Many soldiers were upset because Peter was strangely pro-Prussian. His obsession with Frederick the Great, king of Prussia, was so intense that he forced his soldiers to dress like Prussians.[6] Whereas his predecessor had waged war against Prussia with Austria, one of Peter's first moves was to save Russia's enemy from certain defeat. He could have marched on Berlin but didn't. When Frederick offered him lands to stop the war, he refused to take them. Then, with his troops exhausted from a war from which they didn't seem to gain anything because Peter was unwilling to press Russia's advantage, he decided to prepare for war with Denmark because Denmark had control over Schleswig. That didn't really have anything to do with Russia, but, once again, it was one of Peter's strange obsessions.[7] As a result of these events, many of the soldiers were seething.

Unlike Peter, Catherine was exceptionally good at forging alliances with the powerful at court. From day one in Russia, the German princess had embraced the culture. She learned Russian and did her best to take Russian Orthodoxy seriously. She acted, as she put it, 'so the Russians should love me'.[8] And it's clear that many of those at court did, or at least they preferred her to Peter III. One of their courtiers commented: 'Sympathy for the empress grew in proportion to contempt for her husband.'[9]

Clothed in black, Catherine made her way to the barracks of the Izmailovsky Guards, who were tasked with protecting the royal family. At the barracks, the soldiers kissed her hands, feet and the hem of her dress.[10] After arriving at the Winter Palace, priests, senators and palace guards made it clear that they would support Catherine rather than her husband in the struggle for power.[11] But even with their support, the problem of what to do about her husband remained. Peter might be away from the capital, but he had access to thousands of troops.

When his wife's betrayal had first become apparent, Peter was distraught and confused. Should he try to negotiate? One of his generals advised him to march on St Petersburg.[12] With the military force he had at his command, he could crush his wife and her co-conspirators; he could then reclaim the throne that was rightfully his. But unlike his wife Catherine, Peter didn't have what it took. Instead of making the decisive move as counselled by his general, he dithered.

In St Petersburg, Catherine made the boldest move possible. After changing into the green uniform of the Imperial Guards, she mounted a white stallion and herself led her army to dispose of Peter.[13] In the end, the only thing she was willing to accept was unconditional abdication – in writing. It was the greatest possible humiliation for her husband.

Less than six months after being crowned emperor of Russia, Peter III was imprisoned at Ropsha, a castle some thirty kilometres southwest of St Petersburg. Less than a week after losing power, he died.

Power is relational. You can't be a leader if you don't have followers. But for tyrants, the number of people they must keep happy to stay in charge is small. At the same time, these are also the people most likely to bring them down. The data bear this out: between 1950 and 2012, 473 authoritarian leaders lost power. According to one analysis, 65 per cent of them were removed by regime insiders.[14] Often, the real danger isn't those who openly oppose the leader, but those who see him regularly, smiling while they plot their next move.

To understand how tyrants survive (and fall), think of people in the three groups outlined by Bruce Bueno de Mesquita and Alastair Smith in their *Dictator's Handbook*.[15]

First, there are the people who matter in theory – the group the leaders are supposed to win over to get control. Second, there are the people who actually matter – the group that leaders need to gain control. And third, there's an inner core, the smallest group that tyrants cannot rule without.

The people who matter in theory (called the 'nominal selectorate' by de Mesquita and Smith) have some say in whether a given leader, tyrant or not, gets to stay in power. In a liberal democracy such as the United States, it can be tens of millions of people since most people above the age of eighteen can vote in presidential elections.

The second group of people is the 'real selectorate'. The real selectorate consists of the group that *actually* determines who stays in power. In the United States, that group technically consists of the 538 electors of the Electoral College. Once the people have voted, their representatives choose the president. In modern practice, however, these electors take their mandate from the popular election and vote accordingly. At least that's how it's supposed to work.

This means that the de facto real selectorate consists of the much larger number of voters in a small number of 'swing states' (states where the voting could go either way) that regularly decide the outcome of presidential elections. In addition, there are the lobbyists, donors and other political players who can give you the resources you need to get a meaningful chance of trying to persuade the voters in swing states. To make this more concrete: a voter in Kansas, who is part of the nominal selectorate, is much less important than a voter in Wisconsin because Kansas always goes red (votes Republican) whereas Wisconsin does not. Votes in Wisconsin can make a real difference, whereas votes in Kansas only make a difference in theory. John from Kansas is part of the nominal selectorate, Joanna from Wisconsin is part of the real selectorate.

Then, you have the winning coalition. The winning coalition consists of the smallest number of people from the real selectorate that you need to assemble in order to take or maintain power. In the case of America, this would be the smallest number of voters in swing states needed to win the Electoral College.

The size of all these groups varies hugely depending on the system of government. Most dictators don't need to worry about electoral colleges; some don't even have to worry about voters. The more authoritarian the regime, the smaller these three groups tend to be. At Peter's court in eighteenth-century Russia, the real selectorate was tiny and so was the winning coalition. All it took for Catherine to topple her husband and get him thrown into jail were a small number of the Imperial Guard. Even back in 1762, the Russian Empire had an estimated population of more than 17 million.[16] And yet, losing the support of his wife and a few key military figures made all the difference between sitting on a throne and dying in a grimy dungeon.

It may seem as though the story of Peter and Catherine is a far cry from the dynamics of contemporary politics. The United States didn't exist then, industrialisation hadn't occurred and there was a grand total of zero liberal democracies in the world – but that doesn't mean the general mechanism of how a tyrant functions has ceased to apply. In highly authoritarian countries, the winning coalition can still consist of just a few hundred people. In these countries, the support of a core elite determines everything: if the tyrant can maintain the support of the winning coalition, he stays in power and stays alive. If he loses the winning coalition, he loses power – and perhaps more than that. And for everyone else who lives under these brutal regimes, having a better life means climbing from powerless peasant to someone who actually counts as part of the selectorate.

If they didn't already know this after decades of totalitarian rule, the North Korean regime taught this lesson to its people during the 1990s.[17]

North Korea is mountainous, its winters harsh, its agriculture precarious. Starting in the late 1950s, when much of North Korea lay in ruins as a result of the war with South Korea and its allies, farmers were forced to collectivise. This meant that instead of mostly farming for themselves, people now mostly farmed for the state. As a result, millions of people became totally dependent on the government since they could no longer buy food or grow it in meaningful quantities for themselves. Instead, the government decided who got what. This system only 'worked' to the extent that it did because both the Soviet Union and China provided significant support to North Korea during the Cold War. As the Soviet Union collapsed, China also reduced its support – partly because its own harvest didn't go as planned. It was a massive external shock. The Kim family could have reacted by expanding foreign trade or liberalising the collective system at home; they did neither. When floods hit in 1995, North Koreans were already experiencing famine. The system hadn't worked before the water came rushing in, but now it was totally destroyed.

For many ordinary North Koreans, the situation became so desperate that they began to eat trees. Ji Hyun-ah, who was seventeen at the time, describes what it was like.[18] To start with you had to find the right tree. It had to be pine, and finding it could involve going up mountains or down valleys. Once found, Ji had to chop the tree down, which wasn't an easy task for someone already weakened by hunger.

With the trees chopped, the children (or their parents) had to peel back the outer bark with a knife or a scythe. Beneath the outer bark lay what they called *songgi*, a thin inner layer that separates the outer bark from the wood of the tree. Once enough of the *songgi* had been collected (which was hard work), it then had to be boiled in lye, stretched out and soaked for a night. When all that was done, it had to be beaten with a club and combined with a little bit of corn flour to make a sort of cake. As Ji put it: 'It was barely edible, and having to do with that kind of food was terrible.'[19] For some Korean children, the situation was even more dire, because not even pinetree-bark cake was available regularly. For them, getting to eat the trees was like Christmas.[20] And yet, Ji recalls, 'it never occurred to us to blame North Korea's dictatorial government for our hardships.'[21]

But slowly, as the catastrophe unfolded and more North Koreans became malnourished before dying, the risk of that happening increased. To Kim Jong-il (the father of Kim Jong-un and son of North Korea's first leader, Kim Il-sung), this wasn't just a humanitarian problem, it rapidly became a question of whether the regime would survive. Instead of distributing the little food that was left according to need, it was distributed, at least partly, based on a subject's loyalty to the regime and the extent to which a person was needed to keep the Kims in power. In Pyongyang, where people really mattered to the dictatorship, the rations were comparatively large. Outside the capital, in less important areas of the countryside, countless people starved to death. That wasn't a coincidence. At times during the famine, the rations per person in Pyongyang were almost twice as high as those in some other provinces.[22] As political scientists Daniel Byman and Jennifer Lind have concluded: 'Kim Jong-il shielded his selectorate and concentrated the famine's devastation on the people deemed the least loyal.'[23] And for them, the effect was truly devastating. By some credible estimates, around 3 to 5 per cent of North Korea's pre-famine population died.[24]

Palace elites, whether they are high-ranking party officials, generals or oligarchs, can help or hinder the tyrant's aspirations. In the best-case scenario for the tyrant, a large segment of the elites believes that the continued rule of the dictator is in their own interest. When that is the case, they may not just acquiesce in his rule but act as a crutch during moments of turmoil. But the more likely scenario, and the one that all tyrants must fear, is one in which a significant portion of the real selectorate wants to see the dictator overthrown – either because they want power themselves or because they believe their interests will be better served under different leadership.

To the despot, managing the real selectorate and the country at large is so difficult because these regimes are notoriously opaque, not just to outsiders, but also to the dictator himself. This is known as the 'dictator's dilemma'.[25] To stay in power, the dictator creates a climate of perpetual fear. That fear silences critics, who don't dare to speak their minds. But because most keep silent, the dictator never knows what people – even his advisers – actually think. Is this person genuinely loyal or are they only pretending? Does he or she really support the government's ideology, or is it all theatre designed to buy time until they can stab the tyrant in the back? The tyrant cannot possibly know. He may be the most powerful person in the country, but he can never trust his subordinates to tell him the truth. Every decision a dictator makes, then, is made with information that has been filtered through a fog of fear.

These dynamics feel alien to most of us because we are able to speak our minds without worrying that it'll lead to our untimely deaths, or our families being tortured. An office worker telling their boss an unpleasant truth might lower their chances of promotion. They could even get fired. But who wouldn't lie to a dictator if the truth meant jail or death? In dictatorships, the truth can be deadly.

Most tyrants aren't stupid, so they understand that they don't receive the full picture. Under those circumstances, it's rational for tyrants to assume the worst about the people surrounding them.

But not all tyrants have the same difficulty in dealing with the enemy within because the coalition upon which leaders depend varies hugely. Political scientists Bueno de Mesquita and Alastair Smith have written:

> If a small bloc of backers is needed and it can be drawn from a large pool of potential supporters (as in the small coalition needed in places like Zimbabwe, North Korea, or Afghanistan), then the incumbent doesn't need to spend a huge proportion of the regime's revenue to buy the coalition's loyalty.[26]

Under those conditions, the price of elite 'loyalty' to the incumbent is low because there is plenty of supply. If the minister of the interior demands a larger cut of the money the regime steals from its people, the minister won't get a raise – instead, he will be replaced by one of the many other people who are 'qualified' and willing to do his job. But what de Mesquita and Smith described for Zimbabwe, North Korea and Afghanistan isn't true for all tyrannical regimes. Some incumbents need to work much harder to keep the money-making machine running because the pool from which they can recruit is significantly smaller.

Let's imagine the new head of a military junta. A year ago, he was a colonel worrying about his military role, but now he has seized power and needs to worry about his new role as dictator. He's done his first television broadcast to project authority and calm the nerves of the international community, and now has to get on with his new job. To a large extent, that will mean keeping fellow colonels happy because they are needed for him to stay in office. If the colonels feel as though they could improve their lot with someone else in charge, they will see to it that someone else will take charge. And once that person is in charge, their predecessor will be in immediate danger.

The problem with this situation, from the coup leader's perspective, is that it is difficult to replace people. There are plenty of soldiers, but not a lot of colonels – and he needs to surround himself with high-ranking military officers because privates don't have the experience or stature to help him lead the new government.

In democracies, voters are replaceable; you lose one, you can win back another. But in authoritarian regimes, the supply of elites that make up the real selectorate is finite. In monarchies, for example, there are only so many princes. Alienate one, and there may not be another to take his place. The same is true for many dictatorships. There are only so many generals and so many spy chiefs, and tyrants can't always replace the ones who turn against them. The result of this more limited replacement pool in military regimes or monarchies is that rulers need to work harder to keep the elites on their side. Their price, if you will, goes up. And as annoying as that might be from the tyrant's perspective, not paying is not really an option.

To pay this price, despots need money – lots of it, and that is quite apart from their own private funds, of course. In an ideal situation, tyrants want access to a source of wealth that doesn't depend on skilled labour. If it does, the tyrant depends on the goodwill of large numbers of people and that is a situation they generally want to avoid because it makes them vulnerable. In addition, having the money-machine depend on skilled labour means that money needs to be spent on educating people, which is a waste of money if the same money could also be spent on the things that really matter – such as buying off opponents or building golden statues of yourself that rotate with the sun.

It's no coincidence that many of the world's most vicious regimes have had access to oil, gas or diamonds. Not only is the extraction of these natural resources incredibly lucrative, it can still be done even if just about everybody surrounding the leader is incompetent. Extracting oil is an arduous, difficult process. To get it done, governments need to secure massive investments, besides having access to highly sophisticated technology and a whole lot of expertise. But – and here is the advantage for tyrants – large numbers of people are not required for this process and those who are come ready trained. The reason for this is that oil is such a lucrative commodity that leaders can simply sell an oil field to a foreign major which will take care of everything for them. The drilling? They'll get it done. The refining? They've got it. The shipping? Worry not. Because they know they'll make millions or billions, they'll be happy to take care of everything. In fact, the corporate CEO writing the cheque might even be happy that he's dealing with a tyrant rather than having the annoyance of legislatures, environmental groups or investigative journalists poking around. For tyrants it's the perfect set-up. Oil and dictatorship go hand in hand.

If the incompetence has gone too far or there is no oil to pay off the elites, the dictator has another tool to manage the selectorate: repression. Managing the selectorate is like sitting on top of a pit of ten-foot snakes – every wrong move could be the tyrant's last. Those monsters either have to be fed or they have to be kept down.

But purging, as it were, is as much an art as a science. It is a tough path to take. Tyrants want to move decisively and finish off their enemies instead of just weakening them a little, thereby leaving them in a position where they remain a danger and become radicalised. Niccolò Machiavelli, the Italian diplomat who wrote *The Prince* at the beginning of the sixteenth century, put it as follows:

> You must either pamper people or destroy them; harm them just a little and they'll hit back; harm them seriously and they won't be able to. So if you're going to do people harm, make sure you needn't worry about their reaction.[27]

So why even pay the elites at all, why not just eliminate everyone who presents a minor threat and beat them into submission instead of trying to keep them happy?

Not every despot can go straight to killing because the elites provide a restraint. A purge is, according to one definition, the removal of a member from the ruling coalition.[28] That can mean any number of things. It could be a demotion, it could be imprisonment, it could be forced exile, or execution. Clearly, none of these things are in the interest of the purge's victims but, crucially, such outcomes can be in the interest of the remaining elites.[29] However much money a dictatorship might generate through thievery and extortion, resources are finite. When some members of the elite are banished or killed, the same cake can be distributed differently, leading to others having a bigger slice – or at least, that's what they will expect. The result of this is that elites might not just accept purges but will actively push for them because it's a way for them to advance their position while taking out competitors. Same cake, fewer people.

But there's a tipping point due to what I call the 'Icarus Effect'. According to Greek mythology, Icarus escaped from his unfortunate situation by constructing wings. He was warned not to fly too close to the sea or to the sun, but his hubris led him astray. In the end, he came too close to the sun and his wings began to melt – leading him to fall and die. The situation of palace elites is similar. Initially, there might be excitement about getting a bigger slice of the cake. But at some point, hope for a bigger slice of the cake is outweighed by fear among the elites that they could also be purged. It's one thing if a few high-ranking officials disappear after they've been implicated in an assassination attempt. It's another if person after person is shot for no discernible reason at all. As the seats of the cabinet empty or new faces appear, panic will gradually rise. Sweaty ministers, scared of death, will switch from being supporters of the purge to becoming enemies of the tyrant. As it dawns on more of them that they could be victims of the killings, elites may recognise that they are coming too close to the sun.

As a result, they may try to move against the tyrant before it's too late. If they have an opportunity to coordinate with each other, the ruler runs the risk of creating a further attack on his rule through measures that he implemented in order to strengthen it. But even if despots find the right balance between the carrot and stick, the dictator's dilemma never really disappears. He simply cannot know for certain where his underlings stand.

There is one exception: moments of crisis. When the leader is under attack, for example during an attempted coup, he is able to see through the fog clearly for a brief moment. He sees not just who is genuinely loyal, but also who was merely pretending to be. What's more, he now knows how powerful he is in relation to his enemies. If he survives, he's stronger than them. If not, it's too late to do much about it, but at least he has some certainty.[30] This brief window of transparency is so attractive to leaders that some rulers have deliberately let plots against their regime unfold. Legend has it that Ranavalona I, the Merina queen of Madagascar, did just that. To the extent that Europeans cared about Madagascar at all, Ranavalona was at times portrayed as a savage who mistreated Christians while reversing the more 'enlightened' policies of her predecessor.[31]

That this story was put about was to be expected. The Merina queen's main objectives were the preservation of her power and the safeguarding of Madagascar's independence. Commentators from London or Paris wanted exactly the opposite. The island's neighbours were already under the control of colonisers, and with Madagascar's strategic location, there was money to be made by whoever was able to control it.

That said, there was no denying that Ranavalona I was an exceedingly cruel tyrant – and not just to outsiders but also the indigenous population too. Most infamously, she forced scores of people into a trial by ordeal which involved eating the poisonous seeds of the tangena tree. People were at liberty to accuse each other of being guilty of something – as the queen often did. To prove their 'innocence', the accused had to eat the tree's seeds and stay alive. Those that died were, by definition, guilty. The 'sea mangos', as they are also called, contain cerberin, a type of cardiac glycoside. When a doctor prescribes a cardiac glycoside to a patient with a weak heart, their heart beats slower but stronger. Eating the nuts of the tangena tree initially does the same. But at some point, the poison overwhelms the heart, causing it to beat erratically and way too fast. If left untreated, the heart stops pumping blood altogether. Queen Ranavalona didn't invent the trial by ordeal, but under her reign it peaked. Hundreds of thousands of Malagasies might have died from it while she was on the throne.[32]

In 1855, the queen's place on Madagascar's throne was in danger when a Frenchman named Joseph-François Lambert did a deal with Prince Rakoto, Queen Ranavalona's son and heir. Upon Rakoto's accession to the throne, Lambert would get the right to exploit Madagascar's ample untapped natural resources.[33] Although that was obviously fantastic for the Frenchman, it was terrible for Madagascar, and most of all for the reigning sovereign, particularly so since the deal was only going to come to fruition in the event of Queen Ranavalona being deposed. Initially, Lambert hoped that the French government would take care of this problem for him and get rid of her.[34] It didn't, so Lambert set out to plan a coup.

What happened next is subject to debate. According to one version, the coup ultimately failed because the commander in charge of protecting the palace failed to ensure that the palace guard on the night it was supposed to happen were (dis)loyal to the cause.[35] In another version, the whole thing was a masterclass in deception that involved not just Queen Ranavalona but also Rakoto.[36] According to this version, the queen found out that her power and the nation's independence were endangered, but instead of striking at the first opportunity, she let the plot unfold as long as she could in order to obtain more information on those who had betrayed her.

It goes without saying that this is a high-risk strategy that most rulers don't want to attempt. As a result, they remain in the dark, not knowing who at court stands with them and who is just waiting to attack. That leaves them with a choice: do they prioritise competence or loyalty? Given the stakes, it's rational to surround oneself with sycophants – even if they're stupid or incompetent. In dictatorships, loyalty is paramount. After all, competence can be dangerous. If advisors and officials are too good at their jobs, they might tire of being told what to do and start plotting to take power for themselves. That's why most dictators pick loyalists who don't have any other options. Being dependent on the tyrant breeds loyalty, and loyalty breeds trust.

But, as with all decisions related to regime survival, there is a trade-off. As dictators promote incompetent officials because they seem loyal, the top ranks of government become staffed by people who really shouldn't be anywhere near power. Over time, this becomes a serious problem because even the rulers of highly centralised systems of government must create some positive outcomes for enough people in order to maintain power. Have you ever heard someone say that you should always aim not to be the cleverest person in the room because that allows you to learn? This is the opposite of that. Surrounding himself with incompetent sycophants because they present less of a danger results in a tyrant being the cleverest person in every room by his own design.

Such sycophants are likely to tell the dictator what he wants to hear because, over time, dictators purge the people who tell them unpleasant truths while rewarding those who lie to please. The result of this is a trap that tyrants set for themselves: as their view of reality becomes more distorted due to their own decisions, they become more likely to make catastrophic mistakes based on a version of events that was never real.[37]

There can also be a structural element to this. If the number one priority is security (for the regime, not the population at large), the tyrant is going to spend much of the day surrounded by the people that live in that world: intelligence operatives, military officers, police. These people, in turn, are trained and paid to think about threats all day every day. If you look at Russian President Vladimir Putin, for example, there's a clear trajectory. Initially, he surrounded himself with technocrats who took a serious interest in the well-being of the economy. Before advising the president, they might have been bankers or managers.

Over time, the influence of this group waned while the influence of the *siloviki* increased.[38] The *siloviki* are the men of force. They are people such as Sergei Naryshkin, head of the country's foreign intelligence service;[39] or Alexander Bortnikov, in charge of one of the successors to the infamous Soviet KGB. Naryshkin and Bortnikov have a way of looking at the world that is influenced by their profession. Having spent decades in the world of shadows where everyone and everything is a potential threat, they have a certain way of thinking that rubs off on the man that listens to them.

In 2014, for example, when President Viktor Yanukovych wanted to flee Ukraine, Putin had a decision to make. Would he help? Or would he let Yanukovych face justice in Ukraine, where his government had been responsible for the death of scores of protestors? Whatever path the Russian government took could have massive repercussions for Russia's foreign policy. It was a political, economic and military problem. To make a decision, President Putin convened an all-night meeting that was to last until 7 the following morning. But instead of trying to understand the problem from multiple angles, the people he listened to were soldiers and spies – *siloviki*. As the meeting came to an end, Putin declared: 'We must start working on returning Crimea to Russia.'[40]

The result of this over-reliance on the *siloviki* is a feedback loop that the political scientists Seva Gunitsky and Adam Casey have described as follows:

The President's advisers uniformly see the West as a grave security threat to Russia, which encourages Putin to adopt an increasingly hostile stance. This in turn provokes the United States and Europe to confront Russia, which only increases the influence of Putin's hawks by justifying their pessimistic and often paranoid outlook. Partly as a result, Russian foreign policy has grown more belligerent over time.[41]

Broken people become tyrants, and then tyranny can break them further. Many dictators come to office with experiences that profoundly distort their view of reality. Take Kim Jong-un. He lived his childhood like a character in *The Truman Show*, where the entire world was constructed for him.

The estate of the supreme leader was so large that the children would regularly move around on a golf cart.[42] There were private chefs, gardeners and tutors who catered for every need. One thing that the young Kim really enjoyed was playing with toy planes and ships.[43] He would spend hours at it. And if he had a problem, whatever the time of day or night, he would summon a nautical engineer to help him out. And that nautical engineer would have no choice but to come.[44]

When he was just eight years old, the heir 'wore a general's uniform with stars, and the real generals with real stars bowed to him and paid their respects to the boy'. If the family's then private chef is to be believed, Kim also started to carry a Colt .45 pistol when he was eleven.[45] One journalist remarked in a magazine feature on Kim that it's true of most of us that, as children, we are at the centre of the universe but this changes as we get older. For Kim, it never did. Everything in his surroundings continued to revolve around him.[46]

It doesn't take a psychologist to see that dictatorships aren't conducive to a healthy mind. Most obviously, that's true for the dictator himself – but it's also the case for the average person in the street.

Living under tyranny is inherently stressful. Ordinary people have to watch what they say because saying the wrong thing could have severe consequences. Even if they themselves aren't subject to repression, people around them might be. And when the situation becomes so overwhelming that it requires medical treatment, those unlucky enough to live in non-democratic systems of government might not even be able to trust doctors. Throughout the last century, more than one tyrannical regime used the psychiatric care system to deal with its enemies.

Unlike most (although not all) other forms of medical treatment, psychiatric intervention can be ordered against a patient's will in liberal democracies. But in democracies, drastic measures, such as committing a patient to a psychiatric hospital, are only administered under tightly defined conditions – usually when a patient is a danger to himself or others. In the Soviet Union, in contrast, psychiatrists – themselves afraid or a part of the regime – regularly committed healthy people to mental hospitals.

At the top, where elites and the tyrant dance for power and enrichment opportunities, there's no tranquillity either. The dictator's dilemma means that everyone around the dictator is a potential source of danger.

Psychologically, that can be immensely taxing and as a result, many have attempted to diagnose the mental state of tyrants. Doing so is difficult because few of them are willing to sit down with healthcare professionals – but that hasn't stopped psychologists from trying. Given the extent to which some individual dictators have shaped the world, that's unsurprising. How do you understand what happened in Gaddafi's Libya, for example, without an understanding of Gaddafi's brain? It's impossible. But also, understanding the mental state of a tyrant can help to predict their behaviour. How does he react under pressure? If cornered, is he likely to lash out or make concessions? Does he suffer from any mental illnesses that shape how he governs?

Given the structure of these regimes, 'suffer' might not be the right word. To an extent, an abnormal mind can come in handy when running a dictatorship or a kingdom. Dictators are faced with an abnormal environment in which they have to take abnormal decisions with some frequency. If a healthy person from a normal environment were to wake up as a dictator, they probably wouldn't last long. Staying in power in such a hostile environment for years or even decades requires an element of paranoia: some of those threats will be real. And how does a 'normal' person sleep after ordering the death of a person they had a totally normal conversation with a day or two before?

Dr Jerrold Post, born in Connecticut in 1934, was a prominent psychologist who analysed the minds of dictators. He spent most of his working life advising the Central Intelligence Agency (CIA) and various other parts of the United States government, and one leader he studied particularly closely was Iraqi dictator Saddam Hussein. In his 1991 profile of Hussein, he wrote:

> Saddam's pursuit of power for himself and Iraq is boundless. In fact, in his mind, the destiny of Saddam and Iraq are one and indistinguishable . . . In pursuit of his messianic

dreams, there is no evidence he is constrained by conscience; his only loyalty is to Saddam Hussein. When there is an obstacle in his revolutionary path, Saddam eliminates it, whether it is a previously loyal subordinate or a previously supportive country.[47]

Dr Post believed Saddam Hussein was a 'malignant narcissist'. A severe form of narcissistic personality disorder, this state can be described as follows:

Like classic narcissists, malignant narcissists are grandiose, self-centered, oversensitive to criticism and unable to feel empathy for others. They cover over deep insecurities with an inflated self-image. But malignant narcissists also tend to paranoia and aggression, and share some features of the antisocial personality, including the absence of moral or ethical judgement.[48]

In an ordinary job, all this could be a massive hindrance. But to 'succeed' as a tyrant, it can be of help.

But here's the thing: there's a limit. A certain amount of mental illness can be helpful, but it becomes dangerous to the tyrant's rule if it becomes so extreme that the dictator loses all touch with reality. With Saddam Hussein, that wasn't the case. As Dr Post told the House Armed Services Committee:

Saddam has no wish to be a martyr, and survival is his number one priority. A self-proclaimed revolutionary pragmatist, he does not wish a conflict in which Iraq will be grievously damaged and his stature as a leader destroyed . . . Saddam will not go down to the last flaming bunker if he has a way out, but he can be extremely dangerous and will stop at nothing if he is backed into a corner.[49]

Saddam was not psychotic, and his ultimate aim of survival never changed. When either of these circumstances change for a tyrant, a speedy fall becomes much more likely.

That becomes clear when considering the case of Francisco Macías Nguema. After coming to power in the newly independent Equatorial Guinea in 1968, Nguema got to work. The first person to feel his power was Ondu Edo.[50] Edo, who had fled into exile after losing the presidential elections against Nguema, was reluctant to come back, because he feared that he might not be safe if he did. Nguema promised that nothing would happen to him. Edo made the mistake of believing him.[51]

As he consolidated control over the tiny country, almost the entire population began to suffer. Unlike in some neighbouring countries at the time, Equatorial Guinea actually had functioning electricity lines, but utility companies now ceased to provide electricity.[52] As migrant workers from neighbouring Nigeria were increasingly mistreated, they left the country – leading Nguema to institute a system of compulsory labour.[53] Feeling insecure about his lack of education, Nguema went as far as to ban the word 'intellectual'.[54] The situation became so dire that an estimated two-thirds of Equatorial Guinea's population fled the country.

But nobody in the country was treated worse than Nguema's political enemies. In the country's notorious prisons, they were classified 'Category A', the punishment for which came close to a death sentence.

One of those prisoners was Pedro Ekong Andeme, who became Equatorial Guinea's health minister in 1968, when he was just twenty-seven years old. Ordinarily, that would be a cause for celebration. A minister! At such a young age. But in the case of Ekong, it became a nightmare. In 1971, he was sent to prison in Malabo. Confined to a tiny cell, he wasn't even allowed clothing. He was naked, forced to sleep on the barren concrete floor. Then there was the torture. 'Each Saturday morning, every political prisoner including myself received 150 strokes with a metal rod,' he recounted.[55]

When he wasn't tortured himself, he could hear the other prisoners being beaten. It haunted him, but worst of all was when the pain turned to silence. 'Their screams stopped when their backs were broken.' Whenever that happened and a prisoner had been killed, Ekong scratched a mark into the concrete of his cell. By the time he was released, broken but alive, the marks totalled 157.[56]

Nguema instinctively understood that those closest to him were the biggest threat to his impunity, and that made it extremely dangerous to be around him. Most of the forty-six persons who had been part of the independence negotiations with Spain were killed. Of Nguema's first cabinet of twelve ministers, only two survived. 'In politics,' the dictator reportedly used to say, 'the victor wins and the loser dies.'[57]

For a while, this ruthlessness allowed Nguema to stay in power, and more than that, consolidate it. But he had a weakness: his mental health.

It may well be that Nguema said 'the only madness I have shown has been the madness for freedom,' but he genuinely was a sick man. And having once seen a psychiatrist on a trip abroad, he probably knew as much.[58] Unfortunately for his fellow Equatorial Guineans, he couldn't get his affliction treated while he was at home because there weren't any suitable doctors: they had all either been killed or fled abroad.[59]

Health issues, of course, are always difficult to deal with, and for tyrants, who must project an image of invincibility in order to stay in power, especially so. If they appear physically weak, opponents and regime supporters change their calculus. Enemies will think of it as an opening, a chance to step up.

Supporters will stand back and ask themselves whether their 'loyalty' is still worth extending to the incumbent. If this particular leader is no longer going to be around in a few years' time because the prognosis isn't promising, should they perhaps bet on a different horse? Or even stake a claim themselves?

As Bruce Bueno de Mesquita and Alastair Smith have written, 'no leader can commit to reward supporters from beyond the grave.'[60] The diagnosis of something serious such as heart disease can make the situation vastly more difficult for the dictator because it alerts elites to the fact that the leader is operating on a clock – one perhaps that ticks faster every hour. There's a decent chance that a tyrant will fall quicker than his heart will stop beating.

Nguema's struggles with mental health weren't of this order, because they weren't going to kill him – at least not directly. His intense paranoia became integral to the issue of survival (both of the regime and himself) because it meant he was disconnected from reality.

In the capital, a wall about four metres high was built around the old inner part of the city to protect the presidential palace. Houses that fell within the area were simply dislodged.[61] But despite all these efforts, Malabo still wasn't safe enough for Nguema. He no longer slept in the palace and hadn't done so for more than four years. Even daytime visits to the capital were rare.[62] Instead, he spent most of his time at a specially constructed compound in his home village where much of the national reserves of Equatorial Guinea were kept – in cash – in a wooden hut.[63]

Theoretically, this should have made Nguema feel safer, but Nguema's condition didn't improve. At his compound, he would walk about while crying out the names of the people he had killed.[64] In one particularly disturbing episode, Nguema asked his servants to lay the table for eight guests.[65]

But nobody arrived. Nguema, clearly in urgent need of treatment, talked to his 'guests' as if they were there – but he was all alone.[66] It's not just that Nguema saw threats where there were none, he literally saw people who weren't even alive. He was psychotic, having lost touch with reality. Under those circumstances, he lashed out, killing at random. With the killings now unrelated to whether subjects were loyal to him or not, Guinea's elites no longer had an incentive to stay by his side. It was the Icarus Effect at work, not because Nguema had miscalculated, but because he was no longer capable of doing any calculations at all.

The final straw came when a group of militia leaders travelled to his compound. Their request was mild: they simply wanted some money to pay their fighters. But since Nguema was unable to distinguish between friend and foe, he had all of them killed. Unfortunately for Nguema, one of them was related to Teodoro Obiang, Nguema's nephew and the country's deputy minister of defence.[67] With his brother killed, Obiang decided enough was enough. So many had been killed for no reason at all. What guarantee did he have that he wouldn't be next? None.

Obiang decided to act, and his first move was to go to some of the country's most notorious prisons to free men who had long suffered under Nguema's rule. Then, with men eager for revenge, they fought Nguema loyalists – and won. Nguema himself was able to flee into the jungle for a while, but he was eventually found. After a brief trial in an old cinema, he was shot dead.

The enemy within is the most immediate threat to every tyrant. To survive in power, the tyrant needs to take good care of it. That means channelling money to the rich and powerful to keep them on the tyrant's side. When that doesn't do the trick, the tyrant can try to resort to violence to keep court elites in line. That's a dangerous game and finding the right combination of carrot and stick is exceedingly difficult. While all elites matter insofar as they have an influence on the leader's ability to maintain power, one group stands out among the rest: the men with guns. In the next chapter, we will discover why they matter so much and why they are even more difficult to control than everyone else.

3

Weakening the Warriors

With a single stroke the Revolution has lightened the long
dark night of this reactionary and decadent regime, which
was no more than a hotbed of extortion, faction, treachery
and treason.[1]

Muammar Gaddafi

Papa Faal had made it. Well, not quite – but at least he was
safe. Before dawn broke the previous day, he had been in a
wooded area of Banjul, putting on military gear and getting
ready to launch a coup against the Gambian dictator Yahya
Jammeh.[2] Now he was at the United States Embassy in neighbouring Senegal, eating pizza and telling an FBI agent what
had just happened. 'You know this is a crime, right?' the agent
asked. Papa Faal and his co-conspirators had become some of
the most unlikely instigators of a coup in modern history.[3]

The Gambia is a tiny country in West Africa. Geographically
it appears as little more than a river, with narrow banks on
either side. Senegal engulfs it to the north, east and south. To
the west lies the Atlantic Ocean. When the attempt at a coup
occurred on New Year's Eve 2014, Yahya Jammeh had been
the country's dictator for two decades, based in the capital,
Banjul. In this time, he had pledged to rule for a billion years
and claimed the ability to cure AIDS with his hands. He also
turned the Gambia into a state of fear. Gambians, whether

they had stepped out of line or not, had to worry about the National Intelligence Agency, the Gambian Police Force and Jammeh's 'Jungulers'. Recruited mostly from his Presidential Guard, the unit was responsible for many of the regime's worst crimes. Some Gambians had to endure mock executions or being beaten with metal pipes. 'Sometimes,' a former Junguler told Human Rights Watch, 'they burn plastic bags and drop the burning plastic on the bodies.'[4] Jammeh was a brutal megalomaniac and, like all brutal megalomaniacs, he had created enemies within.

The plot to unseat him began when Banka Manneh, an American-Gambian activist, met Colonel Lamin Sanneh in Dakar. 'There is something I have in mind,' Sanneh told Manneh before they exchanged numbers. Before the regime had expelled him after he refused to fire subordinates without cause, Sanneh had been a high-ranking soldier in Jammeh's guard. The two of them regularly spent time together, sometimes joking over green tea.[5] Now that he was banished from the country, Sanneh told Manneh, he was determined to topple Jammeh – through force, if need be.

Coups pose a serious threat to many dictators because the men with guns have an advantage when it comes to violence. Palace elites may be masters of intrigue, but soldiers have the skills to topple tyrants in the blink of an eye. When it comes to preventing that, tyrants face a Catch-22. To protect the regime from foreign threats and rebels, they need a strong military. But if they empower the military, then the generals and soldiers may become powerful enough to topple the dictator. A weak military can create threats from the outside; a strong military can create threats from within. Some small countries deal with this dilemma by abolishing their military, but that's not a viable option for most countries. And it certainly was not for Yahya Jammeh.

Banka was at a crossroads. He had been a peaceful human rights activist, organising protests and raising money for the opposition in the Gambia. The idea had always been that the dictatorship could be toppled peacefully. Did he still believe that was a possibility? If not, where would he go from here? Would he be willing to compromise his core values and support violence? It was a big decision. Sanneh tried to persuade him that a coup was the right move. 'This is not a joke. You know you are talking about people getting killed, right?' Manneh asked him. 'Yeah,' Sanneh replied. 'Some people will die.'[6]

When I talked to Banka Manneh, he told me that he had changed his mind when things in the Gambia went from bad to worse. 'Everyday you are getting a report of somebody getting tortured or killed,' he said.[7]

Indeed, the situation in the country was dire. Opponents of the regime were arrested arbitrarily, and dissent was repressed at all levels. In one particularly disturbing episode in 2012, the regime had nine death row prisoners executed shortly after the end of Ramadan.[8] When an imam spoke out against it, he was tortured. And he wasn't the only one: according to Amnesty International, the human rights organisation, torture had become routine.[9]

Eventually, Manneh came to justify the coup to himself with reference to John F. Kennedy, who had once said that you make violent revolution inevitable when you make peaceful revolution impossible.[10] In his mind, the violent revolution meant a coup. Manneh knew he wouldn't be able to take part in the coup itself because he was already known in the Gambia for his activism, but having made his choice, he now became a major part in organising it.[11]

In some ways, the planning was detailed and thorough; in other ways, totally chaotic. To coordinate it, there were regular telephone conferences for which the participants had to find excuses because they clearly couldn't tell their families that they were working out how exactly they would over- throw a government.[12] The conspiracy was serious, but the plotters were amateurs. Many of them had trained in the military forces of the Gambia or the United States, but they were now mostly middle-aged men leading ordinary lives; they had families, normal jobs. Banka Manneh, for example, planned part of the overthrow while on breaks from his job in construction.[13] Obviously, they had never overthrown a government before. Some of them had started to conspire together after they grew close while playing the online Scrabble game 'Words with Friends'.[14]

One of the conspirators had a manila folder with the words 'Top Secret' on it with annotated satellite images of the presi- dential compound.[15] To keep track of the budget ($220,798), there was a detailed spreadsheet, noting every detail down to the unit costs of vehicle rentals. Every item had explanatory notes. For two Barrett .50-calibre sniper rifles, it reads 'NOT really necessary but could be very useful'.[16] Many of the guns were bought by Manneh – peaceful activist now turned inter- national arms smuggler – who sent assault rifles hidden in barrels across the Atlantic.

The group was confident. They didn't just have the satel- lite images and the spreadsheets; they also had inside informa- tion. Because the group, now called the Gambia Freedom League, included someone who had guarded the dictator, they knew how Jammeh was protected.[17] Certain of their success, they had even drafted a plan for the Gambia's post- coup future, titled: 'Gambia Reborn: A Charter for Transition from Dictatorship to Democracy and Development'.[18]

In the middle of the night of 30 December 2014, Lamin Sanneh, Papa Faal and six other men were standing in a graveyard near Gambia's State House, the equivalent of the country's presidential palace.[19] There was a moon, but it was still dark. After putting on their protective vests and going over the plan one final time, they prayed together. In a low voice so as not to be heard, they all said: 'Let's go take our country back.'[20]

The plan was simple. The men were divided into two groups, Team Alpha and Team Bravo. Team Alpha, headed by Sanneh, would crash through the front door of the compound and take control of the State House after disarming the guards. Team Bravo, headed by Papa Faal, would secure the rear of the compound.[21] Once the attack started, insiders at the State House sympathetic to the coup would join the plot.

Sanneh and his team got into their hired car, driving towards the front of the compound with their headlights off.[22] As soon as they got close to the first guard post, all but one of the men got out of the car. One of the group pointed his weapon towards two terrified guards. 'We're not going to kill you,' he said. 'Drop your guns.'[23] The guards did so. With the good news radioed to Team Bravo on the other side of the compound, the car set off again, ramming through multiple barriers. Thus far, they had succeeded.

But then, Team Alpha was spotted advancing towards the core of the compound by a guard watching from a tower. He fired. After an attempt to talk him down failed, another round was fired, hitting Sanneh. He dropped to the floor. Another member of Team Alpha tried to drag him into safety, but Sanneh was heavy and the bullets kept flying. To save himself, he had to abort, leaving Sanneh behind.

Alerted by the gunfire, the guards on the other side of the compound took aim at Team Bravo. Using one of the .50-calibre rifles that had been deemed 'optional but useful', Papa Faal fired back, but in the darkness and without night-vision goggles, he wasn't quite sure where to aim. The operation was unravelling quickly. When a member of Team Bravo was killed, they tried to alert Team Alpha, but there was no answer; just static.[24]

By the time the sun came up in Banjul, it was clear to everyone that Gambia wasn't to be reborn. The coup had failed miserably. Despite their official-looking Top Secret folder and months of planning, the conspirators had failed to lay the basic groundwork for the coup. They had fewer than a dozen fighters and insufficient equipment with which to attack a fortified compound in the dark. The insiders who it was thought would join the coup never materialised. But most of all, the entire plan hinged on the idea that Jammeh's protectors, sworn to defend him with their life, would switch sides and join the coup.

'They didn't stand a chance,' Manneh told me. He explained that Jammeh's defenders owed everything to the dictator because they were 'created' by Jammeh.[25] They had been nobody and now they were somebody. Those guards were not going to give up their cushy position when a ragtag group of unknown men arrived with guns.

For the conspirators, the consequences were severe. Out of the eight men who swore to take back their country in a Banjul graveyard, three were shot. And that was just the beginning: in the wave of repression that followed in the Gambia, Jammeh's regime began imprisoning the men's family members who had nothing to do with the attack. Sanneh's elderly mother was put in jail without so much as a charge. The regime's thugs showed up at the school of one of the plotter's daughters. She was seven.

Banka Manneh was 'lucky'. Shortly after the coup, Banka, his wife, two children, mother and mother-in-law were asleep in their house in Georgia.[26] At around 4 o'clock in the morning, armed FBI agents stormed the house to take him into custody.

Manneh was sentenced to six months in a medium-security prison for his role in procuring and sending the weapons. He had also broken something called the Neutrality Act.[27] The act, first passed in 1794, was originally intended to prevent Americans from attacking any prince, state or people 'with whom the United States is at peace'. It was now being used to punish Banka Manneh for trying to overthrow a vicious dictator.[28]

American prison wasn't great – but as punishments for planning a coup against a dictator go, it was comparatively mild.

Jammeh was lucky the coup wasn't better organised. If it had been, he could have been in serious trouble. Other dictators can't bank on incompetence, so they need a strategy to manage the threat. That strategy is divide and weaken. If the tyrant doesn't become active, he can easily fall the moment a general decides he'd rather be in charge. And, almost inevitably, that day will come.

Coups are often defined as 'illegal and overt attempts by the military or other elites within the state apparatus to unseat the sitting executive'.[29] Whatever definition is used, the threat of coups is something all chieftains, kings, sultans and supreme leaders have had to deal with since humans agreed on rules to choose leaders. Even the Bible mentions a military coup of sorts. In the Old Testament, Elah, the fourth king of Israel, is toppled by Zimri, the commander of half of his own chariots. Not content with killing his king while he was drunk, Zimri then slaughtered Elah's entire household. According to the First Book of Kings nobody survived – 'neither of his kinsfolks, nor of his friends'.[30] In the end, Zimri's reign became the shortest ever on a biblical throne.[31] It ended seven days after it started when Omri, another one of Elah's old commanders, besieged the city from which Zimri had ruled, leading Zimri to commit suicide by burning down his own palace.[32]

To get a broader picture, political scientists Jonathan Powell and Clayton Thyne analysed 457 coup attempts over six decades. According to their research, around half of the coup attempts were successful. The distribution of the coup attempts was uneven. In all that time, Europe had only twelve coups, while Africa had 169, more than fourteen times as many. In terms of timing, the coups peaked in the mid-1960s.[33] That was no chance occurrence. During the Cold War, when both sides thought they were engaged in a mortal struggle over control of huge swathes of the world, they sometimes supported challengers to take out disliked incumbents. Coups are generally frowned upon, but that was not the case back then – at least not to the same degree. In addition, many newly independent post-colonial governments weren't stable – in large part because colonial powers had deliberately designed them not to be.

But while fewer coups have occurred since the end of the Cold War, it hasn't escaped the notice of the world's most oppressive rulers that it's their own soldiers who usually present the strongest threat to an early 'retirement'. The 'success rate' of coups even started to increase in the early 2000s, after decreasing towards the end of the Cold War.[34] Indeed, there were coups in Gabon, Niger, Burkina Faso and Mali in the early 2020s. In the case of Mali, it was the third coup in less than a decade.

To understand why it's so difficult to deal with the threat of coups, we must first understand how they work. Coups succeed by creating an impression of inevitability – which is precisely the thing the Gambian conspirators in Banjul failed to do. When they arrived at the presidential palace, they appeared weak.

The mechanisms around coups are easiest to understand if we imagine a simplified attempt involving three groups. The first group are those who carry out the coup. These armed men have got together to overthrow the incumbent through force. Usually, they are a part of the military, but they can also be former soldiers or even mercenaries. Why they do what they do can vary hugely. Most perpetrators of a coup want to bring down a regime for one of three reasons: power, to right a perceived injustice, or money.

At the extreme end of this, there's Simon Mann, an Eton-educated Brit who had spent time in the elite Special Air Service (SAS) after cutting his teeth in counter-insurgency campaigns in Northern Ireland. Mann had a plan to take arms and fighters from Zimbabwe to Equatorial Guinea. There, they would be met by an advance party that had already been on the ground for a while. They would then try to draw out the country's president, Teodoro Obiang, to arrest or kill him. With him out of the way, the country's exiled opposition leader, Severo Moto, would become president.[35] On the face of it, that was a pretty crazy plan. But if someone was going to try it, that someone was Mann. Having founded and worked for his own private military company (PMC), he had relevant experience and the network needed to finance, plan and execute the overthrow of a government.

Teodoro Obiang took control of Equatorial Guinea when he overthrew his uncle Macías Nguema in 1979, creating a highly repressive regime in this country of some 1.6 million people. Obiang is the world's longest-serving, non-monarchical head of state (serving being the right word only insofar as he has served himself). He has managed to stay in power for so long by harassing, imprisoning, torturing and killing his opponents. There's no free media, there are no free elections and while there is an 'opposition' party, it's controlled by the government. In 2002, two years before Mann's attempted coup, President Obiang was 're-elected' with more than 97 per cent of the vote.[36]

But, despite assurances to the contrary, that might not have been too interesting to Mann. What was definitely of interest was the discovery of large oil reserves in Equatorial Guinea in 1996.[37] In 1995, the size of the country's economy divided by its population stood at $1,578. In 2008, it was $35,689 – higher than that of South Korea and close to twice as high as Mexico's.[38] Thanks to that oil, the dictator and his thugs became fabulously rich and Mann hoped to follow in their footsteps. In return for overthrowing him, Mann and his international 'investors' expected millions in cash and access to extremely lucrative oil concessions.

In his autobiography, Mann later wrote: 'I knew I would either make billions or end up getting shot.'[39] Before he could find out which it would be, Mann and his co-conspirators had to recruit the type of men that could be used to over-throw a foreign dictator. Many of them were veterans of the Buffalo Battalion, which meant they had experience of fight-ing a brutal counter-insurgency campaign in Angola on behalf of apartheid South Africa.[40]

When the men flew from Polokwane in South Africa to Harare in Zimbabwe, the 'official' story would be that they were on their way to provide mining security in the Democratic Republic of Congo. But when Mann and the sixty-seven other mercenaries were about to depart Harare International Airport in their Boeing 727 full of military equipment, there was a sense that something was wrong. 'Be calm, it's OK,' Mann said to relax his men. Some believed him and fell asleep. They were woken by a loudspeaker outside the plane: 'You're surrounded.'[41]

All of them were arrested by the Zimbabwean authorities.[42] After serving four years in a Harare jail, Mann was transferred (or kidnapped, as he put it) and incarcerated in Equatorial Guinea's notorious Black Beach Prison.[43] He was sentenced to thirty-four years.[44] When he talked to a British media outlet four years after the ill-fated coup attempt, his wrists and ankles were shackled.[45] 'You know, you go tiger shooting and you sort of don't expect the tiger to win,' Mann said.

But when you go hunting tiger, the world's intelligence agencies usually don't pay attention. It's different when you plan a coup, certainly if the government you're targeting controls vast oil deposits. And since the whole plot was reportedly discussed in restaurants and bars in both London and Cape Town, more than one interested party knew what was planned. The Mugabe regime in Zimbabwe obviously knew. But the British government also knew of the plot – including timelines, arms shipments and who was involved – months before it took place.[46] It's impossible to know whether the attack could have succeeded had the mercenaries made it to Equatorial Guinea undetected, but as it was the coup was doomed before it even began.

Whether the motivation is deposing an unjust ruler or making money, those plotting a coup need to believe that they can succeed. If they don't, they won't take the risk because a failed attempt at overthrowing tyrants will almost certainly have severe consequences. As one American study found recently, more than 60 per cent of such conspirators get executed or imprisoned.[47] They get shot, they get tortured. Mann was eventually released from prison before his sentence was up, but his experience probably wasn't pleasant.

At the other end of the coup, there's the incumbent and his closest allies. Naturally, they want to remain in power – not just because being in power brings all sorts of perks in authoritarian regimes, but also because they have a long way to fall should the coup-plotters succeed.

Both of these groups tend to be small: the former, because recruiting a large group of co-conspirators to participate in a coup is risky. Finding ten people to keep their mouths shut about overthrowing a government might be possible, but finding a hundred? Good luck.

And the latter are small, because authoritarian regimes tend towards a concentration of power at the top. They are like a pyramid, with very few people reaping most of the benefits at the apex.

The biggest relevant group are the men with guns who aren't allied with any political group or faction. During coups, they can be kingmakers if they split the 'right' way. But from their perspective, coups can be terrifying. Put yourself in the boots of an ordinary soldier for a moment. Let's say you're a twenty-seven-year-old infantry officer in the army named John. You have learned how to clean a rifle, throw a grenade and use a tourniquet. Depending on the country you serve, you might have commanded soldiers in battle.

But what you are probably not prepared for is a coup. With a coup underway, you stand in front of the company of men and women you command, trying to make a decision. You can either join the conspirators and try to overthrow the government or join the regime to defend the status quo. What are you going to do? If you pick the losing side, the consequences for you and the hundred or so men and women you command will probably be severe. What's more, the information you have is incomplete; you only see a fraction of the whole picture. In such dynamic situations, it's difficult to tell how strong either faction really is.

The safest bet is often to do nothing. For officers like John, the rational course of action is to wait as long as possible amid all the chaos and confusion to see who is winning. Once that has come into focus, John and his company can side with the winners. If the plotters look as though they will win, soldiers like John join the coup. If they look as though they won't, John and his troops will help to put it down. That is why perceived strength is so important to the tyrant. Perception doesn't just beat reality, it becomes reality.

Savvy coup leaders are aware of this and when a coup is attempted, they will try their best to use their limited power to capture points of high symbolic value to project control. Political scientist Brian Klaas calls this a 'bandwagon effect'.[48] When the rank-and-file soldiers and the military brass believe the coup is going to be successful, they rally around the conspirators. Those carrying out the coup use this to their advantage, aiming to topple the tyrant by making ordinary soldiers believe that they will win – thereby making victory all the more likely.

To make this more concrete, let's imagine overthrowing His Majesty's Government in the United Kingdom. The first shift in perspective is to ignore everything outside London. Coups take place in capital cities. Everything else you can worry about later.

The key to a successful coup would be a quick takeover of key assets: airports, Downing Street, the Houses of Parliament, the Ministry of Defence, the Cabinet Office, key broadcasters such as the BBC, and the country's intelligence headquarters. While your troops arrest anyone who doesn't comply, you force the shocked staff at the BBC's headquarters to tell the country's bewildered citizens that a new government has been formed. Once that announcement is out there, you then make it as hard as possible for people to gain access to other sources of information. Shut down mobile phone networks and make it impossible for people to access social media. Curfew begins at 6 p.m. sharp.

But even if all this works out, which is much easier said than done, what have you achieved? The whole of inner

London is only 319 square kilometres and you only control a fraction of that – some roads, some buildings, a few bridges. Even if you managed to arrive in London with 1,000 men (or women) at arms, that would still leave approximately 151,000 personnel of the British Armed Forces who aren't involved in the attempt to overthrow the government.[49] As well as them and their tanks and artillery and helicopters, there are police officers to contend with. In reality, you don't control all that much. But what you do have is an impression of inevitability. When ordinary people turn on the television, they see your troops. When they listen to the radio, they hear the voice of the king telling them to support the military forces that have taken power to restore order. The previous prime minister is nowhere to be seen because he's been hidden away in some basement. The new regime looks strong, the previous government looks weak.

That's the key to persuade officers like John to join the coup or at least not stand in its way. And just like that, a government can be toppled by a small force of soldiers even if they don't have all that much support among elites or the population. That's precisely what makes the military such a potent threat to every tyrant.

In the United Kingdom, of course, a scenario like this is hard to imagine. That's not because military officers don't have any grievances or because they wouldn't be powerful enough to attempt a coup, but because the political system has for centuries promoted norms according to which the military should stay out of politics. The last time that England experienced something that could be called a coup was when Oliver Cromwell took control of Parliament with the help of forty musketeers. That was in 1653. To put that in context: by the time fifty-six of America's Founding Fathers signed the Declaration of Independence, English rulers had already managed to avoid coups for more than 120 years. That acts as a powerful deterrent. When the first sea lord or His Majesty's minister of defence have an issue with the prime minister of the day, they won't even contemplate a coup. In countries that have a history of coups, civil–military relations are much more complicated. If a country has recent experience of even one coup, new coups become more likely because coups legitimise further coups.[50] The impact of this is so significant that countries can become caught up in a 'coup trap' – one coup begets another, and so on.

What can tyrants do? This is a massive threat that needs to be dealt with as soon as possible. It isn't optional; they have to get to work.

A ruler's first instinct might be to throw money at the problem, since that is often a good way to bind people to the regime. That can be a temporary solution, but simply giving the generals more money or more weapons won't do the trick because every time money is transferred, the generals become more powerful. Just as importantly, money flowing to the generals might make the generals happy, but military coups can also be launched by much more junior figures, who don't benefit from corruption to the same extent. Research from the US Naval War College shows that a great many coups are carried out by soldiers at the lower end of the hierarchy, people like John (captain and below).[51] And whilst they have a lower success rate than coups orchestrated from the middle (48 per cent) or the top (68 per cent), almost a third of them have succeeded. Money alone can't solve the tyrant's problem.

Since there's always the possibility that the military will turn on the dictator, the key is to develop a strategy – an insurance plan. There are three main ways to 'coup-proof' a regime: splitting the military, reducing trust and making sure everyone is in the right place.

Dividing the military into smaller factions that compete with each other is called 'counter-balancing'. Assuming the tyrant isn't ruling a country in which the last coup-like event was carried out using muskets, the military will – at some point or other – consider assuming power. For the military, the best way to overthrow the government is to act together. If the soldiers cooperate, they are overwhelmingly powerful and all they have to worry about is the public (which can be subdued) and perhaps the police (which can be outgunned). To the tyrant, that's the nightmare scenario.

By splitting the military into smaller factions, the palace can create counter-weights to each of the forces. As well as a regular military, there's now a regular military, a parallel military and perhaps also a militarised palace guard. The same goes for intelligence organisations. Instead of having a single intelligence organisation responsible for monitoring domestic threats, split it into three – each of them with separate tasks, but which also overlap. That way, the agents keep an eye on each other and it becomes much more difficult for agents to plot an overthrow of the regime in the shadows.

The aim of all these measures is to influence the calculus of potential plotters. When the officers sit down to think about overthrowing the government, they need to believe that they will encounter stiff resistance. That, in turn, is more believable if the military forces are split and none of its individual parts is so dominant that it can outmanoeuvre the others.

The political scientist James Quinlivan aptly summarised how it works:

The parallel military does not have to be as large as the regular armed forces, nor does it need to be able to defeat the regular army in a full-scale civil war. But it must be large enough, loyal enough, and deployed so that it can engage and perhaps defeat any disloyal forces in the immediate vicinity of the critical points of the regime.[52]

That's the theory. So how does it work in practice? Let's look at the way Iraqi dictator Saddam Hussein dealt with the military. He once said: 'The Iraqi army was the only force capable of conspiring against me. The only power we fear is this army will take over the party's leadership. The army is like a pet tiger.' Clearly, he considered the tiger to be a major threat. Once he came to power, he set out to pull 'out its eyes, teeth, and claws'.[53]

Saddam Hussein's Baathist regime's drive to reduce the threat of the military had multiple pillars. The military was purged of suspect elements, which were replaced by party members who passed the loyalty test. In the words of the Baathists themselves: 'Who does not take our path stays at home with his wife.'[54] They also established the Popular Army and the Republican Guard. The Popular Army was a 'party-based, party-led mass alternative to the regular army'[55] – a militia, in other words. Its members didn't get the best training or the best weapons, but there were a lot of them. The Republican Guard started out as a much smaller organisation specifically designed to protect the regime. With all these structural changes to the security forces, Saddam no longer faced the threat of a unified opponent. Instead, all the smaller factions of the security forces had to consider the strong possibility that they would have to fight each other as well as the dictator if they ever attempted to overthrow Hussein.

This brings us to the second measure despots can use to 'coup-proof' their regime: reducing trust between generals and their soldiers as well as among the generals. Saddam Hussein was constantly shuffling the security agencies around.[56] That's not an anomaly, it's standard practice for despots.

In addition to reducing trust, shuffling people around has the advantage of making it harder for people to talk to, and cooperate with, each other. Dictators definitely don't want the minister of defence, minister of the interior and the head of intelligence to spend a lot of time with one another. If they did, they could sound one another out and begin to make plans. It's best if they are suspicious of each other, always vying for attention from the palace. Divide so you don't get conquered.

Relatedly, coup-proofing works best when there's no single actor (aside from the tyrant) who knows too much or can bring people together. So in place of having a chairman of the joint chiefs of staff who has regular meetings with everyone in charge of the people with guns, have everyone report straight to the dictator's study. That way, they don't trust each other, they don't talk to each other, they don't act behind the tyrant's back. Yasser Arafat was infamous for this: every part of the Palestinian security apparatus reported to him.[57] Arafat's micromanagement was so intense that he would sometimes sign the cheques made out to paramilitary units for amounts as small as $300.[58]

Now that security forces are structured in a way to make coups less likely, it's all about making sure that the right forces are in the right place. Most obviously, tyrants want some loyal forces in the capital near the presidential palace and the other key installations that need to be protected. But since having a force too large in the capital brings risks as well, some tyrants have gone the other way, and moved the regular troops further out. No more manoeuvres anywhere near the capital. Regular military bases in the vicinity? No. When regular troops are no longer near the capital, it's sufficient to place the parallel forces between the tyrant and the main threat (which is their own military).

As a hereditary monarchy with at least one adversarial nation-state nearby, Saudi Arabia has a regular military (the Saudi Arabian Armed Forces), a counter-balancing force (the Saudi Arabian National Guard) and a dedicated force to protect the House of Saud (the Saudi Royal Regiment). In the 1970s, the royal family decided that the existence of a counter-balancing force wasn't sufficient. With the regular military primarily deployed to military cities that the Saudis had built (at great cost) at key trouble spots and invasion routes on the country's periphery, the National Guard were physically placed between the Armed Forces and the royal household.[59] The Saudi Royal Regiment, then, acted as a last-resort guarantor in the event that intending-perpetrators of a coup happened to make it to anywhere near the royal palace in Riyadh.

These structural measures are a way to decrease the ability of conspirators to coordinate, work together and execute a successful coup. It's also a way for tyrants to exploit a paradox: the men with guns, trained to kill, don't actually want to use violence.

There's a public misconception that coups are always intensely violent. Some of them most definitely are. But if you witness a coup in which soldiers clash with other soldiers, or soldiers direct fire at civilians, something isn't going according to plan. After analysing close on four hundred coup attempts, political scientist Erica de Bruin found that under half of them involved fatalities. There's a reluctance to shoot at comrades.[60] In part, this is cultural: soldiers, who are trained to fight external enemies, often resist the use of violence at home and this can lead to a split within the army. On a personal level, it's also about the loss of legitimacy. Defending the country against threats from abroad can be respectable; in some societies, it's seen as heroic. But shooting at their own people – the military or civilians, in particular women and children – to take power? Few will call you a hero. And in the end, that helps cruel governments to stay in power. If leaders can credibly signal that either will be necessary to overthrow them, their chances of staying in power increase considerably.

But there's a catch: this deterrent only works if those plotting to overthrow the regime believe that the parallel security forces will put up a meaningful fight when the coup is carried out. That means they need to be loyal to the dictatorship and effective enough to inflict serious pain on the regular forces. If they're obviously a paper tiger, the real one will simply tear them to pieces.

For dictators, the effectiveness of parallel military forces can be achieved through training, equipment and positioning. If tyrants have done all that, they've taken the first steps towards staying in power. But there's more that needs to be done to prevent unplanned retirement. With the military split and weakened, now is the time to give it a reason to support the status quo. The most straightforward way to achieve the loyalty of the parallel security forces is to spoil them rotten. Give them money, give them toys, increase their opportunities for personal enrichment through corruption. It's no coincidence that parallel security forces tend to be better equipped than their regular counterparts.

Another option is to select soldiers based on a certain identity.

In her excellent book *When Soldiers Rebel*, Kristen Harkness outlines how governments have sought to bind soldiers to the regime. She explains how, during the Middle Ages, European armies were 'rooted in reciprocal feudal ties'.[61] Later on,

France and Germany would transform their officer corps in a way that made it possible for aristocrats without significant land holdings to become officers. In fact, even some non-aristocrats were allowed to become officers – but only in engineering roles and artillery. In Britain, promotions within the military had to be bought. None of these systems was based on merit. But the advantage that they did have was that they bound military elites to the state.

Within Europe, those systems eventually changed as the military was opened up to larger groups of citizens. But long after this happened at home, colonial empires maintained a military recruitment system based on identity in their colonies. In colonial India, the British Empire had an explicit 'martial race doctrine' according to which it differentiated between those ethnicities it saw as capable of warfare and those that were unsuitable or unreliable. In Africa, the colonisers were constantly wary about finding themselves in a situation where the colonised would stand up and fight back. To mitigate that risk, the British Empire ensured that no ethnic group ever gained control of the two core institutions of the colonial state – the civil service and the military. If one was promoted heavily to the administrative class, soldiers were recruited primarily from the other.[62]

Moreover, many colonial units were regional and not based on the territory of future independent states. The King's African Rifles, a British colonial unit, for example, drew soldiers from British East Africa (Kenya), Nyasaland (Malawi) and British Tanganyika (Tanzania).[63] The purpose of this was, once again, to prevent the emergence of unified opposition.

Lastly, all colonial empires in Africa were reluctant to allow local populations into the officer corps. In a military with 25,000 men, the Belgian Congo had not a single African officer.[64] The colonised, in other words, were wanted to make the administration of the colonies cheaper, but they were not required in any leadership role. Even in the case of the British Empire, which was comparatively more inclined to promote from the local population, the numbers were small. By 1960, the entire Nigerian Army had just eighty-two Nigerian offi-cers – and 243 seconded from the British military.[65] As one might imagine, this practice made it difficult for independ-ence leaders to tie their soldiers to their regime. They simply couldn't trust them.

One solution that many post-independence leaders pur-sued was 'ethnic stacking' of security forces. The idea here is that, due to their ethnic identity, these groups have an advan-tage in the current system; if the leader who put them in power were to fall, they might lose the privileges afforded to them. And who would want that? Tyrants speculate that few do.

In a study of Africa since independence, Harkness found evidence for the remarkable extent to which autocratic leaders have engaged in ethnic stacking: around 50 per cent of them implemented stacking methods. (For democratic leaders, it was around 24 per cent.) What's more, the process was clearly advantageous for them. Leaders who didn't engage in ethnic stacking stayed in power for an average of around six years. Those that 'create and personally control coethnic paramilitary units' stayed in power for more than twice as long.[66]

Ethnic stacking is a way to make the status quo appealing to soldiers. They benefit because of their identity, giving them a reason to support the regime. But if the carrot doesn't do the trick, there's also the stick – making all other alterna-tives so dire that the men in camouflage have no other option but to support the status quo. Back in Saddam Hussein's Iraq, security services regularly committed gross human rights violations on behalf of the regime. One of their frequent targets were the Kurds.

The Kurds, an ethnic group spread primarily across Turkey, Iran, Syria and Iraq, were the victims of brutal violence at the hands of the regime for decades. They were harassed, tortured and killed.

The men that committed those crimes? They were hated. And when an opportunity to fight back against them came along, there was no hesitation. In March 1991, Kurdish forces took Sulaimaniya's Central Security Prison, where countless inmates had had to endure beatings, torture and hunger while Hussein and the Baathist regime were in charge.[67] In that small corner of northern Iraq, the tables had now turned. The security forces that did the torturing and killing were weaker, and those they had tormented had the upper hand.

According to Kurdish sources, not one of the 300 secret policemen who defended the prison survived. After the complex was liberated and all of them were dead, a forty-five-year-old headmaster who was tortured in a soundproof chamber at the prison said he wished all of them would come back to life 'so we could kill them again'.[68] Under those circumstances, the loyalty of soldiers and intelligence officers to the regime has to be 'to the death' because they cannot switch sides or lay down arms.[69]

Implementing some combination of these measures can help tyrants survive to fight another day. If they don't tackle the problem, they will almost certainly fall because there will be a day when the generals decide that they, rather than the despot, should be in power. And when they do and are united, they will be very hard to beat because violence is their specialty.

In both Saudi Arabia and Iraq, coup-proofing 'worked' in the sense that there were no successful coups. Saddam Hussein's regime only fell once the United States, an overwhelmingly strong outside power, decided to remove him.

Before that, he held onto power even after a series of hugely embarrassing military defeats. South of the border, the House of Saud continued to rule the country named after their family from Riyadh.

But if coup-proofing is the key to avoiding coups, why doesn't everybody simply reorganise the military and intelligence services once they rise to power? One of the challenges, as Erica de Bruin demonstrates in her book *How to Prevent Coups d'État*, derives from the process itself.[70] Having a coup-proofed military increases the chances of a regime's survival, but once the tyrant starts the process, and before he's finished, his situation is perilous.

Kwame Nkrumah's story shows why that moment can be so dangerous. When Nkrumah first went into Ghanian politics in the late 1940s, Ghana was a British crown colony known as the Gold Coast. Once Ghanaians achieved independence, Nkrumah became the country's first leader. He quickly became worried for his own security. As a result, he began to put some specialised intelligence and security units under his personal command. Since that wasn't enough to make him feel safe, he then started to turn the presidential bodyguards, the President's Own Guard Regiment (POGR), into a fully-fledged fighting force capable of deterring those who might try to destroy him. The size of the force grew rapidly and the benefits the men received were vastly better than those of the regular troops.[71] Nkrumah was initially reluctant to focus on ethnicity as a recruitment tool because he saw 'tribalism' as a 'canker-worm which, unless removed, may destroy the solidity of the body politic, the stability of the government, the efficiency of the bureaucracy and the judiciary, and the effectiveness of the army and police'.[72] But although he did not particularly favour ethnic stacking, officers from some ethnic groups, including his own, were frequently promoted while others were seemingly overlooked. Crucially, Nkrumah didn't stop there but went after the police as well.[73]

The intelligence and security services aside, Nkrumah consolidated his political power by other means also. By 1964, a constitutional amendment had turned Ghana into a one-party state with Nkrumah's Convention People's Party on top.[74] Nkrumah was declared president for life, and many of his political opponents found themselves imprisoned in a fort that had once been used to hold slaves en route for the United States. What's more, soldiers were used in an internal security role to suppress strikes.[75] At this point, all warning signs should have flashed bright red.

In early 1966, the president for life left for a trip to Vietnam and China. With Nkrumah and many of the key defence officials out of the country, it was the perfect time to make a move. At around midnight, Colonel Emmanuel Kotoka, stationed some two hundred kilometres northwest of Ghana's capital Accra, started to move his troops. When they came close to Accra's airport, they were joined by a company of paratroopers who had been training for a few days near the capital. After this, things moved rapidly. By around 2.30 a.m., the conspirators arrived at Flagstaff House, the president's compound. The Ministry of Defence, the radio station and the post office were surrounded. At 6 a.m., Ghanaians heard Colonel Kotoka on the radio declaring that the 'National Liberation Council' had taken power. The President's Own Guard, the force that was intended to fight back in the event of a coup, did put up a fight. But by noon that day, the 'commander of the Presidential Guard marched out with his troops and surrendered'.[76]

Those who orchestrated the coup were undoubtedly unhappy with the overall political and economic situation in the country, but what really motivated them to overthrow

President Nkrumah (who subsequently lived out his days in Guinea) were Nkrumah's moves to counter-balance the military and diminish the role of the police.[77] J. W. K. Harlley, the police commissioner who took part in the coup, explicitly justified his role by saying that Nkrumah had created a 'private army of his own at an annual cost of over half a million pounds in flagrant violation of a constitution which he himself had foisted on the country to serve as a counterpose to the Ghana Armed Forces'.[78]

Nkrumah's attempt at coup-proofing failed because it created an incentive for the regular security forces to strike while the parallel forces were too weak to resist.

The overall problem, then, is that the very things tyrants do to reduce the threat of the military can lead the military to act against them.

In theory, there's a way out of this. If the tyrant can persuade another state to guarantee the security of the regime with its military, the regime can concentrate on coup-proofing without worrying about military effectiveness. It can then reduce its military force to one so weak that it becomes manageable. During the Cold War, for example, the French military sometimes stepped in to save dictators from their own soldiers. In some cases, as with an operation to reinstall Gabonese president Léon M'ba in 1964, French troops were flown in to reverse a coup.[79]

The foreign guarantor is an attractive option for tyrants but it's rarely on offer. Even if it is, it comes at a price: every time a leader becomes so dependent on a foreign power that he cannot survive without it, his room for manoeuvre is severely reduced.

Most difficult is finding another state to provide that service. Not only does another state need to have a motive for intervening, they need to be able to do so. The list of potential security suppliers is short. Coups happen quickly and to have any effect, foreign troops already need to be in the area.[80] It's no good if they are in the Caribbean or a training ground overlooking the Pyrenees. They need to be in the region, or better still, already in the country, in order to make a meaningful difference.

Then tyrants need to find a state with troops that are not just nearby but also strong enough to deter or at least overwhelm the coup-plotters. In Gabon, it was only possible to reverse the coup because the French paratroopers were strong whilst the Gabonese were weak. According to one estimate, the Gabonese security forces at the time, military and police combined, numbered a mere six hundred men.[81] Nowadays, the list of militaries that could theoretically pull off something like this is not long. If there's a coup in Egypt and a European power sends paratroopers to try to reverse it, those paratroopers will probably come home in coffins – if they come home at all.

As can be seen, convincing a foreign power to defend the regime against potential coups d'état is a challenging task. They are being asked to risk the lives of their own troops to defend an unstable dictatorship at huge reputational cost. As a result, most tyrants are on their own when dealing with the military.

The military, as we have now learned, are a potent threat to every despot. Unlike court elites, soldiers have the capacity to use brute force. Tyrants understand this, which is why they work to divide and weaken. And with the military successfully fragmented, a new problem opens up: it becomes plain for all to see that the military isn't built to fight and the situation invites challengers from the hinterland. And before the tyrant knows it, a rebel commander from the regions may be on his way towards the capital.

4

Rebels, Guns and Money

The mere existence of privations is not enough to cause an insurrection; if it were, the masses would always be in revolt.[1]

Leon Trotsky

At 1.30 a.m. on 23 December 1972, residents of Managua were woken from their sleep when the ground below them shook.[2] 'At first the earth seemed to go up and down, then it seemed to go from side to side and everything came down,' a resident recalled.[3] Although the earthquake itself was relatively mild, at 6.25 on the Richter scale, the effect on Nicaragua's capital was devastating.[4]

When the sun came up the following morning, the sky above Managua was concealed by smoke and red dust. On the ground, fires were burning where thousands of buildings had collapsed. Firemen, with their fire engines buried and the water mains burst, were often forced to look on in despair as the flames consumed the structures still standing.[5] Many of the survivors fled the city.[6] And they, their homes and neighbourhoods destroyed, were the lucky ones. So many people died that an official declared an entire section of the city would be covered in lime after being levelled to create a mass grave.[7] When the first foreign journalist arrived in Managua, he said: 'Those of us who knew Managua will never see it again. Managua has disappeared. All is desolation, death and tragedy.'[8]

For Nicaragua, the earthquake was a catastrophe.

When General Anastasio Somoza Debayle, Nicaragua's ruler, looked at the devastation from the presidential palace, he saw opportunity. In a first step, the government declared martial law, thereby expanding the powers of the National Guard, which Somoza controlled. Then, as money for reconstruction poured in from countries around the world, Somoza made sure that he, rather than his country, would be the primary beneficiary. With his brother and father having ruled Nicaragua before him, Somoza had a vast business empire that made him rich in a country in which many had nothing. Now that Managua was in ruins, Somoza made sure it would be 'rebuilt on Somoza land, by Somoza construction companies, with international aid funnelled through Somoza banks'.[9]

For the dictator and his thugs, things could have been perfect. But he went too far. Although Nicaragua's wealthy elites might have accepted that the dictator should get the largest slice of the pie, but not enough was left for them. Many of Managua's rich businessmen, previously supportive of the dictatorship, began to turn against him.[10]

And outside the capital, an insurgency was brewing. The Sandinist National Liberation Front (FSLN), a leftist rebel group founded in 1961 on the back of widespread popular discontent, foresaw that guerrilla war would bring them victory over the regime.[11] They also used some more unusual tactics, when, in 1974, they kidnapped multiple well-known politicians and business figures during a Christmas party. The regime paid a ransom to free the hostages, but then it unleashed a wave of violence on the rebels — as well as on entirely innocent civilians. Much of the repression targeted the population outside Managua. At the time, priests reported that Somoza's National Guard had 'instituted a reign of terror . . . routinely killing and torturing peasant men, raping women, burning homes and stealing crops and property'.[12]

Somoza was sitting on a powder keg.[13] Then, on 10 January 1978, the fuse was lit when three men shot Pedro Joaquín Chamorro Cardenal, a popular journalist-turned-opposition leader, eighteen times.[14] With Chamorro's family and much of the public blaming the Somoza regime for the death, the flame of rebellion was lit. In the capital, Somoza businesses were burned. In other cities, young men and women attacked members of the National Guard with whatever weapons they could muster. In Masaya, not even infantry could put down the unrest. Instead, the regime had to send in tanks and helicopters.[15]

By 1979, Somoza had three problems. First, the different factions of the FSLN managed to bridge their differences to become a homogenous group.[16] Second, the Carter administration withdrew its support for the Nicaraguan dictatorship after the United States had supported the Somozas for decades. Third, many of Nicaragua's neighbours had become convinced that Somoza had to go, and they acted accordingly.

Fidel Castro provided rifles, rocket-propelled grenades and artillery for the rebels.[17] Venezuela provided financing and Costa Rica was used to smuggle weapons into the country. In May 1979, Mexico broke off diplomatic relations with Nicaragua. With Somoza increasingly isolated and the rebels better armed than ever, the Sandinistas announced their final offensive. By July, the Sandinistas had taken control of most of Nicaragua and Somoza realised he had to go.

After losing against the rebels and fleeing to Miami, the former Nicaraguan dictator found a friendly dictator who would take him in: Paraguay's Alfredo Stroessner. In Paraguay, Somoza had a chauffeur, a white Mercedes-Benz and a swimming pool at his suburban home. And although he complained about having lost some $80 million, that still left him with $20 million in the bank. He wasn't exactly destitute. But one day, just a few blocks from his house in Paraguay's capital Asunción, Somoza's previous life caught up with him when his convoy was met with a hail of bullets and a bazooka.[18]

Tyrants can't keep everyone happy. To maintain their grip on power, they usually need to steal from the masses and distribute the gains to insiders of the regime such as the generals, oligarchs and rival politicians. If they don't, they can easily be toppled by palace elites or their own troops. But if they do, the neglected, overlooked masses of the hinterland might rise up. And when that happens, despots who don't pay enough attention to threats outside their capital can be taken by surprise.

Nicaraguan dictator Anastasio Somoza Debayle managed to upset a great many people. Parts of Managua's elites were upset because Somoza stole from the masses without giving them sufficient opportunity for enrichment. Many Nicaraguans outside the capital were upset because they barely had enough income to survive on. The country's Catholic bishops were appalled at the brutal repression the regime used against civilians. Somoza also managed to alienate his most important protector, the United States, while energising his enemies in Latin America.

What happened in Nicaragua was unusual. In the modern world, it is extremely difficult for rebels to topple tyrants. Around five thousand years ago, there were no regular armies. People fought each other, but it was effectively a fight of guerrillas against guerrillas.[19] Big states in ancient Greece had only a few hundred thousand inhabitants. A few hundred years ago, Germany was so fragmented that someone travelling from Brunswick to the French border would cross six duchies, four bishoprics and one free imperial city. That may sound like a lot, but the Holy Roman Empire at the time consisted of 812 more or less sovereign political entities.[20] To a large extent, these were weak, fractured states prone to being defeated by small groups of soldiers, attacking on a whim.

The modern nation-state is a different animal altogether. It's extremely effective at organising a large group of people in the pursuit of a single aim such as waging war. If rebels are going to go to war against one such state, it's going to be much more difficult to beat than ancient Greek city-states or German duchies. This is partly a result of the size and effectiveness of modern states, but it's also the result of advances in technology.

Such advances have made it increasingly difficult to hide. Now that states can mass-manufacture surveillance drones or simply buy them from one of dozens of manufacturers, hiding has become more challenging. Rebels can't just camp on a ridge or make a fire in a forest clearing if they want to remain out of the eyes of the government. The world has become much smaller.

And that's merely the effect of drones. In addition, there are now easily available satellite images, biometric tracking and a multitude of other tools that despots can use to track their enemies. Perhaps the biggest overall difference is due to modern infrastructure. The existence of roads and railways completely changes the balance of power between the state and its people because they allow regular troops to operate in territory that was previously inaccessible.

Obviously, insurgents can benefit from modern technology as well: mobile phones can be used to coordinate, Google Maps can be used to plan attacks, social media networks can be used to find new recruits. But ultimately, at the scale that is required to win rather than just keep fighting, it is difficult to outdo modern nation-states. They are, in comparison to anything humans have seen in the past, incredibly powerful.

That doesn't mean it's impossible for rebels to win, but the bar is now higher. To fight an enemy as powerful as this, rebellions need to be more sophisticated, better funded and better armed. Fighting a rebellion is not an easy thing to do, especially because it requires significantly more time and coordination than a 'simple' military coup. Rebellions are in some ways the opposite of a coup: they require huge numbers of people to succeed, they tend to be extremely bloody, and battlefield strength matters more than perception. When they happen despite the difficulties, it's usually because someone, somewhere has been excluded.

A military officer by training, Idriss Déby spent part of the 1970s in France, where he trained to become a pilot. When he returned to his native Chad in February 1979, the country was at war, with multiple warlords fighting one another. After considering his options, Déby joined Hissène Habré's Armed Forces of the North (FAN). In return for successfully fighting on Habré's side during the insurgency that brought him to power, President Habré made Déby the deputy commander of his military forces.[21]

But the alliance didn't last long and, by 1989, the former allies were close to open conflict. Habré feared that an ethnic group called the Zaghawa presented a threat to his rule and as a result, he used his secret services to target ordinary Zaghawa people as Zaghawa members of the government were killed.[22] Born into a poor herding family that belonged to the Zaghawa, Déby had to wonder whether he might be next. On 1 April 1989, Habré gave a speech in which he accused Déby and his co-conspirators of treachery following an attempted coup. 'They took great advantage of the benefits of our struggle, of the sweat and the blood of our armed forces and our people to enrich themselves, [only] to stab Chad in the back,' he said.[23]

After fleeing to Libya via Sudan, Déby set out to raise an army that could march on Chad's capital. And march (or rather drive) it did, all the way to N'Djamena. As his troops approached, Habré fled to Cameroon and many of his soldiers simply threw away their guns.[24]

Fearing exclusion, Déby used force to topple the man he had brought to power through force less than a decade earlier. But as president, Déby made many of the same moves as Habré and soon enough, he too faced an insurgency of disgruntled military men from across the border in southern Libya. Faced with the threat of being toppled by rebels just as Habré had been, Déby decided to stare danger in the face. In April 2021, he joined his troops on the frontline against the rebels. Shortly thereafter, a general appeared on Chadian state television. Déby, he said, 'breathed his last defending the sovereign nation on the battlefield'.[25]

Both Habré and Déby lost power because they moved to exclude insiders they perceived to be unreliable. Those insiders fled, only to return with fighters, Kalashnikovs and grenades. That isn't unusual, it often happens. So why do so many tyrants do it anyway? The political scientist Philip Roessler argues it's about moving the conflict from within the regime to society at large, 'where the ruler and his allies calculate it poses less of a threat to their political supremacy'.[26]

Every tyrant faces the threat of civil war. But not every tyrant faces the same level of threat. Some of the worst tyrants on earth are relatively popular despite their cruelty. For example, oil-rich dictators are often guilty of obscene corruption and grotesque inequality, but they can pay out enough to the masses to stave off a violent uprising. In a country with massive natural resource reserves and only a few million inhabitants, the population can live in prosperity even if the royal family steals billions. At the other end of the spectrum, there are countries where everyone is extremely poor except for those in the dictator's inner circle. The contrast is so extreme that most of the population have good reason to be dissatisfied with the ruler.

When anger burns hottest, the risk to the tyrant is determined by whether there is the opportunity to rebel.

Rebels fight for all kinds of reasons. Some are motivated by injustice; others are motivated by greed. And, as paradoxical as it may sound, some people decide to join up and fight because they seek safety.[27] If you're reading this book, chances are there are some things you've always taken for granted in your life. First, that there's a state which retains something close to a monopoly on violence within its borders, producing law, order and stability. Then, even though buying property might be more difficult for you than it was for your grandparents, there's work. In an emergency, there's the police and, if a really serious dispute arises, a working court system. But in many of the world's poorest countries, none of that exists. There's little infrastructure, no work, the police extort money from law-abiding citizens and the court system is painfully slow, the bench populated by corrupt judges. If under those circumstances a situation arises in which someone feels threatened, holding a Kalashnikov and joining a rebel organisation might actually be the best way to look after themselves and their families.

And if the ranks of the rebel organisation can't be filled fast enough with voluntary recruits, people can be forced to fight. To provide just one example from the Cold War: according to one estimate, some 80 per cent of the fighters involved in the anti-communist armed group, the National Resistance of Mozambique (RENAMO), didn't choose to fight, they were forced to enlist.[28] A particularly gruesome tactic involves kidnapping 'recruits' and then forcing them to commit atrocities near their home so that they became trapped within the insurgency, never able to return to their families.[29] Not even children are safe. During the Burundian Civil War, rebels bought street children from Kenya and turned them into fighters.[30]

But no tyrant is threatened by unarmed fighters. And if the declared aim of the group is to fight the government, they can't simply walk into a gun shop and pick up the rocket-propelled grenades and heavy machine guns they need. But if the nascent rebel movement has enough money, they can source the weaponry they need on the black market – or from a willing sponsor.

Rebels need money – for guns, certainly, but that's just a down payment. Fighters also need to be fed and equipped over the course of months, or more likely years. They need salaries to justify the risk. That's a dilemma for rebel groups because their activities do not directly generate any revenue.[31] It's not like a business that perpetuates itself through its operations. So, how do rebels generate the cash they need to bring down the tyrant?

The one advantage that insurgents have is the capacity for violence. And violence, in turn, can be turned into cash. If you're involved in organised crime in London or New York or Hong Kong, you can use violence to extort money from people. You're an insurance salesman, of sorts. If people don't pay your insurance, their windows might get smashed because they don't receive your 'protection'. In many of the poor rural areas in which rebel groups tend to operate, that's not really an option because you can't take things away from people who don't have anything.[32] Or you could, because everybody has *something*, but whatever it is you can steal might not be enough to keep going. That said, there are other options. One of them is natural resources.

For someone looking to fund an insurgency, diamonds are perfect. They are often easy to extract, easy to smuggle and extremely expensive once they make their way out of the war zone. We all know the term 'blood diamond' – diamonds that fuel wars. They've been discussed in newspapers, books and on the screen in Edward Zwick's 2007 *Blood Diamond*. Starring Leonardo DiCaprio, the film is set in Sierra Leone during the country's brutal civil war. During that war, the rebels financed their fighting thanks to gems dug straight out of the ground. The gruelling mining work was often done by young men and women with nothing more than a shovel and a sieve. After digging to a depth of up to twenty metres, the excavated gravel was passed in buckets from person to person in a long chain. At the end of that chain, the earth was checked for signs of precious stones. The diggers were poor and easily intimidated. If they managed to find a stone, the rebels could 'tax' them. If they wanted to take a break, the rebels could beat them until they started working again. And if they stopped turning up in the morning, someone else could be forced to do the job. From West Africa, the stones went to London, Paris or Moscow, where they were sold for thousands of dollars in fancy jewellery shops. It is big business. According to some estimates, diamonds from African war zones made up as much as 15 per cent of the world supply during the mid-1990s.[33]

Rebels who sell diamonds can earn eye-watering sums. According to one estimate, UNITA, a rebel faction during the Angolan Civil War, made more than a billion dollars this way. (Some estimates put the figure much higher).[34] For the tyrant, the threat posed by rebels funded by diamonds can be vicious. The rebels make money by extracting diamonds; they then use that money to buy weapons and attract fighters. As they go from strength to strength, they capture more territory and extract more diamonds. The snowball keeps growing.

Using commodities other than diamonds (or drugs) is more difficult because rebels don't usually have access to advanced machinery, large-scale outside investment or sophisticated technology. Extracting oil, for example, is significantly more challenging. But, as difficult as it might be to drill for oil, there are ways to profit from those who do the drilling or some other task related to it. The easiest way to do this is to threaten or kidnap the employees of the multinational companies that often do the work.[35] These companies don't just have deep pockets, they are willing to work in the poor, rural areas where rebels are often strongest. When their engineers or managers are held at gunpoint and then hidden away in a jungle or cave, many of these firms are willing to pay large sums to get them back.

Sometimes, even a single corporate 'benefactor' can make a huge difference. In the early 1980s, the champagne corks must have popped at Mannesmann HQ. The German conglomerate had just won a $160-million contract to build 278 kilometres of pipeline from Colombia's oilfields to the Caribbean coast. There were only three small problems: first, the pipeline had to be built through the Andes mountains. Okay, that's an engineering problem the Germans could solve. Second, the Marxist-Leninist National Liberation Army (ELN) was active in the area. Trickier. Lastly, Mannesmann was supposed to finish the project in a year.[36] It was quite a task.

Then one of the German engineers and two of his Colombian colleagues were kidnapped and the company's managers had a decision to make: would they strike a deal with the rebels to get their employees back and stand a chance of finishing the project on time, or would they try their best to do the work they were hired to do without such an arrangement? Neither was a great option. Making a deal with the rebels would mean paying a lot of money to criminals who had just abducted colleagues; not paying it could lead to their colleagues' deaths and endanger the entire pipeline.

In the end, the company reportedly struck a deal. According to a former manager working on the project, they paid millions in ransom.[37] According to the rebel leader, even those millions were only one part of a series of payments the ELN received from Mannesmann. The relationship became so close that the company was issued with stickers for their cars and lorries. When a Mannesmann lorry drove through a remote settlement, these stickers alerted villagers to the fact that the vehicle was 'protected' by the ELN. This benefited the ELN, in that the stickers also made known to the villagers that the ELN was bringing money into the region.[38] Mannesmann managed to complete the contract, but the ELN, fuelled by German money, went from strength to strength. The rebels would later say that it allowed the group to grow by 500 per cent.[39]

Those are the 'usual' ways of financing a rebellion. More unorthodox ways exist, such as those that political scientist Michael L. Ross calls 'booty futures'. When they are not funding insurgencies, futures are contracts in which one party agrees to buy an asset at a specified time in the future. One of the advantages of these types of contracts is that they can reduce volatility. Imagine an airline company that is worried by fluctuating kerosene prices, for example. The company's managers know that they need to buy a certain amount of fuel in June next year because they know how many flights the company usually does when people go on holiday. If the airline's managers think the price of fuel might go up a lot by then, they can lock in the price now and be sure of what they are going to pay.

Obviously, this type of instrument can be used not only to safeguard against risk but also to speculate. This is where the rebels come in. But instead of entering into a legal agreement through the Chicago Mercantile Exchange to sell a fixed amount of kerosene by next summer, rebels can try to sell a future for the 'booty' they have yet to capture. Through that, they can make the capture more likely. This might sound like something from the Golden Age of Piracy, but it's a little more recent.

Congo's president Pascal Lissouba feared that his predecessor, Denis Sassou-Nguesso, wanted to become president again. Worryingly for Lissouba, Sassou had a private militia. When Lissouba sent government forces to surround Sassou's private compound, his militia fought back and the civil war began.[40] The funding for Sassou's militia reportedly came in part from the sale of future exploitation of Congo's oil to the French company Elf-Aquitaine. Sassou supposedly received $150 million and the firm might have helped him buy arms.[41]

Hard to believe as it is, this episode occurred in 1997.

Whether it be voluntary fighters, forced recruits, diamonds or even booty futures, the rebels now have fighters, arms and enough money to keep the insurgents marching. What they still need in order to topple the tyrant is a place to hide. This is where geography plays a role. If you're near a map, take a look at continental Europe, specifically the Netherlands. Obviously, the Netherlands has been a liberal democracy for decades – the Dutch are among the freest people in the world. But let's say a sizeable number of Dutch people decide to wage an insurgency on account of some grievance or other. How would that work? It wouldn't. Fighting an insurgency in Holland (or in Friesland or in Limburg) would be all but impossible.

Much of the reason this is because hiding is impossible. Driving from Groningen to Eindhoven takes less than three hours and the country's widest point is perhaps two hundred kilometres at most. While there is a mountain of some nine hundred metres within the Kingdom of the Netherlands, it's in the country's overseas territory in the Caribbean. On the mainland, there are no jungles and no remote areas beyond the control of the central government. You could of course try to hide in a neighbouring country. But as it stands, the Netherlands borders on Germany and Belgium, and neither Berlin nor Brussels is likely to be particularly supportive once told that you're planning to march on the Binnenhof. As a result, a Dutch insurgency wouldn't last a day against the Royal Netherlands Army.

It's not true to say that all small, flat and easily accessible countries are governed by democrats, but it's a fact that many autocrats operate in countries that look nothing like the Netherlands. When the Tajik government faced a civil war in 1992 after the Soviet Union imploded, one of its big problems was that the opposition was difficult to pursue because large tracts of the country were covered in snow-capped mountains. The Ismoil Somoni Peak (Stalin Peak until 1962, then Communism Peak until the late 1990s) in Tajikistan has an elevation of 7,495 metres, making it more than twenty-three times higher than the highest 'mountain' in the European Netherlands. And obviously, Ismoil Somoni Peak doesn't stand in isolation – Tajikistan is full of mountains which are difficult to access for outsiders (or even the central government). They were the perfect hiding place not just for fighters but also for their Kalashnikovs and rocket-propelled grenades. Insurgencies work best when the rebels are likely to win a game of hide-and-seek with the government.

Sometimes, not only is a country remote, it borders on other countries which are remote as well. Going back to the Netherlands: Belgium is densely populated, and so are at least some of Germany's regions on the Dutch border. In the case of a hypothetical Dutch rebellion, that would make it extremely difficult to traffic weapons or fighters. But in a country such as the Central African Republic, the government has to contend with a doubly difficult situation. The eastern part of the Central African Republic is underdeveloped and difficult for the central government to reach because of the geography and lack of infrastructure. On top of that, it is surrounded by regions of the Democratic Republic of Congo, South Sudan, Sudan and Chad which are themselves difficult to access. Given the porous borders and extent of the problems in neighbouring areas, that part of the country is almost impossible to control from the capital Bangui. Even the smallest armed opposition group can carve out a little fiefdom for itself and gradually that slice of land can serve as a springboard to a serious challenge.

In large part, civil wars are a contest between the rebels and the government as to who can win over the populace. Civilians are a resource that provides labour, opportunities for 'taxation' and intelligence to friendly troops – or the enemy. Because they are so important, both government and insurgents want to prevent them 'defecting' to the other side. That's a particular concern in contested territories in which civilians regularly come into contact with both sides.[42] And when dealing with that problem, insurgents often have a number of advantages. Government troops tend to be drawn from around the country. When their mission is up or the government changes, they leave. Rebels may well be local in the first place and may never leave. That permanence is an advantage when trying to prevent civilians from defecting. Another disadvantage for governments, both democratic and non-democratic, is that they tend to be more constrained when it comes to violence than rebels.[43] There's a story from the Algerian Civil War about an old man, who, when arrested by the French army for having sawn off some telegraph poles, explains why he has done such a thing:

> Sir, the French come and tell me: you mustn't saw off poles; if you do, you go to prison. I say to myself: I don't want to go to prison, I won't do it. The French leave. At night, the rebel comes and says: saw off the poles from here to there. I answer: no, the French would put me into prison. The rebel tells me: you cut the poles or I cut your throat. I calculate: if I don't cut the poles, he'll surely cut my throat; he has done it to others, in the next village. I prefer going to prison. So, Sir, I cut the poles; you caught me; put me in prison.[44]

This was a war in which French soldiers were exceptionally brutal. They razed villages, tortured, killed. But in the end, the rebel threat to that old man was simply more credible so he did what any rational person would do: he cut the poles.

But violence, even when it is brutal, is most effective when it is discriminate.[45] If those who cut the poles receive no more punishment than those who do not, the locals might as well start cutting poles. To prevent that, the tyrant's soldiers and the rebel army have to work out who is a 'traitor' and who serves the cause. Because of their permanence, connection to the local community and capacity for violence, this is easier for insurgents than it is for the government troops who might not even speak the local language.

As we can see, insurgents have a number of advantages against the tyrant on the battlefield. But importantly, rebels can topple tyrants even if they don't succeed in beating the regime's military. Just like rebels, tyrants need people, money and guns to keep fighting.[46] People are relatively easy to come by if you already have an established fighting force

– but rebels can sever the flow of money and weapons to the regime.

Both tend to depend, at least in some respects, on the tyrant's 'good' standing. When rebels force the tyrant to fight a bloody civil war in which thousands of innocent civilians get killed, they can turn the incumbent into an international pariah.

No sanction will make it impossible to acquire weapons because someone will always sell them, but sanctions can ensure that weapons come at a premium, and that further reduces the effectiveness of a military that's probably already proving ineffective. Sanctions can also cause hardship for the population, although that's usually of little concern to autocrats. From their perspective, the main issue is that they risk running into a redistribution problem when foreign aid gets cut or trade routes are frozen due to civil war. Given that tyrants stay in power by dividing up a cake among the hungry elites that surround them, they generally don't want that cake to be reduced.

There's another problem that tyrants can run into even if the cake isn't reduced. In some conflicts, dictators are able to buy off rebel groups with cash or patronage in the event that suppressing them is either too costly or simply impossible.[47] If it's just the rebels and the dictatorship involved, the considerations for either party aren't too difficult. Is it better to settle (for a price) – the path of least resistance? Or is it preferable to fight? With these being the only options, the price to be paid for the rebels' 'allegiance' is comparatively low. Unfortunately for modern tyrants, twenty-first-century civil wars tend to be incredibly messy and outsiders are almost always involved. Perhaps a neighbouring country has an economic interest in the conflict or they think a rebellion against the next-door neighbour is a good chance to get rid of a hostile leader they've long disliked. Now that this outside power is involved, a two-way negotiation between the dictator and the rebel commander turns into an auction. With the rebel commander able to choose to fight for the dictator, or the foreign power, or neither of them, the price the dictatorship has to pay automatically goes up. In some cases, this has led to truly bizarre outcomes.

These mechanisms were at work during the Darfur conflict of 2003 in western Sudan. When the level of unrest grew during 2002, the Sudanese regime made a miscalculation when they thought that they could buy off armed groups on the cheap. The result was a war for which neither the insurgents nor the government were prepared. Then, because of the violence, other powers became interested. But once peace negotiations began, they didn't succeed in resolving the conflict. Instead, explains Alex de Waal, they 'served perversely to increase political competition, lower the barriers for new entrepreneurs to enter the market, and (in the paradox of security markets) further inflate the price of loyalty'.[48] This obviously doesn't apply to every civil war and every rebel group but it does demonstrate that tyrants can run into trouble even if the size of the 'cake' never gets smaller. It's already problematic enough for them if they have to cut bigger pieces.

All these problems are accentuated by corruption. Most authoritarian systems of government evolve around corruption, and the military is no different – it's an institution where money is to be skimmed off ammunition, salaries and guns. But the two are related: risking your life on a low salary to fight on behalf of an uninspiring autocracy is one thing, but to do it while your commanders steal the very equipment you need to survive? That's another.

Rebel movements are extremely difficult to defeat. Even after suffering severe casualties, they can survive, zombie-like, for a very long time. And as the wars drag on, the costs mount

– not just for the people doing the fighting, but for countries as a whole.

On the morning of 21 March 2018, I was in the Beqaa Valley, a stunningly beautiful part of Lebanon wedged between Mount Lebanon and the anti-Lebanon mountains. Beyond the range to the east lay Assad's Syria. I was sitting on the floor in a large tent, listening to a woman talk about her truly desperate situation. The woman and her immediate family had left their hometown in Syria because of the devastating civil war that Bashar al-Assad was waging after he decided that he would rather burn the country to the ground than leave office. Now she was in an informal refugee camp with her young children. The tents had carpets, electricity, and people could sleep on mattresses. But outside the white United Nations tarpaulin that kept families dry, the ground wasn't paved. I dreaded to think what life was like there when it rained.

The woman and her children were safe in a sense, but they also had no security. Basic healthcare was available, but little beyond this. There was barely enough money to make ends meet. And while her husband had made it to Europe, there was no guarantee that she and the children would be able to follow in the immediate future. Returning to Syria wasn't an option either because all that awaited them would be ruins, repression and yet more violence. So they were stuck in a place where they didn't want to be, because of a war they had no part in waging.

On the flight home, I contemplated the fact that the small Syrian family I had met that day were just three of millions of Syrians who had paid the price for Assad's civil war. Turkey alone hosts more than three million Syrians; Lebanon, almost eight hundred thousand. With over three hundred thousand civilians killed and fourteen million displaced, the Syrian civil war is one of the biggest tragedies of a generation.[49]

Some of these conflicts are so traumatic that they continue to play an outsized role in the public imagination for hundreds or even thousands of years after they end. In Chinese politics today, for example, the Warring States Period that happened some two thousand years ago continues to be a symbol for chaos. But as devastating as these conflicts can be, they don't necessarily lead to the fall of tyrants. Henry Kissinger had it wrong when he said 'the guerrilla wins if he does not lose.'[50] In fact, there are plenty of insurgents who have waged guerrilla war for decades without ever coming close to winning. Using drug money, the Revolutionary Armed Forces of Colombia (FARC) have engaged in a relentless struggle against the central government in Bogotá for decades. They have carried out surprise attacks, fought battles, bombed civilians and taken politicians hostage. In total, the war has perhaps cost more than two hundred thousand lives.[51] FARC didn't lose, yet they eventually signed a ceasefire accord with Colombian president Juan Manuel Santos. It was highly controversial at the time and in a way a major achievement for FARC – but was it victory? No, it was not and it's not an isolated case.

Evidently, it's not sufficient for rebels simply to keep fighting to kill off governments. They need to be able to do more than that: win on the battlefield or beat the regime some other way. Only then does the tyrant fall. The despot's vulnerability off the battlefield largely depends on his susceptibility to outside pressure, and some countries are more vulnerable to outside influence than others. Does the regime have access to an indigenous arms industry that can keep pumping out weapons when foreign suppliers stop their deliveries? Can the dictatorship sell something at high prices even while it stands accused of committing crimes against humanity? Can the economy survive without foreign aid? If the answer to all three questions is yes, it will probably be extremely difficult to beat the regime. As depressing as it is, it will probably keep on fighting – either because it can sustain the fight itself or because others find it valuable and so protect it.

One example of the latter is Chad's Déby. When he came to power in 1982, it was partly because Paris ordered French troops in the country to stand by as Déby's rebel army marched on the capital. At the time, the French foreign minister said: 'The times have passed when France would pick governments or change governments and would maintain others when it so wished.'[52] That was a blatant lie. The French had previously protected Habré, but he had become a little too close to the United States for Paris's liking, and was therefore not worthy of French protection anymore.[53] Things were vastly different when Déby was in power. As late as 2019, French pilots flying French jets took to the air to bomb rebels on Déby's behalf.[54] When the French foreign minister was asked what was going on, he explicitly said France was intervening to protect the regime from a potential *coup d'état*.[55] If that isn't picking and choosing governments, what is?

At the beginning of the fight, rebels have the advantage. Provided they have the right terrain, they can take on their opponents with simple means even if they are vastly outgunned.

When the People's Democratic Party of Afghanistan, the party in government in Afghanistan, started fighting its own people in the late 1970s, the tribesmen of Nuristan, a region remote even by Afghan standards, had next to nothing with which to defend themselves. In some instances, they had to resort to slingshots and axes. But what they did have was the terrain, which they knew better than anyone else and could use to their advantage. The government went on the offensive and sent armoured vehicles to put down the rebellion.

But the mountain roads were so narrow that the vehicles couldn't even turn their gun turrets. And engaging targets above them along those steep ravines? Forget it.[56] And even if the armoured battalions did come close, the Nuristani tribal militias triggered mudslides to halt their advance.[57]

But eventually, neither slingshots nor mudslides will do the trick anymore because taking harder targets requires different tactics and different weapons. Rebels have to fight more like a conventional army. As Mao believed, they need to control territory, to mobilise people and resources like the state. When they control those resources, they can defend any newfound territories from the state's counter-attacks before going on the offensive.[58] But when this happens, the rebels become more vulnerable because they need to concentrate their forces, thereby becoming a bigger target for the tyrant's firepower.[59] That vulnerability has allowed many tyrants to stay in power.

On the battlefield, civil wars and insurgencies are particularly challenging because the flame of rebellion is difficult to extinguish for good. Nevertheless, clever tyrants can manage rebellion. As many armed opposition groups have found out to their cost, winning a civil war is much more difficult than not losing. Even if the government's forces are corrupt and not designed primarily to go to war, they are often enough to overcome any opposition.

If they succeed and the tyrant manages to hold the rebels at bay, there are much bigger monsters across the horizon. For if these cruel leaders make a single wrong move at the wrong time and in the wrong neighbourhood, they will come face to face not with peasants wielding Kalashnikovs, but with other states. And when that happens, all bets are off.

5

Enemies, Foreign and Domestic

First pacify the interior then resist the external [threat].[1]

Chiang Kai-shek

Tyrants are often much weaker than they appear. When an external power tries to unseat them, they don't necessarily have to use a lot of force to knock them off their pedestal. In part, that's because prioritising internal enemies, as many tyrants do, makes them particularly vulnerable to foreign threats.[2]

And yet, there's a common conception that authoritarian regimes have an advantage when it comes to the battlefield. In some respects, that's true. To give one example, democratic leaders have a real problem when they take their nation to war and flag-draped coffins start coming back home. Those casualties have mothers and fathers and siblings and friends, and those are the people whose votes are needed by democratic politicians in order to stay in power. In highly personalised systems of government such as absolute monarchies or personalist dictatorships, family and friends mourn their dead just as they do in democracies, but they aren't the constituents the leader needs to worry about. As long as the regime can repress dissent from the streets, and ensure that the sons and daughters of their allies don't get shot, the autocrat is much less vulnerable to the immediate fallout of battlefield deaths than the democrat. Autocracies, in other words, have a lower 'casualty sensitivity' and that helps them to stay in the fight.[3]

Similarly, twenty-first-century dictatorships are less constrained than liberal democracies when it comes to the use of extreme violence. That's not to say that democracies are incapable of it, of course. But there are two key differences. The first is that even the most bloodthirsty democratic leaders can only go so far before they risk being stopped by the courts or people around them. Secondly, in instances where war crimes are committed, there's a process for them to be brought to light by a free press and often a realistic chance of perpetrators being held accountable. In 2023, for example, a former member of the Australian Special Air Service Regiment was arrested for murder after an independent inquiry found special forces operators had purposely killed Afghan civilians.[4] As part of the process, the Australian state encouraged anyone who had relevant information to come forward.

It's difficult to imagine something like this happening in Putin's Russia or in any other personalist dictatorship. When the Russian Air Force bombs a civilian target and then waits for doctors to arrive before bombing them as well, it will never be reported on Russian television. And even if it is, what is supposed to happen? Nothing.

In combination with a higher capacity for extreme violence, lack of political sensitivity about casualties provides tyrants with a significant advantage on the battlefield. But that's largely where the despot's advantages end, and these are outweighed by the costs of coup-proofing and of having an army weakened by the effects of purges, political promotions and a climate of fear.

On 11 June 1937, Mikhail Tukhachevsky, one of the Soviet Union's most capable generals, was standing in front of a secret court. 'I feel I'm dreaming,' he said.[5] Weeks earlier, he had been demoted and then arrested. In the meantime, he had been tortured by the People's Commissariat for Internal Affairs (NKVD) and beaten into signing a confession.[6] The trial was part of the Great Purges, a wave of terror unleashed by Stalin in the latter half of the 1930s. The Soviet Union had always been a brutal regime, but this was of a totally new order. Stalin saw enemies everywhere, including where there were none.[7] Instead of eliminating the few rivals that might actually threaten him, the regime proceeded to come up with quotas of people to be disposed of. With a single order, 268,950 people were to be arrested: 193,000 of them were to do forced labour, the other 75,950 were to be executed. Thereafter, things only became worse. New lists were drawn up, more people were killed. Nikolai Yezhov, the ghoulish head of the NKVD, would send 'albums' of people's names to Stalin for review. The 383 albums seen by Stalin contained around forty-four thousand names.[8]

By the time General Tukhachevsky went on trial, the purges had become a frenzy. Regional officials were no longer simply fulfilling their quotas but going out of their way to ask Moscow for permission to kill and torture more. No longer content with killing people in the basement of Moscow's infamous Lubyanka prison, Yezhov had a slaughter room set up in a building across the street. On one side of the room were logs so that bullets could be caught after exiting the victims bodies; the floor was sloped to allow for easier drainage of blood.[9] Not even the families of 'enemies of the people' were spared. On the contrary: the regime locked up thousands of women for the crime of being married to the 'wrong' man. Children as young as three could be imprisoned.[10] The revolution also ate its young: Corps Commander Ivan Belov, one of the judges sentencing Tukhachevsky, was so scared at the trial that he wondered whether he might be next.[11] And indeed, a little over a year later, the regime found Belov guilty and had him shot.

By one estimate, Stalin's NKVD arrested 1.5 million people between 1937 and 1938, with most of them never being released again.[12] Shot at 22.35 on 11 June 1937, Mikhail Tukhachevsky was one of them. As well as the distinguished general, others purged were among the Red Army's most talented and experienced officers.[13] The regime even boasted that tens of thousands of officers had been arrested.[14] A consequence of this was that other people who were much less capable than the purged officers were now being promoted into more senior roles due to their perceived 'loyalty' to the regime.

As a result of this bloodshed and the promotion of lackeys, Stalin vastly increased his domestic power. Before the terror, the Communist Party had been the most powerful political actor in the Soviet Union. When the violence began to die down, all power was centred in him. He stood alone at the top of one of the largest empires the world had ever known.

But because the purges were so intense, the disruption of the economy, the administrative state and the Red Army so extreme, Stalin put himself at risk. He, after all, could only survive in power if the Soviet state survived, and that was no longer assured.[15] The situation was especially precarious because the international environment had been deteriorating for quite some time. War would break out shortly and the purge of military leaders was undoubtedly one of the main reasons the Soviet forces initially did so badly when Nazi Germany invaded the Soviet Union in June 1941.[16]

But even if Stalin hadn't purged Tukhachevsky and other competent generals, the Soviet Army would have struggled. Soldiers can't fight properly when they are more scared of their own government than the men they see through their gunsights. Whereas generals in democracies may fight for country and glory, generals in heavily politicised militaries can find themselves in an impossible situation. If they lose too much, they become a liability and that can easily mean death rather than demotion. If they win too much, they become a threat to the tyrant and that can also mean death. With the stakes so high, military leaders have a strong incentive to 'lie, exaggerate, and shift blame to cover their mistakes'.[17]

In 1943, Stalin's Red Army and Nazi Germany fought one of the most decisive battles of the Second World War in Kursk. On the southern front of the battle, several hundred Soviet tanks stood in opposition to about a third as many German tanks. Despite the numerical superiority of the Red Army, the German military won a massive victory. By one estimate, they destroyed 'as many as 15 Soviet tanks for every one they lost'. With the fighting done, it now fell to General Nikolai Vatutin to tell Moscow about the defeat. But he refused, so terrified was he that Stalin would sack or execute him. Instead, according to Kenneth Pollack, he fabricated a fierce battle, claiming that both sides had suffered terrible losses.[18]

That story about the Battle of Kursk was repeated again and again, from battle to battle and soldier to soldier. Everybody lied. And over time, military effectiveness was hindered because lying on this scale is devastating when trying to win a war. It's as if the tyrant's own troops set up such a smokescreen that it becomes impossible for the ruler to see anything at all.

Sometimes the fear can be so intense that officers don't just lie to their superiors but become paralysed outright. During the Gulf War, Saudi forces and American forces fought side by side, and both broke through enemy lines. American Marines, despite facing stronger resistance from the enemy, pushed ahead much quicker than the Saudi soldiers. Why? Mainly because Saudi commanders were unable to make decisions in the heat of the moment, constantly looking for their superiors to decide for them.[19] They were so scared of doing the wrong thing that they did nothing.

And unfortunately for tyrants, open warfare isn't all they have to worry about. There's a world beyond congressional authorisations or prime ministerial speeches – a world of shadows. In that world, external powers can go after the despot despite having said that they never would. There are all kinds of options. External powers can train the opposition, give money to armed groups, keep enemies alive or encourage coup-plotters to take on the incumbent. If we travel back to the Cold War for a moment, we can discover what that threat towards tyrants can look like.

In her book *Covert Regime Change*, the political scientist Lindsey O'Rourke provides a thorough account of the 'secret wars' the United States waged while it was struggling against the Soviet Union.[20] In total, the United States pursued seventy regime-change operations (that we know of). Of these, sixty-four were covert. By O'Rourke's count, twenty-five of them led to a US-backed government taking power. The rest failed.[21]

The goal of these interventions varied greatly. Sometimes, they were meant to push back the influence of the Soviet Union by replacing supposedly pro-Soviet leaders with more amenable ones. At other times, they were meant to take out leaders before they could come anywhere near the Soviet camp. While some of the targets were tyrants, others definitely were not.

As O'Rourke argues, covert action is such a problem for tyrants because it's attractive to policymakers.[22] In a way, that's surprising because staying in the shadows while attacking other states inevitably means that the attacker has to operate without their total strength.[23] If they can go to war openly against another nation, they can use everything they've got to try to topple that unfriendly regime, and that can maximise the chances it will actually happen. The demonstrative show of massive power can be so useful that generals have planned entire military doctrines around the notion that overwhelming force can quickly break the enemies' will to fight. Shock and awe is a little harder to do when nobody is supposed to find out who was behind it.

That said, the decision as to how to topple a foreign leader doesn't happen in a vacuum and there are always other considerations at play. Is there public support to go to war? How expensive is it going to be? What does it mean for the next election if young men and women become crippled because they were sent into harm's way by the government? What will it do to the country's reputation if the government openly admits to toppling established governments?

Using political violence out in the open is, in other words, not that easy to do. That's where covert action comes in. To politicians, it's a convenient middle ground: they do something and it could pay off but even if it doesn't, it's not the end of the world. Indeed, many covert regime-change operations have been signed off despite it being abundantly clear that they were unlikely to succeed. When the CIA director told President Eisenhower that the chance of success in a planned intervention in Guatemala could be below 20 per cent, Eisenhower actually thought a low number made the proposal more convincing. Talking to Allen Dulles, director of the CIA, the president said: 'Allen, the figure of 20 per cent was persuasive. If you had told me the chances would be 90 per cent, I would have had a much more difficult decision.'[24] Covert action from abroad can be particularly dangerous to dictators precisely because the allure of 'plausible deniability' makes action against them more likely.

But the men and women working to overthrow dictators in the shadows aren't omnipotent. More often than not, the high appetite for risk combined with the need for things to remain hidden leads to mistakes. Blunders have saved more than one dictator.

After ruling with an iron fist for decades, Cuba's military dictator was overthrown in 1959 by a young revolutionary named Fidel Castro. Unlike Fulgencio Batista, Castro wasn't content to let rich Americans control much of the island's wealth. Since Castro was a self-declared Marxist-Leninist, the White House was immediately concerned that he could align Cuba with the Soviet Union. After John F. Kennedy won the presidential election against Richard Nixon, American intelligence agents presented their plans. Kennedy was reluctant. If the United States was going to try to overthrow Castro, the operation needed to be covert. Initially, American intelligence set out to train exiled Cubans in Florida and Guatemala. Americans would help, but the Cubans themselves were going to be the tip of the spear.

If they were to have any chance of holding out against the inevitable counter-attack, they needed to disable Castro's air force. To maintain the conspiracy, the CIA painted American B-26 aircraft to try to make them look like units of the Cuban Revolutionary Armed Forces before they took off from Nicaragua to bomb the planes.[25] While there was some division within the government, most pre-assessments of the invasion's chances of success were optimistic. The US Department of Defense and the CIA were of the belief that, at the very least, the invaders would reach the safety of the mountains. And at best, there might be a 'full-fledged civil war in which we could then back the anti-Castro forces openly'.[26]

When the first troops landed in the bay, they saw a B-26 up in the air. 'We assumed it was ours,' one of them explained. 'It even dipped its wing. But then it opened fire on us,' he added.[27] Since they had previously been told that Castro's air force had already been destroyed, they could barely believe what they were seeing. But it was real. The CIA's planes had missed many of their targets and now Castro's planes were dominating the skies.[28] Out at sea, one of the cargo ships carrying ammunition and fuel was hit. In an attempt to avoid a similar scenario, other supply ships turned back.[29] Stranded without adequate supplies and some fifty miles away from the mountains in which they were supposed to find refuge if things went wrong, the attempt to topple Castro through force was doomed. Perhaps the enterprise had been doomed before the first shot was fired. The CIA itself later made a good point which indicates that the invasion plans were probably always destined to fail:

> The bay was also far from large groups of civilians, a necessary commodity for instigating an uprising, which may be a moot point, as the bay was surrounded by the largest swamp in Cuba, making it physically impossible for any Cubans wanting to join the revolt to actually do so.[30]

Would things have played out the same way if Kennedy hadn't insisted on covert action over an open attack? We will never know.

With the invasion an abject failure on all levels, the United States could have stopped further attempts to overthrow Castro. Instead, Kennedy authorised a follow-up operation that proposed more and more absurd plans for getting rid of

Fidel. The man in control of the effort to find 'a solution to the Cuban problem' was Attorney General Robert F. Kennedy, the president's younger brother, who wanted to succeed in order to confirm his position. In one meeting with his team, he said finding a solution to the Cuban problem was the top priority of the United States government. 'No time, money effort, or manpower is to be spared,' he added.[31]

That effort included some truly absurd schemes, including a plan to cover Castro's shoes with thallium salts – which, it was believed, would have made the leader's iconic beard fall out. Someone at the CIA thought the way to get rid of him was to spray his surroundings with a chemical that would induce hallucinations before an important speech. Plans were not limited to discrediting Castro: the United States government was willing to assassinate him. In one scheme, Castro was to be given an explosive cigar; in another, a contaminated diving suit was supposed to give him a 'debilitating skin disease'; and in another, which made use of Fidel's love of scuba diving, he was to be blown up with explosives hidden underwater in an attractively painted seashell.[32] Needless to say, all of these plots were either abandoned or they failed – in blunder after blunder. Fidel eventually died at the age of ninety a few years after handing power to his brother Raúl. The Communist Party of Cuba remained in charge of the island nation.

Secretary of Defense Robert McNamara would later say that they had been hysterical about Castro.[33] What this shows is that it's not only tyrants who make irrational decisions when they feel threatened. Their opponents, whether they be democratic leaders or fellow dictators, can make exactly the same mistakes. But despite all these failures, we tend to imagine intelligence services as omnipotent puppet masters that can shape the world as they see fit. In reality, the Bay of

Pigs is in many ways the norm, not the exception. Toppling foreign governments is difficult, especially if it has to be done in secret.

But obviously, simply hoping for the enemy to blunder is not a rational strategy for autocrats especially – because they face a dual threat. Great powers may target them because they are tyrants, whilst their aggressive manoeuvring also means that they run the risk of coming into conflict with regional rivals.

Not every tyrant faces the same threat. Some hang on by a thread, constantly having to worry about being deposed from abroad. Others are comparatively safe in the saddle. Either way, they all have something in common: defeat doesn't have to be total to lead to a fall. If there's an invasion and the invading army reaches the presidential palace, the dictator will obviously lose power. But tyrants can fall much earlier if they are losing on the battlefield – and many of them do. When a team of researchers looked at the effect of losing a war over a period of more than 150 years, they found that 29.5 per cent of leaders who lost a war also had to deal with violent regime change.[34]

There are multiple ways this can happen – one of them being popular protest as a result of the perceived weakness of the dictator.[35] Let's imagine a scenario in which war breaks out between two regional rivals over a contested province that both claim as theirs. The defending state, which previously controlled the province, is beaten badly. To prevent the attacker from marching even further, the dictator in charge of the defending state makes a concession: going forward, the defending state no longer claims the contested province.

The attacking army is still far from the palace and the dictator is physically safe from them, but there's a decent chance that the dictator could now find himself in serious trouble.

With the public upset over this embarrassing defeat, they might well be out on the streets calling for his head. While that by itself might not matter too much to the dictator, it sends a signal to the dictator's opponents that the regime is weak. It's the perfect time to launch a coup.

To dictators worried about falling, there are two avenues to take to reduce the risk of military defeat: increase the effectiveness of their military, or leave the military as it is and find another way to protect themselves. To those looking to do the former, the most rational strategy is to build up military strength to a point at which an attack from outside is too costly even to be contemplated. In international relations, this is referred to as a 'deterrent'. Once that deterrent has been established – and only then – do they go all out on coup-proofing. The key to this is developing a deterrent that doesn't disappear as the military becomes more and more geared towards taking on internal enemies. For inspiration, dictators can look to twenty-first-century North Korea.

The North Korean People's Army is outdated and in many ways primitive compared to the military of the United States or even that of regional powers such as South Korea or Japan. With more than a million active-duty personnel, it is also among the world's largest. More importantly, North Korea has thousands of artillery systems, many of which are deployed near the demilitarised zone that has divided the peninsula since 1953.[36]

In the event of all-out warfare between North and South, commuters on their way to work in South Korea's capital could suddenly find themselves in a situation which would seem apocalyptic. Skyscrapers would be reduced to rubble, office buildings would burn, windows would shatter. With the ground shaking from the impact of an artillery round, the next round and the one after that would already be on their way.

In 2020, researchers at the RAND Corporation, an American non-profit think tank that works closely with the United States government, estimated just how destructive such an attack would be.[37] To do this, they looked at the positioning of North Korean artillery systems and the South Korean population density, and also at the way targeted populations would react in the event of an attack. How many would panic? How quickly could people take cover in basements or subway tunnels?

One complicating factor is the location and size of South Korea's capital. Lying about fifty kilometres south of the border zone, Seoul proper 'only' has a population of 9.5 million.[38] But once you look at the entire capital area, it becomes a metropolis of some 26 million. To put that in context, that's around the population of Belgium, Greece and Ireland combined. In the worst-case scenario, North Korean artillery would turn Seoul into a 'sea of fire' by sending over around fourteen thousand rounds within a single hour. If that happens, the casualty estimates range from around 87,600 (positive) to around 130,000 (negative).[39]

However much Kim Jong-un coup-proofs the military, those artillery pieces aren't going away. And while they are in place, they have a huge deterrent effect because everyone knows that war against North Korea would inevitably lead to hundreds of thousands of casualties.

There is only one form of deterrent that works better than Kim's artillery: weapons of mass destruction. These weapons, whether they are chemical, biological or nuclear, are so destructive that leaders pursue them because they know that having them will provide their regime with a deterrent that's powerful enough to ward off other states. These weapons also mean that dictatorships don't need to go back on their coup-proofing. All they need is a small number of soldiers, selected on the basis of their loyalty to the regime, to wield the weapons.[40] And even if things go wrong and these soldiers turn on the dictator, they can't do much with these weapons even though they are so destructive. That differs from conventional forces: every extra main battle tank given to the military can be used by the military against the regime. But a nuclear bomb? Exceedingly useful to deter a nation-state but useless to overthrow the government. Nobody is going to nuke their own capital city.

For all these reasons, weapons of mass destruction are a popular 'strategic substitute' for tyrants. In the Middle East, for example, five countries have seriously pursued nuclear weapons programmes (Iran, Iraq, Israel, Libya and Syria), and all of them except Israel were or are highly coup-proofed.[41] That's no coincidence.

But while having nuclear weapons is a massive advantage to dictators, the business of acquiring them is perilous. As the nuclear weapons expert Nicholas Miller told me, it's very difficult to develop nuclear weapons in secret. Once other countries find out (or at least suspect) that a dictator is working on building them, there's a constant threat of economic sanctions or perhaps military action.[42] But even if tyrants could proceed secretly, they'd need sufficient resources to turn their bold plans into nuclear reality.

This, ironically, is where the focus on domestic security can hurt despots yet again: nuclear technology is difficult to master. To do so, countries need competent and functioning institutions. A lot of autocracies, constructed with the singular goal of keeping the incumbent in power, simply don't support such institutions because anything that restrains the incumbent is seen as a threat by the presidential palace. This can make it impossible for some tyrants to acquire nuclear weapons even if they wanted to.

Gaddafi's Libya wasn't just brutal, it was also highly dysfunctional, with every aspect of the system tied to its leader's personality quirks. The resulting incompetence made it challenging to pursue strategic goals, including the development of nuclear weapons.

For a start, the Libyan regime didn't have enough engineers and scientists – partly because Gaddafi was reluctant to invest in higher education in science and technology, which he saw as a source of opposition.[43] At the time of independence, Libya was a deeply impoverished country: in 1948, per-capita income stood at around fifteen pounds a year.[44] Moreover, there was almost no state capacity and much of the population lacked even basic education – 94 per cent of the population was illiterate.[45] Things could have changed after the discovery of oil. The economy grew rapidly and the regime then had the resources to expand the capacity of the state. But that didn't happen. Gaddafi, in fact, wanted the opposite. He explicitly set out to dismantle what little there was of the state because he saw it as a threat to his rule. His goal wasn't shared prosperity, but power.

In her book *Unclear Physics*, Malfrid Braut-Hegghammer explores how the Libyan nuclear programme failed. It makes for devastating reading. According to her, Libya's institutions were not well-equipped for carrying out simple tasks, let alone planning a nuclear weapons project.[46] So the Gaddafi regime tried to buy its way towards becoming a nuclear weapons state. At first, it attempted to persuade Beijing to sell them ready-manufactured nukes. But the Chinese prime minister Zhou Enlai reportedly said: 'Sorry . . . but China obtained the bomb through its own efforts. We believe in self-help.'[47]

That was just the beginning of an odyssey. The regime tried to buy from Argentina, China, France, India, Yugoslavia, the United States, Egypt, Pakistan and the Soviet Union. Nothing brought a breakthrough.[48]

When the regime succeeded in buying relevant equipment or recruiting scientists from abroad, it struggled to make use of them. And when things inevitably went wrong, Gaddafi's personalised system of government made it difficult to understand the full extent of the problem. Gaddafi himself obviously couldn't understand what the nuclear scientists were doing, but then his bare-bones state didn't have any of the institutions required to monitor and understand what the scientists were doing either.[49] As a result, Gaddafi never got close to the nuclear threshold because he had traded protection against external threats for internal security.

If regimes feel threatened by external actors and there's no time to invest in weapons of mass destruction (or it's judged too risky), the only remaining option to increase destructive power is to go back on some of the coup-proofing measures, thereby trading security the other way: less protection against domestic enemies; a more effective military to fight foreign threats.

During the 1980s, Saddam Hussein was at war with neighbouring Iran. For his soldiers, it was an extraordinarily difficult war to wage. The generals were paralysed by fear and the dictator was micromanaging military strategy, even ordering the size of individual trenches.[50] The regime was also flying blind because almost the entire intelligence apparatus was directed at spying on ordinary Iraqis and the military.[51] The focus on domestic enemies was so complete that, on the eve of the war, Iraqi intelligence had only three officers tasked with gathering and analysing intelligence on Iran. Only one of them had actually studied Farsi, the language needed to understand what's going on in Iran.[52] It was the classic case of a coup-proofed military losing on the battlefield because it simply wasn't designed for the job.

But then, Hussein's threat calculus changed. Before the war, the Iraqi military was a much bigger threat to his rule than the Iranian military. But as the Iranians got the upper hand and even Baghdad no longer seemed safe, he changed his mind. 'The true military professionals were never Saddam's favourites, even when they were most important. Increasingly throughout the war, he understood that he needed them, and more often than not, he heeded their advice,' an analysis based on the recollections of an Iraqi general later said.[53] The spies were also redirected: whereas there had previously been almost nobody doing that job, there were more than two and a half thousand people generating intelligence on Iran in the final year of the war.[54]

In the end, going back on some of the coup-proofing measures was enough to achieve a stalemate with Iran – keeping Saddam Hussein in power for another day. It also meant that the military became a bigger threat to the regime, but that was a risk worth taking because the imminent threat to regime survival had been averted.

The Iraqi dictator was able to pivot from internal to external defence because he had a large military, vast quantities of oil and the enemy wasn't overwhelmingly powerful. When that isn't the case and tyrants can't change course, or doing so would make little difference, there are few good options for dictators. They must find a way to deal with external aggressors without using the military.

The immediate option is acquiescence. If an external power that can credibly threaten a tyrant's rule wants something done: do it. Obviously, that's not a great option for the tyrant because it reduces the room for manoeuvre and risks demonstrating weakness. A more elegant solution can sometimes be found in international diplomacy. Perhaps powerful states, whether they are democratic or not, can be talked out of their hostility. Alternatively, there might be a way to give greater powers something else they want. Perhaps that's oil, uranium, market access or indirect control over a strategic maritime route – or 2,498 metres of concrete near Afghanistan. When five al-Qaeda terrorists flew American Airlines Flight 11 into the North Tower of the World Trade Center on 11 September 2001, American foreign policy changed in an instant. Five days later, President Bush spoke of a war on terrorism. To wage that war, the United States needed new friends in an area of the world that most people couldn't find on a map: Central Asia.

At the time, Uzbekistan was ruled by Islam Karimov, the last first secretary of the Communist Party of Uzbekistan. Karimov was a brutal dictator. He became infamous internationally when the bodies of two former inmates of Jaslyk Prison in northwestern Uzbekistan were returned to their families for burial. Muzafar Avazov, a thirty-five-year-old with four children, reportedly didn't just have 'a large, bloody wound on the back of the head', he was also missing his fingernails. On top of that, 'sixty to seventy percent' of his body was burnt. According to Human Rights Watch, a prominent non-governmental organisation, 'doctors who saw the body reported that such burns could only have been caused by immersing Avazov in boiling water.'[55] When the victim's sixty-three-year-old mother dared to complain about her son's brutal torture, she was sent to a maximum-security jail for attempting to 'overthrow the constitutional order'.[56]

But despite this case and others like it, Uzbekistan received tens of millions of dollars in aid after it agreed to let western forces use (and expand) Karshi-Khanabad Air Base for military operations in Afghanistan. In late 2001, American secretary of state Colin Powell visited the Uzbekistan capital Tashkent. Early the following year, President Karimov met President Bush.[57] The two countries signed several agreements to strengthen their relationship. While in Uzbekistan, Powell referred to the country as 'an important member of the coalition against terrorism'.[58] Because America derived so much value from the air base in southern Uzbekistan, the United States government eventually became reluctant to speak out about human rights abuses in the country.[59] Far from seeing the United States as a threat, Karimov turned it into an asset to solidify his grip on power.

An arrangement that is even better for the tyrants is one in which external powers don't just leave them to their own devices but actively shield them against outsiders. This is the strategy pursued by multiple middle eastern petrostates. They may expend billions of dollars on American military equipment, but ultimately the external security of the emir of Qatar isn't guaranteed by the soldiers of the Qatari Armed Forces, but by the men and women of the United States military stationed in the country. Hosting thousands of soldiers, Al Udeid Air Base in Qatar is the largest American military base in the Middle East. If an external power wanted to topple the emir, they would have to face these forces. And who would want to fight the American military? Fighting the Qatari military, maybe. But the American military? No.

For the security provider, it's a delicate situation. On the one hand, the security provider gains a lot of leverage. In exchange for protecting the Qatari royal family, for example, the United States gets not just a lucrative arms customer but also access to a giant hub that can be used to move soldiers and equipment around, or fly sorties against targets in nearby countries, if need be. But these security guarantees are dangerous in at least two ways. First, there's always the risk of escalation. Governments that agree to provide security for autocratic regimes usually do so on the assumption that they won't have to fight on the regime's behalf because their military presence itself provides sufficient deterrence. That, of course, cannot be taken for granted. Whether it's because of miscalculation or accident, things can always go wrong and suddenly there's war.

Second, these security guarantees create a moral hazard and they incentivise 'free-riding'. When countries free-ride, they make use of a benefit without paying for it. Over the last couple of years, for example, the term has repeatedly been used in the context of European defence spending. While all members of NATO benefit from the deterrence value of the alliance, not everyone is contributing to it to the same extent. The countries that contribute less are said to be free-riding because they enjoy protection from Russian attack even though they don't (adequately) contribute to it. Giving security guarantees to autocratic regimes means that the dictatorship has little incentive to guarantee its own external defence. That's contrary to the interests of the security provider because it means if war does break out, the brunt of the fighting (and dying) will have to be borne by the security provider rather than the dictatorship itself.

That's all the more dangerous to the provider because the security guarantee also creates a moral hazard that means the security guarantee can *increase* rather than *decrease* the chance of war. Because the dictatorship thinks it is protected and unlikely to bear the brunt of a possible conflict, it has an incentive to act more aggressively than it usually would.

Without such security guarantees, dictators are alone. They can coup-proof their military or have a military that is as effective as possible to deal with external threats. Having both at the same time is almost an impossibility. Weapons of mass destruction are a potential way out, but obtaining them is difficult. As a result, most tyrants are stuck in the trade-off, moving the needle to one side or another without ever being able to find the perfect balance.

But even if they did – having now defused both internal and external military threats – nothing they've done so far is about good governance. Everything they've done is tied to staving off immediate danger and that means they have probably done a bad job of looking after the needs of most of the population. Without having much choice in the matter, they've exposed themselves to popular anger at a scale that could lead to massive protests, a violent uprising or even a popular revolution.

6

You Shoot, You Lose

Those who were deprived of their freedom or life were not saints, they were not little angels. They tried to alter the established order.[1]

Hugo Banzer, president of Bolivia

When Mao famously said political power grows out of the barrel of a gun, he was wrong.[2] Political power lies with those who don't need to use guns. When regimes turn their guns on their own people, they risk becoming brittle. Tyrants may fall and regimes can collapse when the barrel of the gun ceases to be a metaphor and instead becomes a real-life strategy to retain control.

When the masses erupt and can no longer be controlled without guns, dictators must make an impossible decision. For many of them, it's their last. These uprisings aren't the principal risk to most tyrants, but that doesn't mean they are no threat: around 17 per cent of dictatorships fall as a result of popular uprisings.[3] Given the obsession that all despots have with controlling their population, it's a remarkably high number.

Democracies are extremely good at dealing with dissent. If you want to protest against the government, you can go ahead. Not only will it be allowed, the police will protect demonstrators as they march. It's a sign of strength that many heads of state need not devote a single brain cell to working out what to do about people chanting in the streets. Dictators, however, can't ignore people in the streets. For them, it's a real dilemma: if they allow protests without cracking down, others may be tempted to join. That can create a cascade, in which the protests swell to a level that threatens the regime itself. If protestors can get away with marching even though they have been specifically told not to, what else can they get away with in defiance of the government? It's a dangerous moment.

In the social sciences, the process by which protests spread from one place to another is referred to as 'diffusion'. This spread can happen through a number of mechanisms, such as, for example, emulation. If protestors in one place see that protestors in another don't get beaten by security forces, they might imitate them. But also, they are going to ask themselves whether they can learn anything from the others – thereby making their own resistance more effective. So when these protests break out, they aren't just contagious – they become more effective as they spread from town to town because dissidents learn from each other; they inspire each other.

This learning effect happens all the time. During the Arab Spring, many dissidents consulted a book written by Gene Sharp called *From Dictatorship to Democracy*.[4] Written in 1993, the book outlines 198 methods for popular resistance, ranging from strikes to more unusual forms of protest such as mock funerals for regime officials. Gene Sharp describes methods of resistance falling into two categories; they are either 'acts of commission' or 'acts of omission'.[5] Or, put more directly: doing what you're not supposed to do or no longer doing what you're supposed to do.[6]

Diffusion of protest isn't exclusive to dictatorships, but the effects of diffusion are especially important in them because they contribute to solving a coordination problem faced by people who would like to protest but can't. In every dictatorship, a sizeable percentage of the population hates the regime, but rising up is difficult because the disgruntled don't know whether others would join them, and they can't plan protests because it's illegal and dangerous to do so. Under those circumstances, it is very hard to launch a demonstration. But once people see others protesting in a town down the road, they no longer have to launch a protest, they can simply join in.

That prospect is especially menacing to dictators because it can happen so quickly. According to Erica Chenoweth from Harvard University, one of the key advantages of non-violent civil resistance is its participation advantage.[7] In comparison to a guerrilla movement, for example, non-violent resistance campaigns can mobilise vast numbers of supporters with ease because barriers to participation are much lower. You don't need to be a hardened fighter to join a march – almost everyone can do it, whether they are schoolchildren, the elderly or somewhere in between. As a result, dictators who miscalculate can find themselves besieged by tens of thousands of people in a flash once they have solved their coordination problem. Eventually, the number may become overwhelming, leading the regime to collapse. And indeed, there's a '3.5% rule'. Coined by Chenoweth, it says that 'no revolutions have failed once 3.5% of the population has actively participated in an observable peak event like a battle, a mass demonstration, or some other form of mass non-cooperation.'[8] In 2003, for example, the Georgian people forced President Eduard Shevardnadze to resign. With a certain number of people in the streets, governments are simply overwhelmed and then they either have to make major concessions or they fall. That's not only because there are so many people in active opposition, but also because the protestors will probably have support among an even larger share of the population.[9] That said, only eighteen out of 389 resistance campaigns exceeded the 3.5% threshold between 1945 and 2014.[10] It's comparatively rare – but when it does happen, it can be deadly to governments.*

Despots understand how dangerous popular opposition can be, which is why they are so obsessed with the prospect of protest. These regimes depend on control and public perceptions of invincibility, and the mere existence of overt dissent signals vulnerability. Because of that, tyrants try to nip protests in the bud as soon as they break out. The usual tool to do this is repression. In political science, this is referred to as the 'law of coercive responsiveness'.[11] When the marching starts, the beatings start. This is true even for non-violent opposition movements. When researchers examined more than one hundred non-violent opposition campaigns, they found that almost 90 per cent of them were met with violent repression.[12]

From the dictator's perspective, the problem with beating protestors who are already upset with the government is that it can lead to yet more people in the streets. That's particularly true for non-violent resistance. It's one thing to shoot back at people who shoot at you, but to pro-actively go out and shoot at unarmed demonstrators is another.

In February 2022 Russia launched an illegal large-scale invasion of Ukraine. But Russia's government and the Ukrainian people were already in conflict. In late 2013, the Ukrainian government was about to sign an association agreement with the European Union that would have seen its economy become integrated more closely with the West.

---

* As Chenoweth points out, a 1962 revolt in Brunei and protests in Bahrain between 2011 and 2014 are notable exceptions. Both failed despite active participation by more than 3.5 per cent of the population.

Then, on 21 November 2013, the government of Ukrainian president Viktor Yanukovych announced a stunning U-turn at the last minute. The agreement would be suspended and Ukraine would move closer to Russia instead.

Protestors immediately started pouring towards the Maidan Nezalezhnosti, Kyiv's central square. When it became apparent that Ukraine's rough winter weather wasn't enough to break the protestors' spirit, the government unleashed its security forces. The night of 30 November, instead of sending demonstrators back to their heated homes and re-establishing control, police officers attacked peaceful protestors with batons. According to witness reports, not even protestors who had fallen to the ground were safe: Ukrainian security forces simply kept hitting them.[13]

The use of violence against unarmed students, including women, outraged people. The next day, Pavlo Tumanov, a thirty-eight-year-old doctor, was on the Maidan with 'stripes in the colours of the Ukrainian and EU flags tied to his hands'. 'I came to support the students who were brutally beaten yesterday,' he said.[14] Pavlo wasn't alone. Many who had been on the fence had got off it and sided against the government. The government now faced tens of thousands in the streets as repression had clearly backfired.

But the government hadn't learned its lesson. As the Yanukovych government used repression, the protestors became more motivated and radical. Some of them rioted, used firearms, threw Molotov cocktails. This seesaw of escalation, mobilisation and then escalation continued for months, and the authorities never regained control until the battle between protestors and the government ended in late February the following year.

On 20 February 2014, the Yanukovych government made its final stand as security forces fired live ammunition at demonstrators. Dozens were killed, many of them by special police snipers.[15] But despite the dead and the injured, the protestors did not back down. The next day, as Ukrainians were mopping up blood and reinforcing barricades in the square, President Yanukovych signed a deal with the opposition in the presence of the foreign ministers of Germany and Poland.[16]

But it was too late for a piece of paper to save Viktor Yanukovych and he knew it. Just over twenty-four hours after police snipers had taken aim at the protestors, Yanukovych had no choice but to flee to Russia.

Activists mourned the dead, but they had killed the government. Faced with public protest, the aspiring dictator in Kyiv had continued to make things worse by using physical force that simply made people angrier.

Since this seesaw of repression and radicalisation is a common problem, tyrants often try to prevent people from marching in the first place – because if nobody marches, they don't have to retaliate with violence. And if they don't have to do that, they don't risk a loss of control.

Preventing people from resisting is a serious challenge in dictatorships because the system is so obviously set up in a way that hurts the vast majority of the population. There's nearly always a large number of unhappy people.

And the obvious way of making people happy – giving them more influence – is not an attractive option because it runs counter to the interests of the tyrant and wider elites. Instead, tyrants can focus on other forms of legitimacy.

All governments can be measured according to two forms of legitimacy, which are sometimes split into 'input' vs 'output'. The 'input' refers to democratic procedure, so authoritarian regimes always fail that test. But output legitimacy refers to whether or not the regime delivers prosperity or some other positive outcome that people are looking for. That's an area in which some autocrats can deliver. Every authoritarian regime has a version of this. In their telling, the leaders of the junta in Myanmar put an end to anarchy. The absolute monarchies of the Gulf turned barren deserts into marvels of modern engineering. President Kagame, the dictator of Rwanda, has lifted millions out of poverty. But to go beyond transactional acquiescence and achieve real support, governments need a story to tell; they need to give people an emotional reason to support something that is bigger than themselves. These appeals to a higher ideal come in all shapes and sizes. Il Duce subordinates the individual to the health of the Italian people. God chooses kings and queens to rule their subjects. Ayatollahs defend Allah's will on earth. Communist dictatorships oppress workers to set them free.

One thing that helps to persuade people to tolerate or even support the dictator's rule is to give them the illusion that the dictatorship is supported by others. Ever wonder why non-democratic states spend millions of dollars on elections despite it being clear that they don't mean anything? This is why: 'winning' elections is a way to demonstrate to a country's own people and to foreign states that the regime has popular support.

The classic way to persuade the population of obvious falsehoods is to blast them with propaganda every minute they're awake. When they read the newspaper, they read what the regime wants them to read. When they turn on the television, they watch what the regime wants them to watch. When they listen to the radio ... you get the idea. No form of propaganda is more intense than dictatorial cults of personality.

But even these attempts at legitimation, effective as they can be when amplified by a powerful propaganda apparatus, will never persuade everyone. So instead of fighting all remaining opponents, sophisticated authoritarians give at least some of them a stake in the continued survival of the regime.

A sustainable way of giving people a stake in the survival of the regime is 'co-optation'. If you walk some three hundred metres north from Moscow's Kremlin, you'll find yourself standing in front of a large, symmetrical building that houses Russia's lower house of parliament. In a liberal democracy, this building would be full of opposition parties. Firebrand politicians would use their time at the lectern to hold the government's feet to the fire. Reporters would do television interviews in the lobby, going after the government because this or that latest policy had failed.

In Putin's Russia, all of this still happens but none of it is real. It's a charade, an illusion. Voters get to vote for opposition candidates at the ballot box but all of them are effectively controlled by the government. Journalists are allowed to criticise the regime but only within the parameters set by the shadowy figures who oversee this 'managed democracy' which is actually a dictatorship. If this theatre didn't exist, the journalist and the firebrand might actually oppose the regime. Now that it does, both have a strong interest in its preservation because the preservation of the current order also preserves their high positions and plush salaries. If co-optation is done well, it turns potential enemies into supporters without any bloodshed.

There are also structural factors that tyrants can change in order to make mobilisation more difficult even if a large segment of the population is deeply unhappy. The most effective way of doing this to a leader's advantage is to use the full force of the state in a way that makes it impossible for large groups of people to collaborate even if they do come across triggers that inspire them to take action. That means closing the window to any sort of political opposition as far as is humanly possible: no free media, no free expression, no forms of political organisation outside the control of the dictatorship; as many people as possible spying on each other to detect even the smallest infractions; harsh punishments, if need be across generations, for anyone who dares to defy the supreme leadership. That's how North Korea works and that's why Kim Jong-un doesn't have to worry about protests ever breaking out in Pyongyang.[17] There are plenty of reasons why North Koreans might be upset, but even if they are, they can't do much about it. They might be hungry, they have no space to meet like-minded individuals and even if they managed to bring some people onto the streets, it would be highly unlikely for protests to spread because people elsewhere in the country would simply never know a thing about it. Because how would they? Watching television means watching the government's propaganda, and organisation through social media is impossible. While a few North Koreans have access to foreign media, sharing something as innocent as a South Korean television show can reportedly lead to North Koreans being executed.[18]

Not all authoritarian rulers can sleep as easily as Kim Jong-un. One thing that many of them are obsessed with is the prospect of a 'Colour Revolution'. The term Colour Revolution initially referred to the popular uprisings in Eurasia following the end of the Soviet Union. There was the Georgian Rose Revolution in 2003, the Ukrainian Orange Revolution in 2004 and the Kyrgyz Tulip Revolution in 2005. From the perspective of Moscow and like-minded capitals, these protest movements were not organic signs of dissent with unpopular governments, they were instigated, financed and organised by the United States and other hostile democracies. Faced with the threat of this supposed destabilisation from abroad, the Kremlin moved to bring Russian civil society under its control.

On 4 December 2008, the Moscow employees of Memorial, Russia's oldest and most prominent human rights organisation, were in for a shock. That morning, seven masked men stormed the office. Armed with batons, they prevented all staff members from leaving while they cut the phone lines. Over the course of the next seven hours, the organisation's lawyer was denied access while the men searched the office. In addition to computer hard drives, they seized an archive of Soviet repression stretching back two decades.[19]

The raid caused international uproar, but it was only the opening barrage of a long campaign waged by Putin's regime. In 2012, it escalated as Putin signed the foreign agents law. The law was a frontal assault on the viability of running a non-governmental organisation in the country. It introduced 'a requirement that organizations engaging in political activity and receiving foreign funding must register as foreign agents, even if the foreign funding they receive does not actually pay for political activities'.[20] The American non-governmental organisation Freedom House summarised the situation as follows: 'Once an "apolitical" organization engages in a critique of government policy, its activities could be deemed political as well.'[21] Since that can mean just about anything, nobody was immune and the ensuing regulations were strict. Among other things, 'foreign agents' had to let everyone they dealt with know that they were 'foreign agents'.

Combined with the regime making clear to domestic donors that they should no longer fund such organisations, laws such as this made it more difficult for the organisations to operate. What's more, whipping up the population against human rights organisations (or traitors funded by the country's enemies, in this version of events) served another purpose.

If enough people are angry enough, some of them won't stop at posting mean comments on social media; they will throw fake blood at the doors of the organisations or harass their employees. It made life hell for anyone involved with them, whilst the regime retained plausible deniability because the intimidation was carried out by another party.

The *coup de grâce* came in 2021. Standing beneath Russia's coat of arms, the two-headed golden eagle, the robe-clad Supreme Court judge Alla Nazarova ordered Memorial to close. Its violations of the foreign agent laws had been 'repeated' and 'gross', she said.[22] And just like that, the Kremlin had used the legal system to restrict the work of a critical non-governmental organisation before killing it altogether. But importantly, it had done it with a thin veneer of legality that made it easier to avoid popular opposition.

Another thing that can help to reduce the probability of mass protests with a comparatively low risk of public backlash is surveillance. If the regime knows exactly who wants to topple them – what they think, who they meet, what they plan – they can take them out of the game before they offer any serious opposition.

During the Cold War, conducting that work was a massive challenge. Agents had to camp outside somebody's house, tail them, tap their telephone, open their letters and even then they didn't necessarily have a full picture of everyone the suspect was talking to. That's why, for example, the secret services of the Warsaw Pact states were so massive. In the Soviet Union, there was roughly one full-time secret police officer for every 600 citizens. The Stasi, East Germany's notorious secret police, had an estimated officer for every 180 citizens.[23] It was, by most accounts, the largest surveillance organisation in recorded history. Since then, obtaining information about people has become easier. When I talked to a human rights researcher about the way technology enables authoritarian rule, I was told that working out who someone is talking to can be as easy as scraping publicly available social media data. The work that was once done by dozens of agents can now be done by a single engineer – and that engineer can do it for dozens of people at once.

As odd as it may sound, reducing the number of people on the streets can also be achieved by focusing on streets rather than people. Think of the big protest movements that have rocked authoritarian regimes. What do they have in common? For people to challenge their regimes they need a place to come together: Tahrir Square in Cairo, Taksim Square in Istanbul, Maidan Nezalezhnosti in Kyiv. Even in democracies, people tend to congregate in symbolic places to show their strength: Pariser Platz in front of the Brandenburg Gate, Trafalgar Square in the City of Westminster, the Champs-Élysées and the Arc de Triomphe in Paris.

Contrast that with Burma. As the journalist Matt Ford has pointed out, the country's military junta was rocked by demonstrations in 2007, but protests never took hold in the country's capital city.[24]

Why? At least in part because the generals had earlier moved the capital from Yangon – an organically evolved coastal city – to Naypyidaw, a planned city, described as 'dictatorship by cartography'.[25] Protests in Naypyidaw were unlikely for several reasons. For a start, barely anyone who wasn't connected to the government lived in Naypyidaw. But even if there had been more potential dissidents in the city, it's not clear where they could have gone to protest. As Ford wrote in *The Atlantic*: 'Broad boulevards demarcate the specially designated neighbourhoods where officials live, with no public square or central space for residents, unruly or otherwise, to congregate. A moat even surrounds the presidential palace.'[26]

And while the structure of the capital is a handicap for protestors, it allows the generals' security forces to move around without being impeded by annoying residents. Perhaps you remember the video that went viral of a fitness instructor dancing, inadvertently made in front of a military convoy during the 2021 *coup d'état* in Burma? That was Naypyidaw.

Some opposition movements sustain themselves without the need for individual leaders. Others slowly evolve beyond them as they become more powerful. But either is difficult to achieve under tyranny because tyrants make it so difficult to come together and organise anything. Under those circumstances, prominent individuals can become the opposition's best hope of achieving real change. That's a weakness that can be exploited by tyrants because they can change the entire board simply by taking an individual piece off it.

Such targeted repression can take many forms: intimidation, harassment, detention, imprisonment, forced exile or even physical attacks; in the most extreme form, murder. Since targeting well-known activists inevitably leads to higher costs for the tyrant, the danger is particularly acute for dissidents and opposition figures who present a threat to the regime if they don't have a large public profile to protect them against the worst.

The advantage of targeted repression, from the tyrant's point of view, is twofold. First, there's a risk of backlash but in many cases this is lower than the risk of backlash from targeting a larger group of people. Second, it's a direct way to make an example out of someone to deter others, so aiming at one may silence many.

Targeted repression like this has always happened, but it's changed over the last couple of decades. In the past, fleeing abroad offered significant (albeit not perfect) protection.

Opponents could still be found and killed in a faraway place, but that was costly and difficult.

In the twenty-first century, tyrants can follow their enemies abroad with relative ease. Transnational repression has moved from being an exception to being the norm, and the assassination of Saudi dissident Jamal Khashoggi in Istanbul in 2018 was only the tip of the iceberg. Not only is it easier to travel long distances to visit friends or faraway places, it is also easier for autocratic hit squads to track and murder dissidents.

But often, tyrants don't even need to send their own thugs to follow dissidents abroad, because fellow authoritarian leaders will do the job for them. A recent report on transnational repression found that 'most acts of transnational repression are undertaken through co-optation of or cooperation with authorities in the host country.'[27] Sometimes, that can take the form of an explicit deal wherein one regime takes care of foreign dissidents within its borders in exchange for another doing the same.[28] Other times, dictators don't even have to ask.

But let's say, despite all this, people still protest. If neither beatings nor snipers are the solution, what is? What exactly can tyrants do to prevent their fall? The answer is depressing: they need to go big. If tyrants are going to use severe repression, including bullets, they need to be ready to go all the way. Otherwise, they risk ending up in an escalating cycle, where the repression doesn't do its intended job, protests grow and they have the worst of all worlds.

Some tyrants have, unfortunately, been willing to commit to the 'go big' approach. The most effective way to avoid a backlash when using force is to be so brutal that the barriers to participation increase disproportionately to its mobilisation effect. Put bluntly, people don't join protests if they think they will die. And as the risk of death increases, the participation advantage of popular protest evaporates into thin air.

That's a strategy more than one tyrannical regime has pursued. On 3 June 1989, a Chinese woman named Jia was looking down at a burning bus on the Avenue of Eternal Peace in central Beijing.[29] Having climbed onto the base of a lamp-post to get a better look at the carnage, her heart beat fast. Without being organised or ordered by any leader, the residents of China's capital had brought out whatever they could find into the street in an attempt to halt the advance of the People's Liberation Army. Earlier that evening, Jia had even seen some men roll a milk cart into the street. They thought if they smashed the bottles, the glass might puncture the tyres of the approaching military vehicles.

But faced with the overwhelming might of the Chinese military, they didn't stand a chance. As the soldiers advanced, they fired indiscriminately at peaceful protestors. Jia jumped down from the lamp-post and ran. Before long, a man waved her into an alley where dozens of people were hiding from the troops. Hiding there, Jia could see tank after tank rumble by. In that moment, she asked herself what would happen to the students. 'Are the soldiers going to shoot them as they did us?'[30]

They did. The army had poured into the city from all four directions. Armoured vehicles cleared barricades and the violence went on for hours with extreme brutality. Students, other protestors and innocent bystanders were beaten and shot. Some were even crushed by Type 59 main battle tanks.[31]

Lu Jinghua, a twenty-eight-year-old, was in the square when the tanks rolled in. 'I heard bullets whizz past and people getting shot. One body fell by me, then another. I ran and ran to get out of the way. People were crying for help, calling out for ambulances,' she said. 'Then another person would die,' she added.[32]

The scene the following morning was harrowing. The Avenue of Eternal Peace 'echoed with screams'.[33] The corpses of dead protestors were carried away by friends. Some of the wounded were thrown onto bicycles or rickshaws. As people ran next to them to make sure that they would find their way through the crowds, some cried.

The first Chinese report spoke of 241 dead including twenty-three soldiers. According to multiple outside observers in the city at the time, the true number of dead is likely to have been much higher – perhaps even somewhere around 2,600 to 2,700.[34] But it wasn't just the dead. The soldiers had shot so many protestors that some doctors had run out of blood with which to treat the wounded.[35]

But even that wasn't sufficient, because protests quickly spread to 181 cities across the country.[36] It was a crucial moment for the Chinese Communist Party. China's regime had gone all out on repression. Would they be willing to see it through to the gruesome end?

The answer came soon, as brutal crackdowns took place across the country. In the provincial capital Chengdu alone, 'at least 100 seriously wounded people' were carried out of one square, according to American officials.[37] And that is just a single square in a single city. With protests being put down around the country, it's impossible to tell how many people were killed by their own government.

The depressing truth is that it worked. On 9 June, some three weeks after the government had declared martial law, the chairman of the Central Military Commission, Deng Xiaoping, gave a speech to military commanders in Beijing. In that speech, he thanked the People's Liberation Army for quelling the rebellion that aimed to 'overthrow the Communist Party and topple the socialist system'.[38] In that moment, millions of people certainly opposed the regime. But the regime survived and continues to survive. Ruthless repression can work, but it requires a total commitment to horrific brutality.

After the protests had been crushed, the regime sent a further chilling message to anyone who might consider challenging it. Soldiers who shot innocent civilians were given praise and promotions. Two went on to become minister of defence and one later joined the powerful Politburo Standing Committee of the Chinese Communist Party. There was no mistaking the signal being sent. Challenge us, and we will kill you. Then, we'll find the person who fired the lethal shot and we will pin a medal on their chest and call them a hero. The choice is yours. Sensing an existential threat to its survival, the Chinese regime hadn't taken half measures as the Ukrainian government did decades later. Soldiers were needed, not policemen. Even guns weren't enough, it had to be tanks.

But if shock and awe, using maximum force, is the best way to stay in power when faced with popular discontent, why doesn't every dictator order tanks onto the street? The short answer is that they can't.

The long answer I found much closer to home. In 2023, I drove east to Leipzig to meet sixty-four-year-old Siegbert Schefke. When I got there, he told me that everyone has five or six days in a lifetime where you remember everything: every detail from the moment you get up in the morning to the moment you go to bed at night. For Schefke, 9 October 1989 was one of those days.

Schefke was for years a dissident, and the GDR regime did what it could to make his life miserable. Codenamed 'Satan' by the fearsome Stasi, he was constantly under observation. Interrogations, some extremely long, were frequent. Then, a day after attending a vigil for a political prisoner, the state-owned company at which he worked told him that he was going to lose his job. But instead of getting him to back down, it only radicalised him. He became a full-time revolutionary.[39]

By autumn of 1989, the Socialist Unity Party, which had ruled East Germany since 1949, had already been dealing with popular dissatisfaction for months. Now a major protest was planned in Leipzig and the authorities were on high alert. Before the big day, the regime desperately tried to prevent people from attending. Among other things, they threatened that a Tiananmen Square scenario could be repeated if the population defied the regime's orders. On the day of the planned protest, Schefke woke up in Berlin. His immediate problem were the Stasi agents who followed his every move. He managed to climb onto the roof of his building unseen, before he boarded a tram and then changed to a borrowed car. It worked. After arriving in Leipzig, Siegbert and his friend Aram looked for a place from which they could film the demonstration. It wasn't easy because the city was crawling with security forces.

In their desperation, they eventually asked a local pastor whether they could set up their equipment on top of his church's bell tower. Their request was followed by ten seconds of silence. 'Of course that's possible,' the pastor finally said.[40] A moment of relief, and up they went. The floor of the tower was covered in bird droppings, but the view was perfect.

We don't know how many members of the regime's security forces were in Leipzig that day since troves of documents were 'lost' when the German Democratic Republic collapsed, but what the historian Mary Elise Sarotte could find paints a terrifying picture of the forces Leipzigers had to fear: 'Fifteen hundred army soldiers appear to have been present. An unclear number of Stasi agents and employees had been activated. More than three thousand police officers would be on duty.'[41]

North of the city centre, ten armoured personnel carriers were waiting to engage with their motors running.[42] All of them were equipped with live ammunition powerful enough to shoot down planes three kilometres away. The regime was ready.

As tens of thousands of peaceful Germans marched in defiance of the Socialist Unity Party, the regime had a decision to make: would they give an order to shoot?

On the morning before the showdown, three high-ranking local party leaders joined forces with a celebrated conductor, a theology professor and a cabaret artist to appeal for non-violence on both sides. That appeal was read not only in the churches where the protestors gathered before their march but also to security forces and on the local radio. 'We urge you to exercise prudence so peaceful dialogue becomes possible,' it said.[43] That intervention was so important because it signalled that the regime was split. There was no uniform desire among elites to crush the opposition.

There were signs of rupture within the security forces as well. Morale in the party's local militias was so low that a good many of its reservists simply didn't show up.[44] Among those who did, many openly questioned the orders they were given. Berlin had indicated that protests would not be allowed to go ahead. But what if there were women and children in the crowd? Who would take responsibility after innocent people were gunned down, their blood running in the streets? As protestors talked with security forces throughout the day, soldiers and policemen sympathised with the people they were preparing to kill.[45]

These dynamics explain why tyrants usually try to maximise their chance of 'success' by bringing in troops from the outside when they crack down on civilians. The closer the oppressor is to the intended victims, the more uncertain things become because even the most loyal supporters of a regime cannot be expected to kill their neighbours, friends or family. And how could soldiers be so sure that this isn't what was about to happen? They were facing a crowd of tens of thousands – there was no telling who exactly would be standing in front of their barrels.

Regime planners were aware of the problem, not least because even the Chinese People's Liberation Army had struggled with insubordination when quelling protests on Tiananmen Square. Local units, which had most contacts among the population of the city, were deliberately deployed as the last line of defence rather than being on the front lines where they could cause trouble.[46]

Under those circumstances, one of the regime's key concerns had to be whether an order to shoot unarmed protestors would even be carried out if it were given. Dictators may want to order a brutal crackdown, but someone has to fire the guns. If the people carrying the guns sympathise with the people they are supposed to shoot, a bad situation could spiral out of control and become catastrophic. And indeed, this is how popular resistance can succeed: either the regime looks weak or it risks crumbling under the weight of its own repression.

The clock was now ticking. Protestors were approaching the Eastern Knot, a sharp bend in the street near Leipzig's main train station at which security forces would have to fire to stand any chance of dealing with this many people. In her book *The Collapse*, Sarotte details what happened next. As it became clear that the march couldn't be stopped without massive use of lethal force, Helmut Hackenberg, the local Party leader in charge of implementing the order to quell the protest, called Berlin to get hold of Egon Krenz to ask him what to do. Krenz was a prominent member of the Politburo. More importantly, he was seen as a frontrunner to replace Erich Honecker, the leader of the ruling Socialist Unity Party. When Hackenberg eventually managed to reach Krenz on the phone and told him that it would be best not to intervene because there were simply too many protestors, Krenz was so shocked that he didn't reply. When he finally did, Krenz said he would call back shortly as he had first to talk to somebody else.[47]

And then no further call came. While Hackenberg waited to hear back, the local police chief began to summon more units from outside Leipzig so that they might stand a chance against the sheer mass of bodies.[48] With the protestors coming ever closer to the curve in the road, Krenz had still not called back. Hackenberg was on his own, weighing his options. None of them was good and there was simply no more time. Now or never, shoot or show weakness.

At around half-past six, he ordered the units to fall back and take defensive positions. According to many of those there that night, the order came not a moment too soon. One young policeman later said that he had already had an order to start charging demonstrators. When he got the order to pull back, he was within thirty metres of the protestors.[49]

With the regime unable to agree to mass murder, protestors in Leipzig had won the day. From the perspective of regime survival, an order to shoot that night would probably have been ruinous, but the decision not to shoot was equally catastrophic.

High up on the bell tower, Siegbert Schefke had captured the protest in all its glory. A day later, he was nervously watching television in his living room. He waited and waited and there it was! After being smuggled through Berlin, their images were shown on West German television and since the signal was easily strong enough to reach most of East Germany, millions there could see it in their living rooms as well.

The following week, Leipzigers marched again and protests quickly grew in other cities as well. With Honecker forced out almost immediately, the new Politburo, now under the direction of the man who hadn't called back until it was too late, tried to concede its way out of the misery, but the wheels of history were already spinning too fast. In November, the whole world watched as East Germans celebrated the end of the communist dictatorship on top of the Berlin Wall.

The international dimension has a role to play as well – as can be seen in particular in the linkage and leverage idea posited in a much-cited article by political scientists Steven Levitsky and Lucan A. Way.[50] Liberal democracies in North America and Europe are the most powerful political actors interested in the promotion of international democracy, and most important among those is the United States. Even though the government of the United States may claim to promote universal values around the world, its interest and ability to do so differs hugely from country to country. When Chinese leaders used tanks to clamp down on protests in 1989, China had neither particularly strong connections to the United States (linkage) nor did the White House have much influence over Beijing (leverage). To the Chinese leadership, that meant they couldn't expect much punishment for killing those protestors. Or at least that punishment, whatever it might be, wouldn't make much difference. As a result, they knew they could 'go big' and get away with it – at least when it came to international reactions.

Some regimes, at the point of having to decide whether to crack down on protestors, face a very different situation. They are highly connected to, and highly dependent on, countries which could imperil the survival of their regime if they do what the Chinese government did. The more the public is outraged, the likelier democratic voters are to push their governments into punishing dictators over whom they have influence. And that chance is now higher.

But obviously, the international environment doesn't have to be a constraint when dealing with the masses – it can be an advantage. If dictators can find a friendly foreign dictator to help protect them against their own population, they solve two problems at once. For one, this increases coherence of the regime elites who keep the dictator in power because they now know that victory is much more likely. Secondly, foreign troops are less likely to refuse an order to fire on protestors than the dictator's own soldiers because they are more removed from their targets. Taken together, this can make a significant difference.

But knowing all this, how are tyrants supposed to react if they cannot 'go big' and they don't have a foreign dictator to protect them? As a start, they should say a prayer because the time for 'good' options has long gone. Then they have the final card to play: they can attempt to split the opposition by making concessions that are either unimportant to them or fake. If that works, it will reduce the number of people who need to die – thereby also reducing international costs and the probability that the dictatorship will come apart. As odd as it sounds, offering concessions is often the best way to break protestors before they break the despot.

With the enemy near the gates, this manouevre can go something like this: the despot fires hated government officials, dismisses unpopular ministers and then promises deep constitutional reforms. And just like that, without giving up anything that really matters, the regime may turn people against one another. Some will reluctantly believe the government, others will keep protesting. Those that protest, now a much more manageable number, can be met with beatings, torture or live ammunition. By the time it dawns on the former that they have been deceived, that the concessions aren't going to lead to meaningful change, the regime, it is hoped, has regained enough strength to put their protests down as well.[51]

If a dictator reaches the point where they need to decide whether to shoot their own people, they've almost certainly made multiple mistakes already. Cunning dictators intervene long before they have to make lose–lose decisions because they realise that killing their own people in the street risks breaking even the most cohesive of regimes. Even if such atrocities don't kill the regime there and then, they are so outrageous that they can serve as a point of mobilisation for opponents forever. It's for that reason that the Chinese Communist Party is so scared of dissidents who as much as mention the date of the Tiananmen Square massacre – let alone what actually happened under their command that day. It is an event that cannot be shaken, it will remain forever a mark of shame for the Party.

Popular uprisings are a constant threat for almost all tyrants. When the streets do erupt, despots can't simply ignore them. They need to take action but they usually cannot give an order to shoot because guns are useless if the regime doesn't have enough people to fire them. Most tyrants don't, and that's why they tend to lose their power at the very moment they try to use them. Clever tyrants can reduce the risk of this happening but it never goes away completely. And even if they manage to avoid a scenario in which their palace is over-run by the people who have long suffered from their rule, they aren't out of the woods. Because there are some things even the most powerful rulers cannot prepare for. Nobody can outrun a bullet.

7

No Other Option

I know that there are scores of people plotting to kill me, and this is not difficult to understand. After all, did we not seize power by plotting against our predecessors?[1]

Saddam Hussein

Assassinations have been around forever. The word 'assassination' entered the English language after Crusaders returned home with stories about the Nizaris, an eleventh-century movement in the mountains of modern-day Iran. The Nizaris, lacked the military strength to go to war with their local enemies, so would instead hunt them down and murder them. According to the stories, real or imagined, they consumed hashish before setting out, and, at some point along the way, *hashīshī* (consumer of hashish) turned into 'assassin'.[2]

The debate around the morality of 'tyrannicide' – the killing of a tyrant – is as old as the practise itself. To fight out in the open, to admit to the enemy that you mean him harm, is something that can be seen as honourable. But assassinating anyone, even a cruel leader, has something about it that makes many people shudder. Perhaps it's because operating in the shadows seems cowardly or even treacherous, whereas fighting people head on can be seen as brave.

As times have changed, so have views on tyrannicide. In parts of ancient Greece, tyrannicide was celebrated. When

Harmodius and Aristogeiton tried to kill the local tyrant Hippias during a festival in 514 BC, Athenians erected statues in their honour. Since they failed and were subsequently executed, Harmodius and Aristogeiton didn't get to enjoy the songs that were written about them, but their descendants were given special privileges. Their families received free food and tax-exemptions. They even got to sit in the front row at the theatre. To avoid their names being blemished, slaves could not be named after them.[3] Harmodius and Aristogeiton had tried to kill a cruel leader for the benefit of the entire community, and they were heroes for it.

There were multiple ways in which ancient Greeks justified tyrannicide. Broadly speaking, tyrannicide was acceptable because every citizen was seen as having equal standing under the law and a tyrant would destroy that bond.[4] The Greek philosopher Aristotle argued that tyrannicide was not just defensible, but that the act could bestow great honour on those who did the killing.[5] Plato considered tyranny 'an errant condition of the soul'. The Greek outlook carried over into Roman thinking.[6]

In the Middle Ages, justifying tyrannicide became significantly more difficult because kings and queens were seen as having divine right. They ruled on earth not because they had the support of their subjects but because a deity had chosen them. If you believe that to be the truth, how do you justify killing monarchs given that they stand in direct line to God?

It's not an easy argument, but some did try. One way out was to argue that the killing of God's king could be justified if the king clashed with God. The Christian thinker Augustine, for example, generally took issue with previous justifications of killing tyrants but he made an exception for cases in which a tyrant infringed on God's worship.[7] If that was the case,

God's king was no longer aligned with God, thereby making it easier to justify his death.

John of Salisbury, a twelfth-century bishop of Chartres, carefully distinguished between king and tyrant. In John's view, the king works towards the well-being of the polity. The tyrant, on the other hand, turns his subjects into slaves of his own private desires.[8] And while princes are appointed by God, their subjects also have a 'responsibility to God to act for the well-being of the body politic'.[9] 'Wickedness is always punished by the Lord,' John says, 'but sometimes He uses His own sword and sometimes He uses a sort of human sword in the punishment of the impious.'[10] Acting as God's sword to kill a tyrant would therefore not be a sin but an act of divine inspiration;[11] a duty.[12] Theological arguments are now less relevant in much of the world, but the questions these thinkers sought to answer persist. Is the killing of tyrants defensible? Is it perhaps even desirable?

Multiple factors make the question of tyrannicide complicated. First, 'tyrant' can have two meanings. One is the meaning that is most common: a tyrant is a leader who uses his power not for the collective good of the community but for personal gain. The second is a meaning that used to be more widespread: the tyrant is not a tyrant by virtue of his cruel rule but because he has taken power without having a right to it. He is a 'usurper-tyrant'.[13] This distinction is not purely academic because, depending on the definition, tyrannicide can mean totally different things. It has come to mean the killing of a cruel leader, but as it used to be understood, it may even mean a cruel leader wielding his power to murder a challenger whom he sees as a potential usurper and therefore potential tyrant.

If the assassination of a cruel leader is morally permissible, it raises several other difficult questions. How do you separate those who kill a tyrant because he is a tyrant from those who do it for personal gain? If it isn't for personal gain, how do you differentiate between tyrannicide and terrorism? Terrorists use violence not just because violence itself achieves their aim, but because they want to instil fear in people who aren't directly implicated. Is that also the case for tyrannicides? It depends. Tyrannicide can be about sending a signal to others to let them know that comparable behaviour will not be tolerated. But it can also be purely about removing one despot to return the country to its constitutional order.

Historically, assassinations have not been rare. According to one study there have been 298 assassination attempts on national leaders since 1875. Of those, just under one in five have succeeded.[14] Looking only at dictators, another study found that thirty-three dictators were assassinated between 1946 and 2010, with another 103 failed assassination attempts.[15]

The puzzle for tyrants is this: if a large segment of the population despises them, how do they avoid being killed?

The twenty-first century is familiar with two main types of assassination: the complex, highly coordinated attack and the attacks made by lone wolves.

On 7 July 2021, the president of Haiti, his wife and children were asleep at their private residence in a hilly suburb of Port-au-Prince.[16] But then, calm turned to panic as shots rang out. This wasn't a random robbery gone wrong out in the street; instead it was gunmen, coming for the family themselves. Dozens of officers should have been outside, guarding the president. Where were they now, and why weren't they doing their job? Worried for their survival, Mrs Moïse went to tell the kids to hide. In desperation, Jovenel Moïse tried to get someone, anyone, to come and help. Eventually, the president told his wife to lie down on the floor. 'That's where you will be safe,' he said.[17] It was the last thing she ever heard from her husband. Shortly afterwards, a death squad executed President Jovenel Moïse with twelve bullets.[18]

According to court documents, the whole operation was based on a double deception.* The Colombian mercenaries who did the killing were initially told that they were going to Haiti to provide protection to the president of Haiti, not kill him. Then, as the necessary weapons and equipment were distributed on the day before the mission, they were told that this was a 'C.I.A. operation' to kill Moïse.[19] When the killers arrived at the residence and faced the prospect of having to fight the president's guards, they pretended to be from another arm of the United States government: the Drug Enforcement Agency. 'DEA operation, everybody stay down,' they shouted.[20] Given that none of the guards died, many of them seem to have followed the order.

Clever leaders with a functioning security apparatus can prevent such complex attacks on their life. Since so many people were involved, intelligence agents had a realistic chance of finding out about the attempt before it happened. The weapons could have been intercepted and the presidential compound could have been fortified. And indeed, this is something states have got better at over time: the overall chance of being assassinated has dropped. In the 1910s leaders had roughly a one in a hundred chance of being killed every year. Now it's less than 0.3 per cent.[21]

That's low, but it's not nothing. And a large part of the reason for this is that it's extremely challenging to stop less complex assassination attempts, especially if they don't come from within the regime. In many countries, weapons are relatively easy to come by. Combined with enough zeal, all it

---

* This is an unfolding case and new information continues to come to light. As a result, there is some uncertainty.

takes is being in the right place at the right time. Stopping attacks like this is incredibly difficult, even for rulers who concentrate significant political power in their hands.

The tyrant's chances of being assassinated are related to his success at insulating himself from other threats to his leadership. Oddly enough, the better he gets at preventing the other threats, the more attractive assassinations become because there are simply no other options – even for those who are part of the regime. That's because assassinations, unlike coups or rebellions, don't require a large degree of coordination. As the tyrant concentrates power in his hands and makes other threats to his rule less viable, rivals are forced to turn to assassination as their only option.

When elites are comparatively powerful vis-à-vis the tyrant, they can hope to change the leader while maintaining their own power within the system. As the tyrant becomes more powerful, elites may no longer have the opportunity to reshuffle the leader while keeping the system as it is.[22] Instead, they have to try to dismantle the entire system. At some point, when the despot has consolidated yet more power in his hands, even that can become impossible. When it does, assassination can be the elites' only way out.[23]

The problem, seen from the presidential palace, is that it only takes one. And unfortunately, there are many who could be in the right place at the right time. The pool of potential assassins is as large as the number of people who can carry a rifle or a blade. That makes assassination a pervasive threat to every tyrant.

It's an unfortunate situation to be in. However, tyrants have some options.

Since democratisation (or weakening their protection against other threats) isn't attractive to most dictators, they must find other solutions. One of the more common strategies they choose is to protect themselves with bodyguards.

These bodyguards serve much of the same functions as body-guards in democratic systems: they scout locations to make sure no assassins are hiding in them, work out how to flee in the event of an attack and, if need be, they catch a bullet for the president. But since this isn't just a normal president but a president for life, these men and women need to have some extra qualifications.

The method commonly used is to assemble a force of elite fighters who can defend the dictator against the public at large and also against attacks from within the regime. The issue with this approach is that those elite fighters can easily become political actors in their own right, for example by supporting *coup d'états* against the leader. In ancient Rome, the Praetorian Guard - supposed to protect rulers – regularly helped to overthrow them, the most notorious example being probably the Emperor Caligula, who was assassinated by his Guard during a festival in 41 AD.

The Praetorian Guard were eventually dismantled by one of Caligula's successors. However, the possibility of a personal bodyguard turning traitor is a constant threat to modern rulers. Because of it, some leaders have resorted to recruiting foreigners. By virtue of their being foreign, such guards are seen as less of a coup risk because they have neither the same level of interest in domestic politics nor the legitimacy that is required to run a government.

Today, demand for this 'service' has allowed the Russian government to turn itself into an insurance salesman for auto-crats, especially in Africa. In the Central African Republic, the Russian paramilitary group Wagner, which had close ties to the Kremlin, was used by the regime to protect itself against assassinations. During the country's 2020 election campaign, for example, Russian paramilitaries could be seen protecting Faustin-Archange Touadéra, the country's president. In return for protecting the ruler against threats from within, the mercenaries get mining concessions and lucrative business opportunities in the host country. The Russian government, in turn, gets a foothold in Africa that can be used not just to make money, but also to advance political objectives – for example, getting African countries to vote alongside the Kremlin's interests at the United Nations.

To Central African President Touadéra and leaders like him, the deal is so attractive because the paramilitaries serve a triple function: not only do they protect him without posing as much of a coup risk, they also provide an active deterrent against others who might be plotting against him. What's more, they can also be used against other domestic enemies such as rebels. That's particularly attractive because these 'bodyguards' can make up for at least some of the battlefield effectiveness that a dictatorship loses when it coup-proofs its military. When a special advisor to President Touadéra was asked what he made of Wagner's mutiny against Vladimir Putin's government, he said: 'Russia gave us Wagner, the rest isn't our business . . . If it's not Wagner anymore and they send Beethoven or Mozart, it doesn't matter, we'll take them.'[24]

But even though the regime is keen on Wagner (or any other 'composer'), there is a price to pay: Touadéra isn't just losing mining revenue, but also autonomy. For as foreign fighters become more entrenched in the regime's security apparatus, they increase their influence in the country's economy and politics. Wagner's increase in control has been so vast in the Central African Republic that some analysts have started to refer to it as 'state capture'.[25] And since these fighters are ultimately loyal to Moscow (if even that) and not the regime they are protecting, they might not present a direct coup risk, but they aren't exactly trustworthy either. If the Kremlin finds a leader who gives them better conditions than

Touadéra, the Central African strongman won't survive in power for long.

For that reason, many dictators prefer fighters who are seen as possessing a special loyalty to the leader. But, as we've seen already, all despots face the dictator's dilemma: they don't know who around them is genuinely loyal and who is just pretending. Given that structural constraint, banking on the loyalty of subjects is always a gamble.

When Laurent Kabila rebelled against Mobutu Sese Seko to take control of the Democratic Republic of Congo, he made extensive use of *kadogo* – child soldiers.[26] He trusted them. Talking to a foreign businessman, he once said: 'They will never do anything against me. They have been with me since the beginning.' 'They are my children,' he went on to say. But then one day, when Kabila was discussing an upcoming summit with an advisor, one of his 'children' walked in, pulled out a revolver and shot him four times.[27]

Evidently, there's no truly good option here. When dictators pick foreign fighters, they put themselves at the mercy of another government. When they pick compatriots, they become more vulnerable to coups because in dictatorships, nobody's loyalty to the regime is assured.

Instead of putting bodyguards between the tyrant and others, there's also the option of isolating the dictatorship using space, fences and guard towers. That can be effective because most assassination attempts occur during the leader's public appearances at speeches, rallies or parades, or when he is travelling by car, helicopter or plane.[28] If there are fewer public appearances and the tyrant spends most of his time in the remote fortress constructed specifically to guarantee his safety, he is less likely to be killed.

For democratic leaders, isolating themselves is extremely difficult. Because they need to win (fair) elections, they need to campaign and be seen among the people. It's impossible not to be. Moreover, many of them genuinely enjoy meeting people and listening to their concerns. If they don't, they are probably in the wrong profession. But what makes the work so enjoyable to them makes life hard for those tasked with protecting them.

Dictators have an advantage here because there's no need for them to go out and meet real voters. They can be more isolated than democratic leaders and some have taken this to an extreme, isolating their entire country out of fear for themselves.

Landlocked and difficult to access due to mountains and deserts, Paraguay was always more isolated than Chile, Brazil or Uruguay.[29] But when José Gaspar Rodríguez de Francia became the country's 'Perpetual Dictator' in 1814, he took matters to extremes. Paranoid and fearing that colonial forces or large neighbouring states could undermine Paraguay's independence, he turned his nation into a hermit kingdom. Trade with neighbouring states was reduced and foreigners were barely let into the country. If foreigners did enter de Francia's Paraguay they could soon find themselves in danger. When the celebrated French botanist Aimé Bonpland settled near the Paraná River to cultivate the plant yerba mate, things initially seemed to be going well. Bonpland's connections, and the labour and wisdom of local workers were a winning combination.[30] Then one morning, Bonpland's colony was attacked when hundreds of Paraguayan soldiers, who had crossed the river under cover of night, struck at daybreak. Nineteen men were killed, dozens taken prisoner.[31] For Paraguay's dictator, Bonpland was a problem twice over: first, his cultivation of yerba mate threatened El Supremo's own position in the lucrative trade, and second, the French plant expert was an untrustworthy figure who might be working with foreign powers to undermine the regime.[32] Perhaps the botanist might even try to kill him? To neutralise the threat, de Francia took Bonpland hostage.

Bonpland wasn't the only foreigner treated in this way. Johann Rudolf Rengger, a Swiss doctor, was also taken hostage. Rengger describes what it was like to have an audience with the supremo himself: 'When you meet the dictator, you are not allowed to come closer than six paces until he gives a signal to step forward,' he wrote. Even then, he went on, 'you have to stop at a distance of three paces.' De Francia was so worried about being killed that those meeting him were required to let their arms hang loose with their hands open and facing towards him so he could make sure they didn't carry a weapon. In fact, not even the dictator's own officers or civil servants were allowed to approach him if they had a blade on them. And just in case, de Francia always made sure that he had his own weapons within reach wherever he went.[33]

Following in de Francia's footsteps and turning an entire country into a hermit kingdom is difficult to do in the modern world, but the point persists: unlike democratic leaders, dictators can afford to isolate themselves. If they can't do it with their entire country, they can at least isolate themselves from the people they rule.

In the winter of 2022, Russia's president, Vladimir Putin, was not just isolated but also disconnected from the lived reality of the Russian people. The regime's future was in question. With Ukrainians bravely resisting Russia's war of aggression, the Russian armed forces were slowly running out of soldiers. Since there weren't nearly enough voluntary recruits, young Russian men were forced into the fight. Conditions for these soldiers were horrendous. For tens of thousands of families, the war that they had previously seen on slickly produced propaganda shows had now become reality as sons, fathers and husbands were sent to get killed in Ukraine's cold, unforgiving mud. Some of the conscripted soldiers were so poorly equipped that their families had to buy them medical kits. And if they ever dared to retreat, away from the enemy's artillery shells or anti-tank missiles, they might have to face so-called 'barrier troops', deployed by Moscow (or Grozny) to shoot soldiers who simply wanted to escape from the carnage.[34]

The aunt of one young Russian man from the western region of Lipetsk said her nephew was sent to the frontlines in Ukraine eight days after being mobilised. There weren't even any commanders there. 'They were hit by mortar fire,' she said. 'Why, after one week of training, were they thrown into the woods and left there to die?' she wanted to know.[35]

On 25 November 2022, Putin was sitting in a cream-coloured chair in front of television cameras at his luxurious estate west of Moscow. He spoke to seventeen mothers with sons fighting in Ukraine. 'I want you to know that me [sic] personally and the country's leadership share this pain,' Putin said. 'We understand that nothing can replace the loss of a son, a child,' he added.[36] It finally looked as if Putin had been brave enough to meet popular dissatisfaction head on. But instead, the whole thing was staged. All the mothers were handpicked by the regime: one was a former government official; another the mother of a senior military official from Chechnya; several of them were active in pro-war NGOs financed by the state.[37]

To add insult to injury, Putin didn't just fake the meeting to make it seem as if the war had more public support than it did. He told the women (and more importantly viewers at home) that they shouldn't trust anything he hadn't faked. 'It is clear that life is more complicated and diverse than what is shown on TV screens or even on the internet – you can't trust anything there at all, there are a lot of all sorts of fakes, deception, lies,' Putin said.[38] Obviously, the chance of one of those handpicked women getting up and stabbing Putin was extremely low. But if he hadn't faked the meeting and had met with real mothers instead, could one of them have attempted to kill the man who had sent her beloved child to his death in Bakhmut? Maybe, but Putin will never have to find out because, unlike democratic leaders, he can avoid meeting real people.

Another avenue despots can pursue is an intense cult of personality coupled with extreme repression. This can create an atmosphere 'in which the assassination of a leader is not even contemplated, let alone planned or executed'.[39] There are tyrants in history who have made their people believe that they can literally read minds, that they are a deity. And if the man on the poster in the classroom, on the billboard and in the little book everyone has to carry around with them is no man but a God, challenging him would be madness.

A deity would know about it even before it happened. Even if he were to get fired at, he'd undoubtedly survive. Sitting where we do, this might seem rather strange, but from the perspective of the people in those countries, it makes at least some sense. These are people who have witnessed dictators put up giant golden statues of themselves that rotate to follow the sun, or who have created entire cities in the middle of nowhere, seemingly out of thin air. In schools, on television shows and on the radio they are told that the supreme leader sees all and hears all. Why shouldn't they believe that it's true?

If ordinary Haitians had met their president during the 1960s, they would probably have seen a man wearing a black top hat, thick black glasses and black suit. With his hands rarely visible, he talked slowly and in a high-pitched voice. He almost looked as though he was from another world, and that was no coincidence. François Duvalier, known as 'Papa Doc', due to his background in medicine, deliberately modelled his image on Baron Samedi, a voodoo spirit of the dead.

Knowing that millions of Haitians had strong connections to voodoo, he used it to his advantage. At one point he allegedly ordered his men to cut off a rival's head and bring it to him because he wanted to talk to his 'spirit'.[40] Duvalier cast himself as a seemingly omnipotent being out of the reach of mere mortals. 'My enemies cannot get me,' he used to say. 'I am already an immaterial being.'[41]

And to drive home the point of his God-like status, he relentlessly bombarded the population with images of his omnipotence. He even went so far as to introduce a Papa Doc version of the Lord's Prayer: 'Our Doc, who art in the National Palace for life, Hallowed be Thy name by present and future generations. Thy will be done at Port-au-Prince and in the provinces.'[42]

If that wasn't enough to achieve compliance, Papa Doc still had his bogeymen. The Tontons Macoute would often wear dark uniforms and sunglasses while they killed and tortured Haitians who stepped out of line. As was intended, some of Duvalier's opponents came to believe that Duvalier knew where they were and what they did.[43] He stayed in power for more than thirteen years until he died a natural death.[44]

But even if tyrants manage to keep their own people from killing them, that's not the only actor they have to worry about.

In September 1990, United States Air Force chief of staff Michael J. Dugan gave an interview to a *Washington Post* reporter named Rick Atkinson. This was a time of high tension, as Iraq, under the control of Saddam Hussein, had just invaded and occupied neighbouring Kuwait. The Gulf War was about to begin. In the interview, Dugan suggested the United States would target Saddam Hussein and those close to him, including his personal guard and his mistress. Since Saddam Hussein was 'a one-man show', Dugan said, 'if and when we choose violence he ought to be at the focus of our efforts.' A little later in the interview the general went on to say that he didn't expect to be concerned with political constraints.[45] As it turned out, Dugan was wrong. Shortly after his comments, he was fired by Vice-President Dick Cheney.

His firing was related to a 1976 executive order which stated: 'No person employed by or acting on behalf of the United States Government shall engage in, or conspire to engage in, assassination.'[46] It was issued by President Gerald Ford, after American intelligence agencies were found to be implicated in several plots to assassinate foreign leaders. Most notable of these was the supplying of weapons to dissidents trying to kill Rafael Trujillo in the Dominican Republic, and also the attempts to kill Fidel Castro, which went on for years. Less well-known is the case of CIA operatives tasked with assassinating the Congolese nationalist Patrice Lumumba in Zaire.[47]

The commission reporting on the matter had argued that assassination was 'incompatible with American principles, international order and morality'.[48] But it also left a loophole by saying that this only applied outside war – meaning that the assassination of foreign leaders could be acceptable if their nation was at war with the United States.

The United States isn't the only country that allows for the assassination of foreign heads of state. The Democratic People's Republic of North Korea, one of the countries against which the United States might attempt targeted killing in the future, has a history of assassinations.

In early 1968, twenty-seven-year-old Kim Shin-jo was in

the mountains. It was January when, in the mountains of Korea, it is desperately cold. Sent by Pyongyang, he and his comrades were on their way to Seoul to kill South Korea's President. Whether by mistake or pure chance, Shin-jo was spotted by some villagers. He knew what he had to do: kill them and bury them. He had a mission and if he didn't kill them now, the whole plan could be imperilled. But the ground was frozen. If he had to bury them here, he would be at it forever.

After some deliberation, he told them not to tell anyone who they had encountered. As Shin-jo left them, they immediately contacted the police, which informed the military. South Korean soldiers were now on the lookout for Shin-jo and the other infiltrators. Against all odds, they continued advancing towards South Korea's presidential palace, where they were to assassinate President Park Chung-hee. In the end, they made it to within 100 metres of the Blue House. And although the attack itself failed, it took more than a week and hundreds of soldiers to find and deal with the North Korean death squad. Even then, one of the commandos somehow managed to make it back across the border to North Korea alive. Only discovered by chance, the killers had come very close to achieving their object, which was a major embarrassment to the South Korean regime.[49]

Three months later, the South Korean government's answer was being prepared on an islet named Silmido in the Yellow Sea. Thirty-one men, the 'type that often got into street fights', were being trained by South Korean security forces.[50] The most important lesson they were being taught, as one of their trainers put it, was that you must kill to live.[51] The men's mission was to go up to North Korea, across the demilitarised zone, to kill Kim Il-sung. It was time for payback for the Blue House raid and they were about to slit Kim Il-sung's throat.[52]

On the islet of Silmido, life was hard. Isolated, Unit 684 had to battle not just their training routines and the sea, but also their superiors. After a few months on the island, they simply stopped getting paid. The food they were getting was poor. On top of all that, contact with the outside world was strictly prohibited. When two of them tried to escape in June 1968, they were beaten to death. Another recruit died during sea-survival training.[53]

Early in August 1971, Yang Don-soo, one of the trainers on Silmido, was getting ready for his regular supply run off the island. He heard gunfire. Confused, he thought that it could be North Korean special forces out to attack them. Before he knew what was happening, he was shot in the neck. But it wasn't the enemy, it was his own men. 'When I woke up, I was bleeding from my neck and everywhere the trainers were being killed by the recruits or running away, or were being shot again by recruits who were making sure that they were dead,' he said.[54] Bleeding heavily, he crawled to the beach. He prayed to God, hoping that his recruits wouldn't find him.

Luckily for him, they had bigger plans. After making their way off the island in their paratrooper uniforms, the death squad commandeered a bus and made their way to Seoul armed with carbines and grenades.[55] Instead of going to Pyongyang to kill Kim Il-sung, they were now on their way to the Blue House to kill South Korean dictator Park Chung-hee whom they held responsible for their suffering.[56] In the capital, they fought South Korean security forces that had been gathered hastily to intercept them.[57] When it became clear that they were outgunned and with no chance of escape, some of the recruits blew themselves up with hand grenades.[58] Of the initial twenty-four recruits who had taken part in the rebellion, only four survived – until 1972, when they were executed.[59]

But why did Unit 684 crack? The harsh conditions in the Yellow Sea undoubtedly played a role, but there was also speculation that the South Korean government, then still a military dictatorship, was about to murder the death squad to make sure nobody ever knew they existed in the first place. But according to one of their trainers, the real reason why the assassins acted the way they did is because they were without hope.[60] The communist North and capitalist South had recently and unexpectedly improved their ties, so the attack on Pyongyang was called off. Because of that, the killers seemingly thought that they would never get off Silmido. As one observer put it, the trainees increasingly saw themselves as 'prisoners with indefinite sentences'.[61]

Yet, despite this experience, 'decapitation' of North Korea's leadership is still part of South Korea's strategy. 'The best deterrence we can have, next to having our own nukes, is to make Kim Jong-un fear for his life,' a former South Korean general said in 2015.[62] To that end, South Korea pursues a double strategy: if conflict with North Korea were to escalate, the South Korean military would unleash a flurry of precision missiles to target the North Korean leadership. In addition, a special military unit would be dispatched to find and kill Kim Jong-un before he was able to order the launch of North Korea's nuclear weapons.[63]

Nuclear weapons expert Ankit Panda, author of *Kim Jong Un and the Bomb*, describes the logic behind this strategy:

As a personalistic dictatorship whose nuclear forces and military are under control of one person, North Korea may be undeterred from nuclear escalation in the course of a limited conflict by threats of damage against military or economically valuable targets. Accordingly, it must be deterred by threatening to punish the leadership directly.[64]

In other words, since Kim Jong-un is not greatly concerned with the destruction of North Korea, South Korea has to find something else he cares about. And that is his own life.

Though this strategy is logical, it is also highly dangerous and there are many ways it can go wrong. To illustrate just one, imagine the following scenario. Tensions between South and North Korea escalate.[65] Unaware of Kim Jong-un's exact whereabouts, South Korean missiles target a North Korean munitions dump that happens to be close to one of the dictator's many hideouts. Kim Jong-un is in there, cowering, and he misinterprets the attack on the military facility as an attack on his life. In that scenario, he now has a huge incentive to use nuclear weapons before he gets killed.

Beyond that, it gives the dictator a reason to change the way the use of nuclear weapons is authorised, and that creates a massive structural risk. The South Korean strategy is based on the idea that the threat of North Korean nuclear weapons can be averted if Kim Jong-un is killed before they can be launched. In democracies, there would be an easy solution to this problem. If the president of the United States, who ordinarily controls the launch of nuclear weapons, were to die, that power would automatically be transferred to the vice-president.[66] This model of command structure is called 'devolution' and for democracies, it works well.

But for dictators, this is not an attractive model because establishing a line of succession risks creating alternative power centres.[67] And since the principal threat to most tyrants, including Kim Jong-un, is internal rather than external, the North Korean dictator did something else. In 2022, the North Korean regime declared:

> In case the command and control systems over the state nuclear forces is placed in danger owing to an attack by

hostile forces, a nuclear strike shall be launched automatically and immediately to destroy the hostile forces including the starting point of provocation and the command according to the operation plan decided in advance.[68]

Faced with the threat of foreign assassins, Kim Jong-un had put things on nuclear autopilot and that autopilot brought all kinds of risks.[69] What if it malfunctioned, for example because Kim was alive but could not be reached? Would the officers panic and assume that Kim was dead? Nuclear war could easily break out despite neither side wanting it. Questions of morality and law aside, that's precisely the problem with threatening dictators with assassination from abroad: the moment 'decapitation' becomes a realistic threat, every form of conflict risks becoming existential for the dictator. And when that's the case, the stakes immediately become so high that the risk of all-out war drastically increases. That's a massive problem for all of us, especially when the dictator doesn't just have access to conventional forces but also weapons of mass destruction.

Whilst the threat of assassination has been a problem with which tyrants have had to deal from time immemorial, the nature and severity of the threat has recently changed.

At 5:41 in the afternoon local time, Venezuelan president Nicolás Maduro was standing on a stage, giving a speech, when suddenly he stopped speaking and looked up. He was nervous because something in the sky above didn't look quite right.[70] Nevertheless, he stayed where he was and, two minutes later, he was talking about economic recovery. Its time had arrived, he said. In front of him were thousands of soldiers marching along Avenida Bolívar, one of Caracas' grandest thoroughfares.

Suddenly, a loud explosion was heard above. In the blink of an eye, an explosive charge on a drone went off, leading to dark clouds of kinetic energy being released below and above the aircraft. Obviously confused by what was happening, Maduro stopped his speech and the state broadcast cut away from the stage. Shortly after, the tyrant's bodyguards scrambled to get in front of him. Just fourteen seconds after the first explosion, another drone crashed and exploded within audible distance.

Whereas the first explosion was met by confusion, this one was met by utter panic. Instead of defending Maduro against whatever enemy this was, the uniformed men and women who had marched on Avenida Bolívar were now running for their lives.

Maduro wasn't harmed, but the way the attack was carried out should serve as an alarm signal to all tyrants. The Venezuelan president could have been killed using a commercial drone that can be bought on Amazon. As these drones proliferate, they solve one of the big problems that non-state actors have when planning to kill a tyrant: the need to be in physical proximity to their target to poison, stab or shoot him.[71] Because of the need for physical proximity, such attacks are extremely risky for the tyrant and for the attacker.

Seconds after a shot is fired, the tyrant may be dead or dying, and the attacker will probably die as well, or at least be on their way to prison. Think of famous assassins: John Wilkes Booth, the man who killed United States president Abraham Lincoln, was shot; Gavrilo Princip, who assassinated Archduke Franz Ferdinand in Sarajevo, died a horrible death in prison. With modern drones, it doesn't have to be that way: attackers can be kilometres away, waiting for the perfect opportunity to launch their shot. And when they do so, they might now get away with it. To dictators, who stake their survival on fear, it's a horrifying prospect.

Assassination is something of a wildcard. Tyrants can do everything 'right' to stay in power: manage elites, weaken the men with guns and deal with the masses while deterring foreign powers so they don't 'decapitate' their regime. But no leader can control everything, and that's precisely the problem when it comes to tyrannicide. Complex assassination attempts can often be prevented, but lone wolves are hard to stop. How well tyrants can respond to the threat depends in large part on the extent of their power. The more powerful, the more of an attractive target they are, but the power they hold also means that they can protect themselves better.

But let's say things go wrong and the leader dies. A new dawn begins. With the tyrant out of the way, what happens next? Will things get better? Will they get worse? We will find out in the next chapter.

8

Be Careful What You Wish For

There are dictators a bit worse than me, no? I'm the lesser
evil already.[1]

Alexander Lukashenko, president of Belarus

After close to half a century in power, the tyrant has fallen.
He seemed to be immortal to many, but his rule and life have
finally come to an end. At the hastily arranged funeral, the
regime's flags fly everywhere and even though half of the
attendees despised the old man for his impulsiveness and
cruelty, they do their best to hide it.

Out on the streets and in front of the nation's television
screens, the dictator's enemies rejoice – those that had been
tortured, those that had been harassed. It hadn't just been a
rumour; the decades-long nightmare was over.

But is it? Sometimes, the answer is yes. The bad dream ends
and as the tyrant no longer has a grip over the country, there's
a chance that democracy may get a foot in the door. But more
often than not, the answer is no. When tyrants fall – whether
they are exiled abroad, are in a coffin or a jail cell – things
frequently stay the same or get even worse. Most are replaced
by new dictators. Only 20 per cent of fallen autocratic leaders
from 1950 to 2012 were followed by democracy.[2]

In the worst case, the result of a fallen tyrant isn't just
another tyrant but violent conflict and chaos. But if the

dictator is the source of a country's suffering, shouldn't his removal from power be a step in the right direction?

Not necessarily. Islam Karimov, the Uzbek dictator who became infamous for a regime that boiled people alive, reportedly liked to say 'no man, no problem'.[3] When it comes to dictatorial succession, the opposite is often true: no man, many problems. That's because the reality isn't 'no man': it's many men now fighting to become the man.

When a democratic leader dies in office or loses an election, everybody knows what happens next. There's a process; there are rules and institutions that oversee both. Immediate successors might be chosen in backroom deals, but sooner or later new leaders must face voters at the ballot box. If they manage to persuade a majority of voters, or at least the voters that matter, the successors then stay in power for a limited amount of time – until, that is, the next election, when, the democratic cycle is repeated.

In political systems with limits on the time any one person can govern, such as the United States, where presidents can serve a maximum of eight years, the rules are even more stringent and frequent turnover is not just the norm but a legal requirement. In personalised dictatorships, none of this exists. There might be some rules on paper that are supposed to matter when a dictator is on his way out, but they don't matter when it actually happens.

Tyrants, power permitting, aim to create a system that revolves entirely around themselves. Functioning institutions, for example in the form of an effective civil service or independent judiciary, are merely a hindrance. To the extent that other centres of power continue to exist, tyrants try to insert themselves into their disputes as the adjudicating force.[4] Instead of forging a compromise that different groups can live with, the tyrant picks winners and losers and enforces his judgement though repression. That doesn't mean that the interests of competing power centres have gone away, but there's a lid on top of it all that prevents the intrigues and the scheming from descending into shooting.

When it looks as if the dictator could fall, that lid is blown off, tensions boil over, and everyone starts conspiring to make sure that their interests come out on top. Conflict behind the scenes turns into fighting in the palace – or on the streets.

And when tyrants fall, euphoria can turn to tragedy. Shouts of victory quickly become screams for help.

In the spring of 2019, people were dancing in the streets of Khartoum.[5] Women were singing, civilians were riding on tanks alongside men in uniform to celebrate their freedom and the promise that things could get better. What started as a peaceful uprising over the price of bread had, through twists and turns, led to the end of the rule of Omar al-Bashir, who had been in charge of the Nile dictatorship for more than three decades. It was a moment of triumph.

But even though peaceful protestors had caused Bashir to stagger, it was the military that brought about his fall. And now that the military was in charge, they weren't going to give up power easily.

Young Sudanese men and women, hopeful for their country's future, decided to stage a sit-in on Buri Road in central Khartoum, right next to the headquarters of the Sudanese military. There were protestors there at all hours of the day for weeks on end; the demonstrators had even set up tents. It was intense, but also cheerful. The protestors sang, danced, played instruments. Sometimes the soldiers joined in. At one point, a man in khaki could be seen playing a saxophone.

But then, on 3 June, darkness fell over the camp as the power cut out. Armed men on pick-up trucks started arriving and the rumours started flying. Then, the violence started.

With the chaos that day, it was difficult even for people in the vicinity of Buri Road to work out what was happening, but open-source intelligence researchers at the BBC have reconstructed the day's events.[6] The men who arrived on pick-ups were part of the Rapid Support Forces (RSF). Under the control of Mohamed Hamdan Dagalo, the RSF grew out of militia forces that were used by al-Bashir to put down rebellions on Sudan's periphery. With Omar al-Bashir gone, Dagalo and his men were now part of the Transitional Military Council (TMC) whom the protestors wanted to push towards accepting civilian control.

As the security forces advanced, they took aim at unarmed protestors. 'Kill them! Kill them,' they shouted. As the TMC's forces moved forward, they started beating and looting. Some of the tents that protestors had erected were burned down.[7]

In the footage livestreamed that day, a man films the ground as gunfire can be heard. As the camera moves, it comes across the lifeless body of a young man, lying with his face on the ground. 'Somebody has been shot,' the cameraman shouts. 'They killed someone! They killed someone here, people,' he goes on. While he shouts, a third man in a blue shirt attempts to drag the body away, but he quickly lets go. And although the cameraman keeps shouting at the top of his voice, nobody seems to pay him any attention.

As the camera pans again, it becomes clear why not: the lifeless young man wasn't the only one being shot. In this new camera angle, another person is being dragged away by two protestors while others flee in panic. Perhaps realising that there was nothing he could do to help, or because he knew that he himself could get shot at any moment, the cameraman begins to run. With the camera shaking from his long strides, he runs shouting: 'They are killing us, people.'

As the protestors ran for their lives, the security forces

continued to shoot. Some 'lucky' protestors were able to get to a clinic, where the doctors and nurses saw serious injuries caused by gunshot, whipping, beating with metal and bayonets.[8] Even a doctor treating the injured was shot.[9] Unfortunately, the horror didn't end there. In a city famous for the confluence of the White and Blue Nile, protestors' corpses were later retrieved from the river – in some cases, with concrete bricks tied to their feet.[10]

As if this was not bad enough, things in Sudan then got even worse. After a brief period in which the military men agreed to share power with civilians, they took full control of the country on 25 October 2021, shattering the dream of democracy.[11]

Even then, the generals didn't deliver stability. Instead, the men in uniform fought each other with increasingly devastating consequences for the rest of the country. In the spring of 2023, conflict between the general in charge of Sudan's ruling council and his deputy turned deadly as their forces clashed with each other in the centre of the capital, where protestors had once danced to celebrate the end of the al-Bashir dictatorship.[12] Only this time, the fighting wasn't limited to small arms fire. Instead, Dagalo's Rapid Support Forces and the regular military fought each other with rocket launchers and artillery. Even airstrikes started to rain down on Khartoum. The open warfare between Dagalo, the man in control of the RSF, and Abdel Fattah al-Burhan, the military's top general, dragged an entire country down with them. It is likely that thousands of civilians were killed and more than five million fled.[13]

Dictatorships have a tendency not simply to collapse upon themselves but to go up in flames, burning everyone and everything along the way. And even though countries could theoretically emerge from the chaos like a phoenix from the ashes, chaos is frequently followed by more of the same. The tyrant might have come to an end, but tyranny has not. It's not a linear transition, but a cycle that simply seems to repeat itself. In this way, many countries live under constant tyranny, only interrupted by the brief moments when one dictator walks out of the back door of the palace only for another to walk in through the gates shortly after. A large part of this dictatorial succession problem is due to the interests of the incumbent. Left to their own devices, dictators are rarely keen on designating a successor or deciding on a meaningful process to find one once they are no longer around. As we have learned above, the survival of autocrats depends on the perception of their strength. Once they designate a successor, they risk weakening themselves while empowering someone else who now has a strong interest in replacing them.

If done badly, planning for succession can be the equivalent of handing the murder weapon to an opponent who wants to stab the tyrant in the back. Tyrants, then, often resist organising the succession because they believe it will accelerate their fall. Whether the country goes up in flames or not after they're no longer in office is, at best, of secondary importance.

When tyrants lose power, it's a chance for those who were a part of the regime but who were previously kept down to improve their position. Perhaps they even want to take the lead themselves? These challengers want change, but they only want it insofar as it advances their interests. That means they don't want democracy or to give power to the people. They aren't opposed to the system itself, simply protective of their position within it. Then there are elites that already occupy the apex of the regime's system. These people, enjoying the favour of the previous ruler, seek to defend their position in order to maintain access to power and money.

Their priority isn't changing the system, it's preventing it from collapse so they can continue to enjoy its benefits.

When the despot is unseated, the interests of the masses will be diametrically opposed to those of the old guard and the challengers within the regime. The masses don't want a redistribution of power and money within the regime, but from the regime to its citizens. The best way to achieve this is through democratisation, for as the country becomes more democratic, the size of the winning coalition expands. And the more people are required to maintain power, the more resources must be devoted to keeping them happy.[14]

Finding a compromise is all but impossible and the stakes are high. Under those circumstances, any group that thinks it can gain an upper hand by using violence will be tempted to do so. And at once, backroom conflict can turn into real-world shooting. When that happens, the masses tend to lose out because their competitive advantage doesn't lie in the use of violence.

A version of this dictatorial succession problem is also what derailed the transition in Sudan. Plenty of people wanted Omar al-Bashir to go – the protestors, the military generals, as well as the RSF leaders, all wanted him to go. What they couldn't agree on was what was supposed to come next. The former wanted a transition to democracy, the latter wanted a man in uniform to be in charge – although even they couldn't agree which man it should be.

As a general rule, the more personalised a regime is, the more disruptive the fall of the tyrant will be.[15] If the system revolves around a single leader, his being out of the picture can easily bring the entire machine to a halt.

That stands in contrast to one-party dictatorships, which have built-in mechanisms for succession. One-party dictatorships systems are also geared towards keeping the leader in power, but there are institutions other than the leader himself that can stabilise the regime when the leader is gone. And in many cases, these party-based systems have mechanisms to deal with the inevitable disputes that will arise when a new leader has to be chosen.

Whether or not effective succession rules are in place depends in large part on the power of the palace elites versus the incumbent. The dictator, king or sultan might not be keen on naming a successor, but palace elites often are. They don't care about the individual tyrant so much as about the continuation of tyranny, because it is the affiliation with the regime rather than the despot himself that gives them their power. Their nightmare scenario is a free-for-all in which challengers openly fight it out for the top position, thereby causing a civil war that threatens the survival of the entire political order. The fear is justified.

Back in the European Middle Ages, autocratic succession substantially increased the risk of civil war.[16] But then, over time, succession rules in these absolute monarchies became more codified and rigid. Around the year 1000, it was perfectly normal for European kings to be succeeded by their brothers.[17] This system, known as 'agnatic seniority', and is a nightmare for tyrants because it means that time is against them: the age difference between the king and his brother tends to be small and the younger brother, knowing that he will be next in line to the throne, has a huge interest in seeing the monarch die so he can succeed him. From the perspective of the king, that's certainly suboptimal.

A better system for the king, and one that more and more of these monarchies moved to, is 'primogeniture'. Under that system, the person to succeed a ruler after death is his eldest son rather than his brother.[18] Because the age difference between crown prince and king tends to be large, the crown prince can afford to remain loyal until his father's death in the confidence that he will outlive him.[19]

But if that's the case, why not just pass the throne to the youngest rather than the eldest child to maximise the age difference? That system is called 'ultimogeniture' and it has one big flaw that is connected to the elites who keep the machine running. Unlike the oldest son, who has had more time to build his own power base over time, the youngest son cannot guarantee that he will be able to reward the elite after he comes to the throne.[20] These little tweaks as to who gets left out in the cold and who gets to ascend the throne, make a gigantic difference to the survival of leaders and regimes. The main beneficiary of this are the palace elites who can continue to reap the benefits of their position as the country avoids a devastating struggle for the throne. Moreover, if the succession is properly organised, it can also increase the tenure of the tyrants themselves.

As over the centuries more and more European monarchies switched from the medieval system of agnatic seniority to primogeniture, their ability to handle the succession massively increased. A study of 960 monarchs reigning in forty-two European states from 1000 to 1800 found that monarchs operating under the rule of primogeniture were more than twice as likely to survive in power as those who ruled in states with other systems of succession.[21]

Powerful members of the court want to benefit from supporting the regime for as long as they can. If they feel that the king's death could lead to the end of their privileges since it will also lead to the end of the regime, they are less likely to continue providing that support and more likely to support moves against the monarch. But if they think that the chance of a (potentially devastating) civil conflict is reduced through the existence of a designated successor, the incumbent might be in less peril. Obviously, this also extends to the successor itself. Now that he or she is appointed to become the next ruler there's a sizeable incentive to maintain the current system as opposed to subverting it. All they have to do is wait in order to ascend to the throne. And indeed, appointing a successor can extend the ruler's reign by virtue of creating someone to shield the regime from its opponents.[22]

Many rulers of non-democracies thus see clear succession rules as a way to make their rule more stable.[23] In Syria, Hafez al-Assad planned to pass power to his eldest son Basil.[24] When Basil died in a car crash, Bashar, Basil's younger brother, became the chosen one. The circumstances were unusual. Whereas Basil had long been groomed to take over, Bashar was training in ophthalmology at a London hospital and was said to have little interest in politics. Nevertheless, Syria's Baath Party leaders agreed to support Bashar as the best way of preserving the system and avoiding internal feuding.[25] Bashar might not have been perfect, but he was viewed as the least bad option. As it was, all the other serious contenders were systematically removed from the political scene by Hafez al-Assad in the years before his death.[26]

There's another factor that has a big influence on what happens after a tyrant falls: the manner of his fall. The consequences of varying forms of 'leadership exit' differ hugely.

When a journalist asked a fruit seller a year after Armenia's Velvet Revolution how things had changed, she replied that only an idiot would think a revolution would change everything. The white-haired woman, sitting in front of cardboard boxes full of onions, apples and tomatoes, added: 'A revolution is like getting an empty new house; you still have to fix it up and furnish it.'[27] That woman was right. A peaceful uprising is a chance to create something better, but it doesn't solve every problem at once. It doesn't give teachers the resources they need to educate the next generation; it doesn't bring back factories that have long disappeared; it doesn't bring down the price of bread or milk.[28] And indeed, life in Armenia remained difficult after Nikol Pashinyan brought down the previous government in 2018. To some, it might have even felt worse. But after years of authoritarian rule in Yerevan, it was at least an opening, a chance for a new beginning.

Generally speaking, there's the best chance of breaking through the cycle of tyranny if tyrants can be toppled through non-violent protest. In their book *Why Civil Resistance Works*, Erica Chenoweth and Maria Stephan found that a full 57 per cent of successful non-violent campaigns led to democracy. Of the changes that involved violence, it was less than 6 per cent.[29] The reasons for this are varied – among them, legitimacy. Toppling an entrenched authoritarian regime that may have survived for many decades by non-violent means necessitates the involvement of a large segment of the population. Now that the old regime has fallen, the new regime has a popular mandate to do things differently.

Because such a large number of people are involved, peaceful ways to adjudicate conflict have to be established. In power, they can use that precedent to deal with other political actors without resorting to violence. That's essential for the functioning of a democracy and it means that movements that have come to power through non-violence tend to be good at the business of politics.[30] Because they are, they have an incentive to keep operating in a system in which those skills are valuable. That differentiates them from groups that take power by force. They have the opposite skillset: they are good at using violence, but not negotiating. Since that's where they have their advantage, why should they stop now that they have power? They won't. They'll keep wielding the sword rather than sheathing it.

In more autocratic regimes in which it is harder for the masses to mobilise, *coups d'état* tend to pose the biggest threat to dictators. When the men with guns take power, there are three main options: military dictatorship, a military-backed ruler, or democratisation. In dictatorships, about two out of three coups lead to a collapse of the entire political system and the birth of a new one.[31] Now, that could mean democracy, another dictatorship or something in between. Interestingly, the numbers on this have seen a significant change: only 14 per cent of coups against dictatorships led to democracy during the Cold War, but during the next twenty-five years, that number shot up to 40 per cent.[32]

Another drawback to coups, though, is that they rarely come in ones. There's a tendency for countries to become caught in a 'coup trap' once they experience even a single coup. In Thailand, for example, there were attempted coups in 1981, 1985, 1991, 1992 (twice), 2006 and 2014.[33] In part, this can be explained by societal norms. In a liberal democratic society such as Norway, a coup is almost unimaginable. Power matters in politics, but so does legitimacy – and the Norwegian government has plenty. Not only has it provided the Norwegian people with a high standard of living, it has also been elected in free and fair elections. And since there's no recent history of coups, the soldiers of the Norwegian armed forces are unlikely seriously to consider the possibility of taking power. By contrast, a military junta, having recently come to power through a *coup d'état*, has very little claim to it.[34] Because a *coup d'état* can be carried out by a small number of armed men and women, it's difficult to tell whether the junta has popular legitimacy. In addition, the junta doesn't yet have the advantage of being accepted simply because it has been in place for a long time.[35] In combination, this makes the junta (and their successors) much more vulnerable to yet another coup, and then another. Escaping from the coup trap is not easy.

Nevertheless, there is an argument to be made that some coups against some types of leaders might not be so bad.[36] Coups are one of the few viable ways to get rid of some of the world's worst dictators. They are unlikely to lead to a flourishing democracy but there are some contexts in which there simply aren't a lot of other options. Moreover, aren't there situations in which getting rid of a particular tyrant would be desirable even if the country doesn't turn into a democracy thereafter? It's not difficult to imagine some scenarios in which that's the case.

Benjamin Disraeli claimed that 'assassination has never changed the history of the world.'[37] Anecdotal evidence (the outbreak of the First World War, for example) aside, there's some hard evidence to suggest that he was wrong. Killing tyrants can be fruitful. In a study on the effect of assassinations on institutions and war, the economists Benjamin Jones and Benjamin Olken found that killing non-democratic leaders can increase the chances of democratisation in a given country. Killing democratic leaders, on the other hand, made comparatively little difference.[38] It's an intuitive finding. In a personalised dictatorship, the death of a single man makes a much greater difference than it does in a mature liberal democracy.

Whereas assassinations are targeted only at the dictator or perhaps also his immediate circle, civil wars can be all-encompassing – often leading to hundreds of thousands, sometimes even millions, of deaths. The destructive force of these conflicts is in a league of its own. And often, the fall of the tyrant in a civil war is not even the end of the war (or tyranny). For example, when Idriss Déby died at the hands of rebels in Chad in 2021, the regime didn't fall and the war didn't end. There wasn't even a dictator with a new last name; his thirty-seven-year-old son simply took over, so Chad continued to be ruled by a Déby.

Like coups, civil wars have a tendency to repeat themselves. Some two out of ten civil wars flare up again within five years.[39] So the tyrant falls, a new leader comes in and the destruction continues. Often, this is because the underlying reason for the conflicts tends to persist. When the disaffected population on the periphery of a country rises up because the inhabitants are poor and without opportunity, their grievances don't simply disappear when a ceasefire has been agreed.

But also, the new leader will will be tempted to keep fighting because he has a strong incentive not to be the leader who loses the war, especially if he is also part of the ruling elite which had a hand in starting it in the first place.[40] Nobody wants to be responsible for losing, so they just keep fighting.

But even if the new leader did want to make peace with the rebels, he would have a hard time doing so. One of the reasons why it's so difficult for authoritarian regimes to make peace with rebels, even after one dictator has died, is that they struggle to make a credible promise to their opponents.[41]

To illustrate this, we have to travel to the northern shore of Africa's second largest lake, Tanganyika. On the night of 13 August 2004, the residents of Gatumba, a Burundian settlement on the border with the Democratic Republic of Congo, heard something unusual.[42] To the west, from across the marsh, there were sounds of drums, bells and whistles. As the sounds came closer, singing became audible. 'God will show us how to get to you and where to find you,' the shadowy figures sang.

Some, but not all, of the figures who were coming closer, wore military uniforms. Unbeknown to the residents of

Gatumba, many of whom were refugees, the drummers and singers belonged to the Forces Nationales de Libération (FNL). Most of them were men, but some were just children, so small that their weapons dragged along the ground.[43]

The FNL was a Hutu rebel group active in the Burundian civil war which began after the assassination of Melchior Ndadaye, Burundi's first democratically elected president. By August 2000, after countless Burundians had lost their lives to the violence, the government of Burundi signed a peace treaty with most of the country's armed groups – but not with the FNL. The FNL, under the leadership of then forty-nine-year-old Agathon Rwasa, kept fighting.

That night in Gatumba, the FNL's fighters started firing. Most of their victims were Banyamulenge, an ethnic group from the Congo frequently categorised with Tutsi. Between the shots, the fires and the screaming, it was utter chaos. But despite the violence, some people thought they were going to be saved since the attackers shouted 'come, come, we're going to save you.'[44]

But nobody came to help. Instead, the rebels shot people who left their tents. Many of those who did not take that chance died inside them, burned to death. The *Washington Post* later reported that one sixteen-year-old girl saw her mother die from a gunshot to the head, her brother decapitated and her father burned alive.[45] In total, FNL fighters slaughtered more than 150 Congolese civilians and another 106 were wounded. According to the United Nations most of the victims were women, children and babies; they were shot dead and burned.[46]

When I talked to Agathon Rwasa about the massacre in Gatumba, he refused to admit responsibility and said the way he'd been treated as a result of the accusations had been an injustice. But despite maintaining his innocence, he made a point of saying that he was a Christian. 'I believe in the strength of forgiveness,' he added.[47]

The case of Rwasa demonstrates why it can be so difficult to put an end to civil wars. In 2004, Burundian authorities issued an arrest warrant for him over the massacre.[48] But for someone like that who is accused of war crimes, to stop fighting, he needs to believe not just that military victory is impossible, but also that the government will not go after him once he lays down arms. That isn't easy, because not going after a rebel leader whose troops created so much suffering is an outrage. Two decades later, Rwasa hadn't spent a single day in jail over the Gatumba massacre. Instead, he managed to become deputy speaker of the Parliament of Burundi and even ran for the presidency.[49] He is far from being an outcast.

Democratic leaders are heavily constrained when it comes to cooperating with people like Rwasa because they need to keep voters on their side but tyrants can promise rebel leaders just about anything. They want amnesty? Sure. They want their soldiers to be integrated into the regular military? Not a problem. They can make all the promises. However, laying down arms in exchange for a promise from a dictator can be suicidal – it means nothing. Idriss Déby is a good example of this. When a rebel leader signed an accord and returned from exile because he thought he was safe, he was killed in his N'Djamena home.[50] Civil wars are not just extraordinarily deadly and destructive, they are also difficult to end – especially for dictators.

That brings us to a change of regime imposed from abroad. In late March 2003, George W. Bush said: 'These are opening stages of what will be a broad and concerted campaign.'[51] Three weeks later, civilians and American soldiers pulled down a statue of Saddam Hussein in Baghdad's Al-Firdos Square. Later that year, a dishevelled Saddam Hussein was found hiding in a hole near Tikrit. A vicious, brutal dictator was toppled, found and executed.

But at what price? Thousands of American soldiers and contractors were killed. The war cost the American taxpayer billions. More importantly, it cost tens of thousands of Iraqi lives and the country was devastated by the war and an ensuing insurgency. Not only that, it destabilised the entire region and contributed to the rise of the Islamic State (IS) as a serious military risk. So why did the operation fail? Was it about America and Iraq in particular, or is there something about foreign-imposed regime change more generally that always made failure likely? Both.

One of the big problems of replacing a foreign regime through force from abroad is that the attacker needs to decide what to do with the remnants of the old regime. Do you purge? If you do, you destroy the people who know how to govern and you give them an incentive to torpedo the transition to a new system of government. If you don't, the transition is at risk because the loyalty of those who have previously worked for the dictator cannot be taken for granted.

In Iraq, the Americans decided in favour of purging. Between 12 May 2003 and 28 June 2004, Paul Bremer was the man in charge of the Coalition Provisional Authority (CPA).[52] In that role, he was something of a governor for the country, except that he wasn't elected by the Iraqi people or held accountable by any type of Iraqi legislature. Bremer issued his first order as CPA administrator within four days of being in the role. In section 1, paragraph 2 and 3, it stated that many members of the Baath Party and government officials were to be removed from their positions. Some of them were also banned from being employed in the public sector in the future.[53] In a second order, issued later that month, Bremer formally disbanded the Iraqi security forces.[54]

At first, both of these orders might sound like a good idea. The Baath Party had been responsible for human rights violations in Iraq for decades. Surely nobody who had been close to them should now have access to the levers of power? It's more complicated than that. The order on de-Baathification might have affected around eighty-five thousand Iraqis, many thousands of whom weren't enthusiastic supporters of Saddam Hussein, but had simply joined the party to keep their work. Some of them were teachers, others crucial to keep the lights on or the water flowing.[55] The CIA station chief in Baghdad at the time warned Bremer: 'By nightfall, you'll have driven 30,000 to 50,000 Baathists underground. And in six months, you'll really regret this.'[56]

With the disbandment of Iraqi security forces, hundreds of thousands of Iraqis with previous military training went from being someone to being unemployed. Now without income and angry, many of them had no incentive to accept the new status quo. A later report would find that 'these two orders severely undermined the capacity of the occupying forces to maintain security and continue the ordinary functioning of the Iraq government.'[57]

And so it turned out. Some of Saddam Hussein's former soldiers quickly began to organise armed resistance and by the autumn of 2003, the occupying forces had a serious insurgency on their hands.[58] In October 2006, the Pentagon assessed that US forces were losing.[59] By the following year, the situation had become so dire that President Bush decided to deploy an additional 30,000 troops to Iraq to try to contain the violence.[60]

It's a problem that's difficult to solve more generally. After defeating Nazi Germany in the Second World War, for example, some of the Allies took the opposite course. Instead of trying to weed out everyone who had been involved with the

Nazi regime, the occupiers west of the Elbe deliberately let former generals, judges and administrators continue working because they were more worried about a dysfunctional Germany than one that contained remnants of the former regime. This had an impact on German politics all the way to the top: in 1969, the chancellor of the Federal Republic was a man who had joined the National Socialist German Workers' Party in 1933. It would be an understatement to say that denazification was incomplete.

When we examine foreign-imposed regime change more generally, the track record is abysmal and not only because it's difficult to deal with former elites. A study published in 2013 found that around 11 per cent of United States regime-change operations over a century ended up creating democracy;[61] barely more than one in ten. Despite democracy often being stated as the priority of the intervening state, it usually isn't.[62] Democratic leaders want to stay in power and using force against another state is a massive risk. To most, it's simply not worth taking that risk unless national security is at stake. Advancing democracy is seen as a bonus, but it's not reason enough to go to war. And if democracy is not even the primary reason to go to war, why would democracy result from war?

President Kennedy understood these dynamics perfectly. During the Cold War, when Washington wanted to remove Ramfis Trujillo from power in the Dominican Republic, Kennedy said:

> There are three possibilities of descending order of prefer-ence: a decent democratic regime, a continuation of the Trujillo regime, or a Castro regime. We ought to aim at the first, but we really can't renounce the second until we are sure we can avoid the third.[63]

When democratic leaders go on television and the news anchor asks them about their motivations for intervening, that's not what they'll say – but back in the situation room, that's how they'll act.

On top of that, there are cases where democracy isn't just seen as less important than national security, but where it is seen as a net negative.[64] If a tyrant is replaced with a democratic leader, that democratic leader will have more of an interest in winning elections than in doing the bidding of a foreign power. Indeed, democracy exporters could end up in a situation in which they expend blood and treasure to install a democratic government only to find that government turns around and acts against them.

There's something of a paradox here. If foreign-imposed regime change is (partly) about creating a sustainable democracy, there are two main factors to consider. The first is the likelihood of success, which differs greatly since some countries are vastly more likely to turn into democracies than others. All else being equal, it's much easier to turn a rich country with a history of democratic rule into a democracy than it is to transform a poor personalised dictatorship in which no popular vote has ever been held.[65]

The other factor to consider is the complexity of the military intervention necessary to bring down the regime. Deposing leaders at the top of stable countries with functioning institutions (such as Imperial Japan), which have the best chance of democratising, tends to be costly because those institutions generate military effectiveness. Deposing leaders at the top of poor personalised dictatorships might be easier, but the chances of success are lower because there's no foundation for a democracy.[66] Democracy exporters can thus either win an 'easy war' for a low chance of a sustainable outcome or a 'hard war' with a high chance of more positive results. Since hard war can mean hundreds of thousands of deaths, it's rarely worth it.

So given the terrible odds, why do attempts to change a regime through force happen as often as they do? It's partly hubris. Politicians tend to believe that this time round, things will go differently. Perhaps they think they are particularly intelligent, that they won't fall into the traps to which their predecessors succumbed.

But also, the alternatives are often dire. In the abstract, you might know that the use of force is unlikely to create a flourishing democracy. But in that moment, when the head of foreign intelligence tells you that a dictator is about to barrel-bomb hospitals and street markets, would the numbers really guide your decision-making? Or would you take a chance and try to destroy the dictator's attack helicopters before they lift off? Even with all the data in the world, it would be an impossible decision.

All these scenarios envisage dictators being toppled, but there's also the option that they go to bed, never to wake up again. And indeed, this happens not infrequently because plenty of dictators are long-lived. Cameroon's Paul Biya was still in power at the age of ninety; in Equatorial Guinea next door, Teodoro Obiang, at eighty-one. Fidel Castro died aged ninety. Robert Mugabe made it to the ripe age of ninety-five before dying in a Singaporean hospital.

Oddly enough, not much tends to happen when dictators 'just fall asleep'. In a report that analysed the aftermath of seventy-nine dictators dying in office, it was found that only 8 per cent of these deaths led to a collapse of the previous regime.[67] And democracy almost never follows. Some might consider these numbers surprising. The dictator is dead. Surely that's the best opening there could possibly be to take the country in a different direction? By and large, that's not what happens.

Speaking of soldiers, people sometimes say: 'Beware of an old man in a profession where men usually die young.' What applies to warriors also applies to dictators. Despots who die in office have usually staved off their fair share of threats throughout their rule. When they fall asleep in their golden bed, the regime is not likely to collapse because the system is entrenched and ready for the change. Everyone knows their place and the machinery hums along under these extraordinary circumstances. In comes the new leader.

Even if the new leader wants to make drastic changes, it will be difficult for him to do so because ruling without the old guard will be next to impossible. And why would the men and women who surrounded the old leader want to dismantle the system that has served them so well? They usually don't, so they will pick someone who doesn't want to rock the boat. If, contrary to expectations, their choice tries to do things differently, he is unlikely to get far.

A researcher at Harvard University recently argued that leaders are only 'allowed' to die in their sleep if the elites are already set on a successor.[68] If they weren't, someone would try to get the advantage by moving against the incumbent while he was still alive. Since that hasn't happened and the dictator has been allowed to die in peace, it's likely there's been some agreement between regime insiders that makes drastic changes less likely.

There's one more angle to this. The way a new leader comes to power doesn't just tell us what type of political system we can expect, it also gives us a clue as to how stable it will be. When a new leader takes power, he is often in a comparatively vulnerable position.[69] The situation is in flux and people don't yet know their roles – they might even be tempted to challenge the new leader if they believe he is weak. But some modes of 'leadership entry' create much more stability than others.[70]

Assassinating someone is comparatively easy and it doesn't telegraph much strength. Dismantling an entire political order through a regime-changing coup, a rebellion or massive protests, on the other hand, requires a much higher degree of support. When new leaders come to power through those means, everyone understands that they are comparatively strong. As a result, those new leaders are less likely to face serious, immediate challenges to their rule because nobody wants to start a fight they will lose.

When tyrants fall and regimes collapse, the outcome is often catastrophic. Tyrants maintain power by picking winners and losers, and whilst intrigue and backroom scheming do occur, all-out conflict is unlikely while they are firmly in the saddle. But as soon as they struggle and it looks as if they might fall, the situation escalates. Regime elites want to keep the regime alive to maintain their benefits; challengers want to rise to the top, expanding their power and access to stolen money; the masses want to redirect resources from the regime to the population at large, but they are usually too weak to compete with the insiders.

When the dust has settled and the bloodletting has stopped, people are often left to wonder whether it has all been worth it, given that the tyranny has not ended but merely assumed another name. This cycle of dictatorship–conflict–dictatorship is difficult to break, but sometimes it does happen if tyrants have been toppled the 'right' way. Now that we know how tyrants fall and what happens when they do, how do we make it happen? And is it wise to try to make tyrants fall?

9

How to Topple a Tyrant

> History proves that all dictatorships, all authoritarian forms
> of government are transient. Only democratic systems are
> not transient. Whatever the shortcomings, mankind has
> not devised anything superior.[1]
>
> Vladimir Putin, president of Russia

Few things in politics are as hard as toppling tyrants, but that
doesn't mean all attempts are doomed to fail.

Given that it's so difficult, what influence do outsiders realistically have? For better or worse, outside influence is often
limited. Toppling tyrants mostly falls to the people themselves, and then to a narrow sub-set of the population. The
general rule is this: the closer to the tyrant, the more influence that person will have. The minister of defence will
usually have more power than a mid-ranking civil servant and
the power of the mandarin will usually exceed that of a shop-
keeper on the periphery.

Just as staying in power involves trade-offs for despots,
toppling tyrants involves difficult decisions for the people
trying to make it happen. To topple tyrants without creating
a catastrophe the dictatorial cycle has to be broken.

There are two principal ways to do this: the first involves
chipping away at his pedestal to weaken it over time, so that a
strong gust of wind is enough to topple him. The second

strategy is more immediate, aiming to take out the tyrant more directly.

When it comes to toppling tyrants, not all countries will have the same set of tools. Some, such as the United States, have all of them – so many you can barely find the one you want, from political pressure to economic coercion to force. In 2019, after disputed Venezuelan elections, the United States moved to recognise Juan Guaidó as president, to weaken Nicolás Maduro, who continued to have de facto control over the country.[2] When President Carter decided that Nicaraguan dictator Somoza had to go in 1978, Washington used its influence over the International Monetary Fund to prevent it from granting the government in Managua credit.[3] And Carter, besides suspending military aid to the regime, blocked others from shipping arms to it as well.[4] In the early 1960s, President Kennedy went a step further when he ordered one of America's fleets off the coast of the Dominican capital. With the threat of invasion imminent, Ramfis Trujillo was told that it was time to step down. He didn't want to take his chances, so he did.[5] In 2003 the United States toppled Saddam Hussein in Iraq and, in 2011, Muammar Gaddafi in Libya. For a country such as the United States, there are plenty of tools in the box.

Others have access only to specialised tools. Their banks might be where dictatorial cash is stored. Or they manufacture equipment that keeps the regime's jets in the air. Or they might just be in geographic proximity, which can come in handy for opponents of the regime who are looking for a safe place from which to organise resistance.

If outsiders choose the slower, more subtle method – to chip away and wait for the storm – the first order of business should be careful analysis and planning. Who really keeps the tyrant in power? Which are the groups the despot absolutely cannot afford to lose? What gets them out of bed on a Monday morning? How can their calculus be influenced? Since authoritarian regimes can be so opaque, it can be difficult to tell – especially in the world's most closed countries. But despite these obvious difficulties, people are more similar than they are different. True, cultures differ widely and people have vastly different ideologies, especially if they live in regimes that have indoctrinated them for decades. That said, a lot of people in these key positions want similar things: power, money, safety for themselves and their families, respect.

Once this analysis is done, the aim of outsiders should be to damage the pedestal faster than the dictator can repair it. To do that, there needs to be not just an analysis of the strengths and weaknesses of the regime but also of the actor now trying to bring it down. What are you good at? What are you not?

There are three advantages to taking this more cautious approach. Since the tyrant isn't toppled by the outsider itself, it can be comparatively cheap. And because this approach is about helping people help themselves, the chances of it going catastrophically wrong are much lower than they could be. (It's theoretically possible for 100,000 people to die because an outside power has held workshops for independent journalists – but thus far, it hasn't happened.) Moreover, if cautious support from outside contributes to the fall of the regime, the outcome has a chance of being sustainable. As we have learned over the course of this book, non-violent transitions, if they succeed, are more likely to bring about democracy than violent transitions.

Tyrants need money, weapons and people to stay in power. Importantly, the people around them need to expect that they will continue to have all three in the future. If that's not the impression they have, elites may recalibrate the support they provide to the leader because they don't want to bet on the wrong horse. When that happens, the tyrant becomes vulnerable, inviting challengers to take him on. Outsiders can have an influence on all three. If they want to contribute to toppling a tyrant, they should aim to weaken the ruler, strengthen alternative elites and empower the masses. The former tactics make the fall more likely, the latter increases the chance that the cycle of tyranny can be broken.

As a first step, outside powers should stop doing all the things that actively keep the tyrant alive. Many a dictator receives military equipment worth billions of dollars. These arms exports aren't all alike, of course. A submarine's torpedoes are unlikely to be used in the internal defence of the regime because neither coups nor popular protests tend to happen out at sea. But a main battle tank capable of killing dozens of protestors in seconds? That's a different story altogether. To make life harder for dictators, the export of military equipment that can be used by the tyrant against his own people needs to be stopped. Details depend on the regime in question, but it certainly means no more armoured vehicles, no more small arms, no more helicopters.

The next step is to make it harder for the dictator to find and control opponents. Nowadays, the key to this is digital surveillance of computers, tablets and phones. When it comes to the surveillance of mobile phones, there's one software that stands out.

In the spring of 2011, executives of the NSO Group, makers of the spyware Pegasus, were sitting in a room used for storing cleaning materials on a massive military base outside Mexico City.[6] Even though this was already inside a secure perimeter, an armed guard stood outside the door. This wasn't an ordinary engineering team and as few people as possible were supposed to find out about the visit. After their wait ended and the guard stepped aside, the presentation began. In attendance were the Mexican president Felipe Calderón and his secretary of defence, Guillermo Galván Galván. The company's chief technology officer gave attendees a BlackBerry.

The phone looked and acted as normal. There were no warning signs, no flashing lights, no error messages. But as the Mexican officials used the phone, they could watch on a large screen as data from the phone were transmitted live. It was the perfect attack: not only was the phone completely compromised, the victim wouldn't know a thing about it.

With the hack completed, the attacker gains access to just about everything on the phone: contacts, text messages, call logs, the microphone. Shortly thereafter, NSO Group had their first major customer: the state of Mexico. The country had long been fighting powerful drug dealers, and software such as this would be perfect to fight cartels. If the authorities knew where they were, who they spoke to and what they planned, they could fight back much more effectively.

But over the next couple of years, more and more governments became interested in the technology, and it wasn't just to fight organised crime. In 2013, the United Arab Emirates (UAE) was offered access to the software. In the hands of the UAE, the software was reportedly used as part of a broad and intense campaign to target Ahmed Mansoor, an Emirati engineer who had committed no wrong other than to criticise his government. As the *New York Times* reported:

> His car was stolen, his email account was hacked, his location was monitored, his passport was taken from him, $140,000 was stolen from his bank account, he was fired from his job and strangers beat him on the street several times.[7]

In addition to all this, he was reportedly targeted by the NSO Group's software. All in all, it was terrifying. As Mansoor himself put it: 'You start to believe your every move is watched. Your family starts to panic. I have to live with that.'[8] Eventually, he was also forced to live with sleeping on the floor of the desert prison into which the regime threw him.[9]

If you had never heard of this software before, you might assume that it was developed in a dictatorship before being sold to other dictatorships. Far from it. NSO Group developed their software in democratic Israel before selling it abroad. It's big business, but more than that it also became a tool of Israeli foreign policy. Since the government controlled the countries to which the software could and couldn't be exported, it could use it to forge new partnerships or cement existing alliances. In the case of the United Arab Emirates, the export licence was reportedly granted after Israeli foreign intelligence agents assassinated a high-ranking member of Hamas in Dubai. The spy software was an 'olive branch'.[10]

If democracies genuinely want tyrants to fall, they shouldn't make such peace offerings.

Dictatorships collect less information about their opponents when they don't have access to these tools and as a result, it becomes more difficult to use repression discriminately. And indiscriminate repression vastly increases the chance of a backlash: if people are punished despite not having done anything 'wrong', what incentive do they have not to start opposing the ruler?

Next, it needs to be harder for the incumbent to please the selectorate. In theory, one way to do that is sanctions. Sanctions against authoritarian regimes are popular with policy makers because they allow them to 'do something' when they don't want to take much risk. As a result, the number of sanctions has ballooned: during the 1990s, more than 50 per cent of the world's population was under sanctions and President Bill Clinton complained that the country had become 'sanctions happy'.[11] Since then, it has only become more so. When President Trump was in office, the administration reached 'an average of almost four sanctions designations every working day'.[12]

But do they work? That depends what we mean by 'work'. Sanctions are intended to apply economic pressure on another country so that it changes its behaviour.[13] In practice, that's almost impossible to do when it comes to incentivising tyrants to step down. 'Asking a tyrant to step down is like asking him to sign his own death warrant,' Agathe Demarais, a sanctions expert of the European Council on Foreign Relations, told me.[14] To the extent that economic coercion does work, it's not by changing the mind of the dictator but the minds of those around him. Sanctions can work by reducing the ability of the dictator to distribute cash to elites which the regime has derived through trade or foreign aid. But how much of a difference sanctions make partly depends on the type of regime that is being targeted. A 2010 study showed that personalist regimes and monarchies are comparatively more vulnerable to sanctions in that they rely particularly on revenue from outside – for example, foreign aid – to fund patronage.[15]

In theory, a collapsing economy should lead to problems for authoritarian regimes by angering both powerbrokers and the masses. The former become less rich, the latter poorer. To try to overcome this unfortunate situation, a personalist dictator might be tempted to use repression. But if he attempts it, there's no certainty that his generals will follow through it because they will probably be aggrieved as well.

In comparison to personalist dictatorships, both military dictatorships and one-party states have an advantage in this situation.[16] Juntas, on average, have an easier time using repression to deal with the fallout of sanctions because their forces are less likely to splinter under the weight of their own repression. Party-based dictatorships, on the other hand, can often co-opt elites by giving them something other than money because they tend to have more functional institutions. So even though this or that important political figure may no longer receive a steady delivery of wads of cash, they can be promoted to become a delegate to a national congress or the head of a publicly owned conglomerate.

The effectiveness of sanctions also relates to geography. If a country has significant oil resources, they have a huge advantage.[17] Oil is such a valuable commodity that it will be sold one way or another. If some countries sanction an oil exporter, others will step in to buy the oil. They might get a discount, but money will keep flowing and dictatorships can often stave off threats to the regime by distributing that money around their capital's villas.

Evidently, a lot of non-democratic states against which sanctions might be imposed with the aim of destabilising their governments fit one or other of these criteria. Does that mean these states should never be targeted because sanctions won't work?

Not necessarily. Economic coercion can also make sense when targeting petrostates, for example, because they make life harder for people who shouldn't have it easy. Asked about sanctions against Russia, a political economist recently told the *Washington Post*: 'The way I think about sanctions is that we are shaking the tree on which the regime sits.' 'We are not shaking it enough for it to fall down,' he went on to say, 'but we're creating problems for them.'[18] That's not perfect, but depending on the situation, it can be better than nothing.

There are other options to keep tyrants on their toes. One way of doing it is to drop external defence guarantees. That's not necessarily because an external actor is likely to topple said tyrant, but because it forces the dictatorship to devote more of its limited resources to military effectiveness, thereby increasing the risk of coups. As that risk increases, so a new problem arises, then another, forming a distraction that invites the tyrant to make unforced errors.

In conclusion, the strategy to weaken the tyrant begins with withdrawing external support. It continues by making it harder to use repression while reducing his ability to redistribute the gains of tyranny to the people that keep him in power. All these measures weaken the tyrant vis-à-vis others who could replace him.

To increase the pressure, outsiders can then encourage rivals and strengthen their hand while the incumbent struggles. Yoweri Museveni became Uganda's ninth president in 1986, a time when the Cold War was still raging. In the twenty-first century, his biggest political problem has been the activist Bobi Wine. A musician turned presidential candidate, his hallmark a red beret with the outline of Uganda on it, Wine excites people. When he landed at Entebbe International Airport on 5 October 2023, his supporters had planned something special.[19] Since he had been abroad for two weeks, they wanted to march him all the way to his home, some fifty kilometres to the northeast in Kampala.

But instead of a welcome home party, Bobi Wine was met by unknown men who twisted his arms behind his back as he got off the plane. Instead of marching along with his supporters, he was driven off in a car before being kicked in the head. And when he arrived home, there was no peace there either because of the dozens of security officers inside and outside the compound. 'I am surrounded by the military, and nobody is allowed to leave and no one is allowed to come,' Bobi Wine told a journalist.[20]

Wine was effectively detained, but at least he wasn't killed. And, as one activist close to Bobi told me, that was no coincidence. According to him, Wine could be harassed and put under house arrest by the regime, but he couldn't be killed. Despots might be happy to kill a foe, but no dictator wants a negative headline in the *New York Times* or the *Washington Post*. And Bobi Wine, being so charismatic, commands incredible attention. On Instagram, Bobi Wine has more than 700,000 followers; on what used to be Twitter, more than 2 million. Uganda isn't exactly the focus of the world's media, but when something happens to Bobi Wine, the BBC, CNN and other major media organisations take note. All that makes it significantly more difficult for Uganda's dictator to eliminate the opposition leader.

Clearly, support for alternative leaders can go way beyond medical care, exile or sympathetic media interviews. High-ranking regime insiders can be encouraged to defect or turn against their boss. They can be bribed or given money to build their own power base within the country. Maybe they can also be given compromising information at the right time.

But simply weakening tyrants and strengthening their rivals is not enough. The masses have to be empowered, because while the principal threat to most tyrants comes from other elites and not the streets, popular uprisings can bring down leaders within the blink of an eye. Just as importantly, they can help alternative elites to put pressure on the leader. Even in highly authoritarian regimes, popular support (or lack of it) still matters – if only because it can tell other elites that the current leader might be at serious risk of falling.

The people can also exert pressure on the incumbent's

rivals in the event that they succeed. In that way a change in leadership can, at least potentially, lead to a meaningful change in policy. If this isn't done, there's the risk that chopping down the tyrant will simply produce a new one – that the cycle of tyranny, chaos, tyranny will simply keep turning.

One of the main difficulties of discussing the utility of outside support with people engaged in trying to promote democracy is that these groups face a dilemma. On the one hand, they clearly believe in the work because if they didn't, they wouldn't be doing it. It's not as though these people drive fancy cars or live in big houses. But on the other hand, they are reluctant to talk up its value too much because it would take away from the people who have effected change on the ground. That would be all the more upsetting because it's these people who face the greatest risk. Additionally, tyrants themselves love to talk up foreign influence when they face any opposition. If the people trying to promote democracy from abroad are too vocal about their contribution, they risk playing into the hands of the rulers they seek to weaken.

Nevertheless, there are a few things that can be learnt from talking to people who do this every day. To strengthen the masses in their conflict with the incumbent and regime elites, outsiders can create networks, train activists, support mobilisation outside the regime's control, allow them to gather force in exile and support the free flow of information.

When activists are struggling against a seemingly omnipotent regime that does everything it can to keep opponents in the dark, it can feel to them as if they are alone; that nobody else thinks the way they do and that the responsibility is theirs to work it out. This, of course, is exactly what tyrants want to achieve because it reinforces the coordination problem that prevents protests from being launched. Outsiders can help to bridge this gap by bringing people together.

In some cases, that also means mediating between people's conflicting interests. Before the amateurish coup that failed to bring down Yahya Jammeh, the Gambian opposition struggled to unite in the face of an overwhelmingly cruel regime. After the attempted coup, they came together with the support of outside non-governmental organisations after realising that they could no longer go on the way they had.[21] In an ideal scenario, bringing people together also leads them to learn from each other. How do you mobilise people? How does one go about organising a nationwide strike? These are questions about which generations of activists have thought so there's no need to reinvent the wheel.

Every dictatorship is different but they're similar enough for it to be possible to provide practical advice to people organising opposition. Outside actors can provide support to domestic groups as they train supporters in strategy and tactics. With the twenty-first century came entirely new categories of things to learn. How does one create viral content for social media? What messengers are safe; which definitely aren't? These are the practical lessons that activists can learn from each other. Outsiders can help by facilitating networks and training.

The people together are harder to beat than any collection of individuals. For that reason, anything that makes it easy for people to come together and mobilise can increase the power of the masses. Where laws don't yet make it impossible to support civil society organisations which are critical of the regime, that should be the focus. Where they do, the next best option is to provide support to organisations that aren't directly engaged in holding the government accountable but still allow large groups of people to coordinate with each other. If that can be done as part of a church, so be it; if it's a trade union, so be it; if it's a disability advocacy group, so be it. Anything that allows for coordination and popular mobilisation that isn't controlled by the government may provide an advantage.

Strengthening opposition movements can also include support of political exile. Political opposition movements don't just consist of figureheads, they are communities. There are people who organise, raise funds, get the message out to journalists and so forth. When things become too dangerous, not one, but many of them will often be forced to leave. Over the last couple of years, as transnational repression has become the norm rather than the exception, a significant number of these communities have come under increasing pressure from their authoritarian tormentors because many democracies have pushed refugees away from their own borders to countries that are more susceptible to pressure from dictators. Reversing this would undoubtedly create significant political challenges, but if the intention is to make life harder for tyrants, it could well be helpful.[22]

A further aid must be the free flow of information. The internet, as much as tyrants have attempted to use it for their own ends, continues to be of use to activists. Not only can they use it to coordinate and spread their message, when the moment comes and it looks as if the regime is staggering, they can use it to mobilise. And existing democracies can help activists help themselves: for example, they can support the development of safe messenger applications and help activists circumvent governmental censorship.

If these measures are implemented and the stability of the tyrant's fiefdom is in serious question, outsiders will then have to decide about a different kind of exile: that of the despot rather than his opponents. As discussed with reference to Philippine dictator Ferdinand Marcos, this is a difficult problem. If democracies don't grant exile, innocent civilians will die because the dictator will have an incentive to do all he can to remain in power. He may give an order to torture, he may give an order to shoot. Those orders might not be followed, but there's always the chance that they are. If democracies grant exile, a truly vile person will get to live out his days in Hawaii or on the Côte d'Azur. Not only that, but it will also undermine international justice and account-ability efforts, and send a signal to others that they are free to torture and kill.

Taken together, these measures will be corrosive enough to destabilise many dictatorships. It might not happen overnight, but it will happen. Some will fall and most will struggle as soon as even a little opposition arises. In the cases in which tyrants do fall, there's a decent chance that the dictatorial cycle will be broken.

But there's a limit to these strategies because many of the most powerful and most damaging despots will have antici-pated an attack on their rule; they are prepared. As a result, there might not be enough people within the country who, even when supported, could make a meaningful difference. As the historian Rory Cormac noted, 'covert action doesn't create opposition groups.'[23] That is to say that you can only support something that is already in existence because even the most powerful external actors cannot create partners out of thin air; or it might be that opponents of the current regime could be supported, but they are worse than the people in charge; or finally, the regime itself might also be so established that it is difficult to break even if opponents can be supported. This is more likely to happen after the regime has already survived for a while; if the machine works better than it initially did.[24]

Under those circumstances, the best one can realistically achieve as an outsider is to accelerate the fall of the tyrant. An end to tyranny is unlikely. The key problem is that the most destructive regimes are the least likely to fall in ways that are likely to generate a good outcome. To bring down those regimes, the measures outlined above might well be insufficient.

In situations like this, policymakers find themselves at a crossroads. If they take one route, need a different set of tools. If they take another, they will need to wait until the moment arises when they can make a difference.

Changing tools means changing aims: instead of trying to weaken the dictator over time, the goal is now to take him out directly. Out goes the hammer, in comes the dynamite. The advantage of using dynamite to topple the dictator from his pedestal is that dynamite is exceptionally effective and the effect is quick. But not everybody has access to it and that's probably a good thing because using dynamite can result in things going very wrong. In other words, these are measures that are more likely to topple tyrants but less likely to lead to a sustainable outcome if the tyrant does fall. They are also vastly more expensive.

Whereas none of the previous measures involved violence, this one does – at least indirectly. The aim should be to make life as miserable as possible for regime elites while giving them the opportunity to break free. If someone can be found who is willing to remove the incumbent from power, help them. If we are talking about a petrostate, encourage sabotage of pipelines or refineries. Identify armed opposition groups and provide them with the weapons they need to wreak havoc. Tell the generals that you would be supportive of a *coup d'état*. If an assassin needs a safehouse, provide it.

Is that going to work? In the sense of toppling the tyrant – perhaps; in the sense of creating an outcome that's good in any sense of the word – unlikely. These measures are hugely destructive and can easily spiral into war. And as we know after discussing the advantages and disadvantages of covert action, such actions are unlikely to stay hidden. Chances are the information about who provided that safehouse or those weapons will eventually see the light of day, with all the consequences that entails for the party that provided them.

The only thing that's even more escalatory than putting dynamite in the hands of others and telling them to use it is to light the fuse yourself. As a German who enjoyed freedom from the moment he was born, I am not going to argue that force should never be used to topple tyrants.

The famous cases of Japan and Germany aside, there are other cases in which it has worked. Yahya Jammeh, the man Banka Manneh wanted to bring down when he orchestrated a coup attempt in the Gambia, was eventually deposed through the use of force when a regional coalition marched on the dictator's home village. The forces – drawn from Senegal, Ghana and Nigeria – met barely any opposition. The Gambia is not a perfect democracy now, but it certainly became a lot freer after the military intervention. And the intervention itself wasn't costly precisely because there wasn't much opposition. But, as we have seen in the last couple of chapters, most foreign regime-change operations are not like that of the Economic Community of West African States in the Gambia. They tend to fail.

Since this is a route few want to go down, the tools are put back in the box as decision makers bide their time until there's an opening to destabilise the despot at an acceptable cost. This is the 'monitor and prepare' approach.

Even the most powerful tyrants cannot prevent crises from breaking out forever. The cleverest leaders can anticipate public grievances and blunt the effects of recessions and so forth, but something unforeseen always happens. Perhaps a spontaneous protest quickly turns into a nationwide uprising; a part of the military mutinies because they haven't been paid, or perhaps the effects of a natural disaster are exacerbated by the regime's corruption. Even if none of those things happens, tyrants are still mortal. They will eventually get ill or fall asleep and never wake up. When a narrow window of opportunity arises, outsiders have to be ready to prise it wide open.

Until that happens, efforts must be made to minimise the damage the dictator can do while in office. That begins at home. Authoritarians have found plenty of suit-wearing allies within liberal democracies. A whole army of accountants, bankers, lawyers and public relations specialists in cities such as London or New York are busy turning dictatorial cash into political power. The dictators sell oil to the United Kingdom (or the United States or Germany or France . . .) and then invest the proceeds in key industries or relationships with influential political factions. Ten and a half per cent of Volkswagen, one of Germany's most important companies, is owned by Qatar Holding LLC.[25] The Saudi royal family has reportedly invested hundreds of millions, and in some cases even billions, of dollars in American companies Google, Zoom and Activision Blizzard.[26] There's barely a high-ranking European football club that doesn't have some involvement from shady autocrats. Hostile authoritarians are also hoovering up ports, telecommunications infrastructure and other critical installations on which modern life depends. Is all this good business? Hard to tell. But it's definitely a good way to buy influence and protect distasteful regimes from external pressure. Where this is still preventable, it needs to be prevented. Where it has already occurred, democratic states need to roll it back – to find the points of leverage that autocrats can use and systematically reduce the risk.

Now that we are on our way to minimising the damage that these people can do, the next thing we need is a big loud siren. When a relevant regime is in serious trouble, we need to be well prepared. This will involve serious planning.

What would be the warning signs for a falling leader? Who might be next in line if the incumbent falls? What happens when the entire regime collapses, and how might you react? Many developments can be planned for before they happen. When the siren goes off, everyone needs to be at their station, ready to respond.

One of the most curious examples of this was uncovered by journalists at the Associated Press in 2014. Four years earlier, a Cuban journalism student named Saimi Reyes Carmona at the University of Havana had signed up to ZunZuneo, a social network, under her nickname Saimita.[27] Originally small, ZunZuneo (slang for a hummingbird's tweet) rapidly grew in size over the next couple of months. Before she knew it, Saimita had thousands of followers. When she texted them to let them know that it was her birthday, she got so many replies that she excitedly told her boyfriend that it was the coolest thing she had ever seen.[28]

What neither she nor any of ZunZuneo's tens of thousands of other users knew was that the entire network had been dreamt up and planned by a big Washington government contractor and the United States Agency for International Development. Since they obviously couldn't come right out and admit it, the whole operation was made to look as if it was something else. It involved stolen phone numbers, fake companies in the United Kingdom, Spain and the Cayman Islands as well as a bank account in a tax haven. The purpose of this, according to an internal memo, was to ensure that it could not be traced back to America. To fool the users, one proposal went as far as suggesting that fake ad banners should be placed on the website in order to make ZunZuneo look more like a normal business than a political influence campaign.[29]

The aim of ZunZuneo wasn't to turn a profit or make life easier for its users, but to weaken the Cuban government by mobilising citizens against it. At first, it was to be unpolitical. Its users might talk about concerts or their birthday or all their other day-to-day concerns. But if a moment of crisis had ever occurred, the American government could have blasted all of ZunZuneo's users with messages critical of the Cuban regime. Not only that, the same users could have used the site to coordinate with one another. Could that little extra push have made the decisive difference at a moment of serious instability? We will never find out because the project failed before the plan could be put into action.

ZunZuneo involved a number of thorny ethical questions since the people who it supposedly aimed to help were deceived. On a purely practical level, it was also incredibly risky. It's one thing to try to destabilise an adversarial foreign government using a foreign intelligence service, but this work was carried out by a development agency and their contractors. If they claim to drill wells but instead engage in this type of work, even once, everyone working for the agency across the globe is in danger. It was such a 'bold' move that Democratic senator Patrick Leahy called it 'dumb, dumb, dumb'.[30] But it was creative, at least.

When that siren sounds, governments need to take action. The flashing red should lead to an activation of contingency plans to deal with the likely fallout of a sudden change in leadership, or the threat of it. These are volatile moments. In the best-case scenario, a struggling leader simply steps down to pave the way for a better future, but, given everything we know, that's always unlikely. Perhaps a natural death leads to a vacuum of power as multiple figures present themselves as 'worthy' heirs to the tyrant. Maybe an uprising is suppressed as a struggling autocrat manages to retain power. Worst of all, maybe the uprising turns into full-blown civil war. That would mean compatriots would have to be evacuated, people would need to flee and sides would have to be picked. When that moment comes, plans already need to be in the drawer, ready to be implemented at a moment's notice.

But just because we *can* topple tyrants and we now know *how* to topple tyrants doesn't mean that we necessarily *should* topple tyrants.

There are plenty of good arguments against becoming involved. To start with, there's the uncertainty.

If you were in the right place at the right time in the continental United States on 4 October 1957, you could have seen an object moving across the night sky. It wasn't a shooting star or some other natural occurrence. For the very first time in history, humans had succeeded in building and launching something that left the earth's atmosphere. It was Sputnik, an eighty-three-kilogram satellite, the size of a beach ball, launched from a cosmodrome in the Kazakh Soviet Socialist Republic. Sputnik wasn't just visible to the human eye under the right conditions, you could actually hear it 'beep' as it went over-head.[31] While American intelligence agencies and President Eisenhower had known that this was going to happen for quite some time, the wider public was shocked.[32] Had the Soviet threat been underestimated? Were they now more advanced than the free world? The space race was in full swing.

In a development that probably wasn't foreseen by the Soviet rocket engineers working on that launch, satellites are now used by social scientists to get a better idea of the economic strength of authoritarian regimes.[33] Looking at a night-time satellite image of the Korean peninsula, the contrast between North and South couldn't be starker. The democratic South is bright, with Seoul and the surrounding area looking like a giant ball of light. Across the demilitarised zone only a few spots, such as Pyongyang, are visible.

To use that data, economists overlay the images with a grid before recording the light intensity for every square. Factories create light. Once you know how much light is emitted in a given area, you can determine how much economic activity is going on. It's an impressive use of data. And it's not just data from satellites: the availability of large datasets on everything from civil wars to assassinations to coup-proofing mechanisms and protests has increased substantially. The advances in methods and computational power have been huge, and governments and international organisations have tried their best to capitalise on it. The CIA is sponsoring research on coups, the United Nations is trying to forecast instability and many European states use quantitative analysis to complement their assessments of election-related violence. All this has led to a more accurate understanding of the way tyrants fall. On top of these systematic attempts to generate insights, there's been an explosion of open-source intelligence. Given the ubiquity of images and videos coming out of even closed societies, it can feel as if we see everything and understand everything.

In reality, much remains in the dark – and what feels like perfect vision is really just a fraction of the whole image. Economists only use (inaccurate) satellite data as a proxy because basic indicators about economic activity can't be taken at face value in many countries around the world. Authoritarian regimes, whether they be military juntas, hereditary monarchies or one-party states, are more opaque than liberal democracies. So much of these regimes is based on backroom deals and informal rules that it's difficult to work out who matters and who doesn't, and how stable the situation is at any given moment. When it comes to understanding authoritarian regimes, not even hindsight is 20/20.

That leads to one of the principal arguments against attempts to topple tyrants: predicting what will happen afterwards is nearly impossible. Such falls are rare events, and even experts have a poor track record at predicting them accurately. And while what happens next could be better, it might also be worse. Almost everything we discussed in the previous chapters is based on probabilities. Is one type of regime change more likely to achieve sustainable results? Yes. But if that type of regime change has historically had a success rate of two out of three and the stakes are this high, should we really roll the dice? There's a good case to be made that we should not.

The practical arguments are perhaps even more convincing. To begin with, overthrowing a foreign leader can be costly. The cost, of course, is dependent on the extent of outside involvement. At the lower end of the scale, it's not usually too expensive (either financially or politically) to provide limited monetary support to non-violent opposition figures in an unfriendly authoritarian regime. To go to war to topple a foreign leader, on the other hand, is extremely costly – both in blood and in treasure.

Then there's the question of competing interests. In the real world, politicians must juggle a thousand different considerations when devising policy towards a country. What are the commercial ties to the region? Do they need to maintain supplies of a crucial natural resource that they cannot easily replace? How about that military base – could they really do without it if things go wrong? On paper, democracy is often at the top of the list. But when it comes to policy, it's usually trumped by less abstract concerns. And if in doubt, 'stability' wins out. That this stability is often merely a mirage is of secondary importance.

There are other considerations also – one of them being ethical. Most of us would, it is to be hoped, agree that people everywhere should have a meaningful say in the way they are governed. Nobody deserves to live in a one-party dictatorship, an absolute monarchy or under a military junta. But just as we wouldn't want a foreign country to choose leaders for us, most are probably not keen to have their political leaders chosen (or removed) by us. They might want to get rid of their politicians, but that's different from having someone else do it – even if things go well.

In the real world, toppling tyrants also involves other challenging moral questions. That becomes clear when we look back at the North Korean famine of the 1990s.

The situation was so bad that the Kim regime asked for international aid even though its entire ideology was based on the idea that North Korea could be independent from, or even superior to, the countries it was now asking for help. At the same time, the North Korean regime wanted to ensure that the aid came with minimum strings attached. They wanted food, money and medicine, but they didn't want aid organisations to monitor how it was distributed. The movement of aid workers was heavily restricted and the regime went as far as banning staff who spoke Korean.[34] Sometimes hospital patients, including children, simply disappeared.[35]

It was a nightmarish problem. Should regimes like North Korea, under those conditions, be provided with aid?

Providing aid to North Korea was a difficult option. Kim Sung-il was working on nuclear weapons and much of the suffering of the Korean people was his fault. He could have opened the economy and prioritised the wellbeing of his people above his personal power. But he didn't, and providing aid to his regime would almost inevitably strengthen it.

Not being able to feed its people was an obvious sign of the regime's failure that would be mitigated by supplying aid. In addition, aid is fungible. Once food is under Pyongyang's control, it can be sold. If the aid is not sold, the regime still profits: now that it has to spend less money on feeding ordinary North Koreans, it can spend more money on something else, such as soldiers.

And indeed, some aid organisations eventually decided to withdraw. Médecins Sans Frontières, an international charity providing medical care, announced that it would no longer work in North Korea. It judged that food was being diverted from people in need and instead given to the military and other politically important groups.[36]

It's an understandable choice. But with millions of North Koreans starving and Pyongyang asking for aid, can democracies turn the request down and let even more people die? They could and have, of course, but toppling a regime with this tactic is far from assured. In the end, hundreds of millions of dollars' worth of aid poured into North Korea to alleviate the effects of the famine the North Korean regime had created – because sometimes, some things are more important than toppling tyrants.[37]

But despite all these arguments and the difficulties of going through with an attempt to topple tyrants, there must be a tipping point. At some point, despite all the risks that come with it, the price of letting these men run rampant simply becomes too high. Where exactly that tipping point is varies: as the risks of these strategies differ, so do the thresholds at which they become worth pursuing.

Whatever happens, toppling tyrants requires patience. In 1972, when asked about the impact of the French Revolution,

Chinese premier Zhou Enlai is supposed to have replied: 'Too early to say.'[38] As good as the quote might be, that's not how it happened. According to an American diplomat in the room 'there was a misunderstanding that was too delicious to invite correction.'[39] Zhou was referring not to the French Revolution of 1789 but the unrest that had erupted in Paris in 1968.[40] It's a popular misquote because it contains a grain of truth: it is difficult to judge what success looks like in the aftermath of such disruptive events. Something can look like success after a day, failure after a decade and success again a hundred years after it happened.

When former dictator Ben Ali fled to Jeddah less than a month after a vegetable vendor set himself on fire in protest at his regime, the entire world was hopeful. Even as other transitions quickly petered out or went into reverse, Tunisia became the international symbol of success of the Arab Spring. Then, after a few years, things changed again. A little more than a decade after Ben Ali's fall, Tunisia's future did not look so bright as the government consolidated power in its own hands once again. The deaths and the bravery of the Tunisian people might have been for nothing; wasted.

But who can tell what the situation will be like in the future? Perhaps Tunisia will turn into another dictatorship. It even seems probable. But there's also the possibility that the ousting of Ben Ali, and the subsequent years of freedom, laid the groundwork for Tunisia's future development as a successful and prosperous liberal democracy. For all we know, the Tunisians could surprise us. History isn't linear. The French Revolution itself (the one Zhou Enlai wasn't referring to) was not exactly smooth sailing. France experienced violent repression and even war. During the Reign of Terror, some 17,000 people were executed by guillotine. The whole episode ended with a *coup d'état* around ten years after it started. And yet, we now remember it as a pivotal moment on the path to French democracy. Staying engaged under conditions of such uncertainty doesn't come naturally to governments, but it's the reality of the world we live in. There's no single answer to tyranny, no button to press to make the problem go away. Instead, we have to chip away at the institutions that keep despots in power and be ready to pounce once an opening presents itself. And when it does happen, it might not go from bad to better but from bad to worse before it gets better. We have to live with that.

Tyrants are powerful, but they are constantly haunted by the fear of death. And despite all the bluster and seeming insanity, most of these leaders are rational. Due to the structure of the regimes they depend on, their biggest threat comes from the people around them – the palace elites, generals and advisors. Sometimes, even members of their own families are willing to destroy them to make it to the top. To survive under such hostile conditions, despots have to manage elites through riches and repression. And to avoid death, jail and exile, they need to pay particular attention to the men with guns. Trained in violence and equipped to kill, these men and women need to be managed. Everything else that threatens dictators comes from managing these two groups. With the military weakened and the masses systematically excluded to provide benefits for the tiny number of powerbrokers at the top, both military conflict and popular protest are a constant threat. And when the masses rise up, tyrants can't just shoot their way out of the problem because it risks fracturing the regime to such an extent that it falls apart. Assassination is something of a wildcard: difficult to prepare for and something that is always a possibility. Not just that, it can actually become more likely when dictators are successful at protecting themselves from other risks, because that means there aren't any other options to effect change. When the dictator is dead or simply out of office, chaos often follows. Most non-democratic systems of government are bad at managing succession – partly because tyrants usually don't want to appoint a successor.

Democracy hasn't yet reached every place on earth and perhaps it never will, but the precedent has been set and there is every chance that it will continue to spread. There remain some cartoonish leaders with seemingly limitless power over their domain, but they have gone from being the norm to being the exception. These tyrants look like strong men, but they are right to be afraid.

Acknowledgements

Writing a book, especially on a topic as complicated as this, is hard.

I couldn't have done it without Joe Zigmond, my brilliant editor. It would be a lie to say I was excited when I saw his first feedback, but his wisdom has made the book immeasurably better. It's been a privilege working together and I've learned a great deal. In the final months of writing, when words seemed to assume a daunting finality, Lauren Howard's sharp ideas were tremendously helpful. I'm also thankful to Siam Hatzaw for guiding me through the publication process.

Talking to practitioners and activists has been exceedingly useful. To the government officials, thank you for trusting me. To those who have stood up against overwhelming cruelty at great personal risk: you are the inspiration that allows the rest of us to believe in a better world.

The book has benefited hugely from the expertise of many authorities on their subjects, who have talked to me about everything from the economics of dictatorship to the Parthian Empire and the proliferation of nuclear weapons. I am grateful to Allard Duursma, Curtis Bell, Seva Gunitsky, Kristen Harkness, Joseph Wright, Daron Acemoglu, Erica Frantz, Nicholas Miller, Jake Nabel, Ian Garner, Aleksandr Herasimenka, Clayton Besaw, Agathe Demarais, Anton Barbashin and Larry Diamond.

I'd also like to mention the following, who have provided invaluable advice and encouragement. A special thank you to: Salvator Cusimano, Anchalee Rüland, Jürgen Brandsch, Livia Puglisi, Caspar Schliephack, Dinah Elisa Kreutz, Reid Standish, Julia Zulver, Nic Cheeseman, Oliver Moody, Imre Gelens, Inga Kristina Trauthig, Rowan Hamill-McMahon, Philip Mühl, Victor Cruz Aceves, Michael Jacobi, Dave Wakerley and my doctoral supervisor Christian Martin. None of this would have been possible without David Landry and Brian Klaas.

My biggest debt of all is owed to friends and family. Thank you for everything.

Notes

Introduction: The Golden Gun

1. Oriana Fallaci, *Interview with History*, Liveright, 1976, p. 267.
2. For more information about Gaddafi's time in Paris, see Isabelle Gautier, 'Quand Paris recevait Kadhafi en grande pompe', France Télévisions, 6 April 2015, and David Pujadas, 'Interview du colonel Kadhafi', France 2, 11 December 2007.
3. 'Gaddafi absolviert das Touristenprogramm', *Welt*, 15 December 2007.
4. Alex Duval Smith, 'Gaddafi Ups Tent, to Relief in Paris', *New Zealand Herald*, 16 December 2007.
5. Helena Bachmann, 'Gaddafi's Oddest Idea: Abolish Switzerland', *Time*, 25 September 2009.
6. Daniel Nasaw and Adam Gabbatt, 'Gaddafi Speaks for More Than an Hour at General Assembly', *Guardian*, 23 September 2009.
7. 'Libya: Abu Salim Prison Massacre Remembered', Human Rights Watch, 27 June 2012.
8. Ulf Laessing, *Understanding Libya Since Gaddafi*, Hurst, 2020, p. 29.
9. 'Inside Gaddafi's Bunker – in Pictures', *Guardian*, 26 August 2011.
10. Alex Thomson, 'Inside Gaddafi's Secret Tunnels', *Channel 4 News*, 30 August 2011, https://www.youtube.com/watch?v=I3Nng9dHFLw

11. Sue Torton, 'Inside a Gaddafi Compound in Tripoli', Al Jazeera English, 21 September 2011, https://www.youtube.com/watch?v=fuAYeZE-b2U

12. 'Libya Protests: Second City Benghazi Hit by Violence', BBC, 16 February 2011, https://www.bbc.com/news/world-africa-12477275

13. Mark Memmott, 'Gadhafi Blames "Rats" and Foreign "Agents"; Says He Will be a "Martyr"', National Public Radio, 22 February 2011, https://www.npr.org/sections/thetwo-way/2011/02/22/133960871/gadhafi-blames-rats-and-foreign-agents-says-he-will-be-a-martyr

14. 'Muammar Gaddafi Remains Defiant', Al Jazeera, 22 February 2011, https://www.youtube.com/watch?v=wElsHiTcz-4

15. 'Timeline – Libya's Uprising Against Muammar Gaddafi', Reuters, 31 May 2011, https://www.reuters.com/article/uk-libya-events-idUKTRE74U3NT20110531/

16. Kevin Sullivan, 'A Tough Call on Libya That Still Haunts', *Washington Post*, 3 February 2016.

17. 'Libya: UN Backs Action Against Colonel Gaddafi', BBC, 18 March 2011, https://www.bbc.com/news/world-africa-12781009

18. Associated Press, 'Coalition Launches Military Action Against Libya', France 24, 19 March 2011, https://www.france24.com/en/20110319-coalition-takes-military-action-against-libya

19. Kareem Fahim, 'In His Last Days, Gaddafi Wearied of Fugitive's Life', *New York Times*, 22 October 2011.

20. Martin Chulov, 'Gaddafi's Last Moments: "I Saw the Hand Holding the Gun and I Saw it Fire"', *Guardian*, 20 October 2012.

21. Ibid.

22. Ibid.

23. For more information on the gun, see Gabriel Gatehouse, 'My Search for Gaddafi's Golden Gun', BBC, 3 February 2016.

24. Fahim, 'In His Last Days'.

25. Barry Malone, 'Gaddafi Body Handed to NTC Loyalists for Burial', Reuters, 25 October 2011.
26. Author's calculations based on Henk Goemans, Kristian Skrede Gleditsch and Giacomo Chiozza, 'Introducing Archigo's: A Dataset of Political Leaders', *Journal of Peace Research* 46, no. 2 (2009), p. 275.
27. Barbara Geddes, Joseph Wright and Erica Frantz, 'Autocratic Breakdown and Regime Transitions: A New Data Set', *Perspectives on Politics* 12, no. 2 (2014), p. 321.
28. David Smith, 'Congo TV Talkshow Stormed by Armed Intruders', *Guardian*, 30 December 2011.
29. Ibid.
30. Peter Fabricius, 'DRC's Mukungubila: A "Prophet" Stuck Down in a Nowhere Land, Just Where Kabila Wants Him', *Daily Maverick*, 28 May 2017.
31. Winston Churchill, 'The Lights Are Going Out (We Must Arm), 1938', America's National Churchill Museum, 16 October 1938.
32. Elisabeth Bumiller, 'Was a Tyrant Prefigured by Baby Saddam?', *New York Times*, 15 May 2004.
33. For more on Mao's early years, see Jung Chang and Jon Halliday, *Mao: The Unknown Story*, Jonathan Cape, 2005.
34. Political scientist Joseph Wright, interviewed by the author, 24 May 2023.
35. Adam Przeworski, 'Some Problems in the Study of the Transition to Democracy', in Guillermo O'Donnell, Philippe C. Schmitter and Laurence Whitehead (eds), *Transitions from Authoritarian Rule*, vol. III, Johns Hopkins University Press, 1986 cited in Barbara Geddes, Joseph Wright and Erica Frantz, *How Dictatorships Work*, Cambridge University Press, 2018, p. 185.
36. For a full discussion of varying definitions of regime see Geddes, Wright and Frantz, 'Autocratic Breakdown and Regime Transitions', pp. 314–16.
37. For Schefke's book with the same name, see Siegbert Schefke, *Als die Angst die Seite wechselte*, Transit, 2019.

38. Marat Gurt, 'Turkmenistan to Move Gold Statue', Reuters, 3 May 2008, https://www.reuters.com/article/us-turkmenistan-statue-idUSL0355546520080503/

39. Justin McCurry, 'North Korea Executes Officials with Anti-Aircraft Gun in New Purge – Report', *Guardian*, 30 August 2016.

40. Colm O'Regan, 'The Rise of Inflated Job Titles', BBC, 17 July 2012, https://www.bbc.com/news/magazine-18855099

41. Bastian Herre, Esteban Ortiz-Ospina and Max Roser, 'Democracy', Our World in Data, 2013, https://ourworldindata.org/democracy

42. 'Growth in United Nations Membership', United Nations, https://www.un.org/en/about-us/growth-in-un-membership#1945

43. Milan W. Svolik, *The Politics of Authoritarian Rule*, Cambridge University Press, 2012, p. 25.

44. Herre, Ortiz-Ospina and Roser, 'Democracy'.

45. See Francis Fukuyama, *The End of History and the Last Man*, Free Press, 1992.

46. See, for example, Michaela Wrong, *Do Not Disturb*, Fourth Estate, 2021.

47. John Pomfret and Matt Pottinger, 'Xi Jinping Says He Is Preparing China for War', *Foreign Affairs*, 29 March 2023.

48. Geddes, Wright and Frantz, 'Autocratic Breakdown and Regime Transitions', p. 327.

Chapter 1: The Dictator's Treadmill

1. Howard W. French, 'A Personal Side to War in Zaire', *New York Times*, 6 April 1997.

2. Richard Engel, 'There is Something I call the Dictator's Treadmill', Twitter (renamed 'X'), 25 October 2019, https://x.com/RichardEngel/status/1187520692738240513?s=20

3. 'Median Wealth in the US Congress from 2008 to 2018, by Chamber', Statista, 3 November 2023, https://www.statista.

com/statistics/274581/median-wealth-per-member-of-us-congress-by-chamber/

4. 'Boris Johnson Earns Nearly £1m in One Month – and Matt Hancock's I'm a Celeb Fee Revealed', Sky News, 27 January 2023, https://news.sky.com/story/boris-johnson-earns-nearly-1m-in-one-month-in-outside-earnings-bringing-his-total-since-2019-to-2-3m-12796180

5. 'Country Profile', World Bank, 2023, https://pip.worldbank.org/country-profiles/TKM

6. 'The World Bank in Turkmenistan', World Bank, https://www.worldbank.org/en/country/turkmenistan/overview

7. See 'The Personality Cult of Turkmenbashi', Guardian, 21 December 2006.

8. Robert G. Kaiser, 'Personality Cult Buoys "Father of All Turkmen"', Washington Post, 8 July 2002.

9. Gulnoza Saidazimova, 'Turkmenistan: Where is Turkmenbashi's Money?', Radio Free Europe/Radio Liberty, 19 November 2007.

10. The depiction of Asel's story here is mostly based on Abdujalil Abdurasulov, 'Kazakhstan Unrest: "If You Protest Again, We'll Kill You"', BBC, 21 January 2022, https://www.bbc.com/news/world-asia-60058972

11. Andrew Roth, 'Kazakhstan President Nazarbayev Steps Down After 30 Years in Power', Guardian, 19 March 2019.

12. Almaz Kumenov, 'Kazakhstan: Street Named After President (Predictably)', eurasianet, 30 November 2017.

13. Guy Faulconbridge, 'West Must Stand Up to Russia in Kazakhstan, Opposition Leader Says', Reuters, 7 January 2022, https://www.reuters.com/world/exclusive-west-must-stand-up-russia-kazakhstan-dissident-former-banker-says-2022-01-07/

14. Joanna Lillis, 'Who Really is Kazakhstan's Leader of the Nation?', eurasianet, 25 October 2019, https://eurasianet.org/who-really-is-kazakhstans-leader-of-the-nation

15. Alexander Gabuev and Temur Umarov, 'Turmoil in Kazkahstan Heralds the End of the Nazarbayev Era', Carnegie Endowment

for International Peace, 10 January 2022, https://carnegiemoscow.
org/commentary/86163

16. Vyacheslav Abramov and Ilya Lozovsky, 'Oliver Stone Documentary About Kazakhstan's Former Leader Nazarbayev Was Funded by a Nazarbayev Foundation', Organized Crime and Corruption Reporting Project, 10 October 2022, https://www.occrp.org/en/investigations/sidebar/oliver-stone-documentary-about-kazakhstans-former-leader-nazarbayev-was-funded-by-a-nazarbayev-foundation

17. Paolo Sorbello, 'Kazakhstan's Parliament Aims to Take Away Nazarbayev's Privileges', *The Diplomat*, 28 December 2022, https://thediplomat.com/2022/12/kazakhstans-parliament-aims-to-take-away-nazarbayevs-privileges/

18. Abramov and Lozovsky, 'Oliver Stone Documentary'.

19. Anatolij Weisskopf and Roman Goncharenko, 'A New Era for Kazakhstan's Reelected President?', Deutsche Welle, 21 November 2022, https://www.dw.com/en/new-era-for-kazakhstans-reelected-president/a-63822032

20. Tom Burgis, 'Nazarbayev and the Power Struggle Over Kazakhstan's Future', *Financial Times*, 13 January 2022.

21. Barbara Geddes, Joseph Wright and Erica Frantz, 'Autocratic Breakdown and Regime Transitions: A New Data Set', *Perspectives on Politics* 12, no. 2 (2014), p. 321.

22. Cecile Mantovani, 'Swiss Reject Initiative to Ban Factory Farming', Reuters, 25 September 2022, https://www.reuters.com/world/europe/swiss-course-reject-initiative-ban-factory-farming-2022-09-25/

23. Geddes, Wright and Frantz, 'Autocratic Breakdown and Regime Transitions', p. 321.

24. This scenario is based on the argument of Kristen A. Harkness in her *When Soldiers Rebel*, Cambridge University Press, 2018, pp. 171-2.

25. Daniel Treisman, 'Democracy by Mistake: How the Errors of Autocrats Trigger Transitions to Freer Government', *American Political Science Review* 114, no. 3 (2020), 792–810.

26. Agence France-Presse, 'Argentina's Dictatorship Dug its Own Grave in Falklands War', France 24, 30 March 2022, https://www.france24.com/en/live-news/20220330-argentina-s-dictatorship-dug-its-own-grave-in-falklands-war

27. David Rock, *Argentina, 1516–1987*, University of California Press, 1987, p. 378 cited in Treisman, 'Democracy by Mistake'.

28. 'Thatcher Archive Reveals Deep Divisions on the Road to Falklands War', University of Cambridge, 22 March 2013, https://www.cam.ac.uk/research/news/thatcher-archive-reveals-deep-divisions-on-the-road-to-falklands-war

29. 'A Short History of the Falklands Conflict', Imperial War Museums, https://www.iwm.org.uk/history/a-short-history-of-the-falklands-conflict

30. Agence France-Presse, 'Argentina's Dictatorship Dug its Own Grave in Falklands War', France 24, 30 March 2022, https://www.france24.com/en/live-news/20220330-argentina-s-dictatorship-dug-its-own-grave-in-falklands-war

31. Abel Escribà-Folch and Daniel Krcmaric, 'Dictators in Exile', *Journal of Politics* 79, no. 2 (2017), p. 560.

32. 'Alberto Fujimori Profile: Deeply Divisive Peruvian Leader', BBC, 20 February 2018.

33. Escribà-Folch and Krcmaric, 'Dictators in Exile', p. 562.

34. Ibid., p. 563.

35. 'Interview: Former "Newsweek" Correspondent Recalls Life and Death in Ceauşescu's Romania', Radio Free Europe/Radio Liberty, 16 December 2009, https://www.rferl.org/a/Interview_Former_Newsweek_Correspondent_Recalls_Life_And_Death_In_Ceausescus_Romania/1905712.html

36. The depiction of Ceauşescu's flight from Bucharest is mostly based on Clyde Haberman's article, 'Upheaval in the East: Dictator's Flight; Pilot of Helicopter Describes Ceauşescu's Escape Attempt', *New York Times*, 1 January 1990.

37. Emma Graham-Harrison, ' "I'm Still Nervous," Says Soldier Who Shot Nicolae Ceauşescu', *Guardian*, 7 December 2014.

38. Ibid.

39. Ibid.
40. Alan Greenblatt, 'A Dictator's Choice: Cushy Exile or Go Underground', National Public Radio, 26 August 2011, https://www.npr.org/2011/08/26/139952385/a-dictators-choice-cushy-exile-or-go-underground
41. For a discussion about the importance of geographic proximity, see Escribà-Folch and Krcmaric, 'Dictators in Exile', pp. 563–4.
42. Daniel Krcmaric, 'Should I Stay or Should I Go? Leaders, Exile, and the Dilemmas of International Justice', *American Journal of Political Science* 62, no. 2 (2018), p. 489.
43. Ibid.
44. 'Liberia's Taylor Begins Exile in Nigeria', Public Broadcasting Service NewsHour, 13 August 2013, https://www.pbs.org/newshour/politics/africa-july-dec03-nigeria_08-13
45. Xan Rice, 'Liberia's Ex-leader Handed Over for War Crimes Trial', *Guardian*, 30 March 2006.
46. Owen Bowcott, 'War Criminal Charles Taylor to Serve 50-year Sentence in British Prison', *Guardian*, 10 October 2013.
47. Escribà-Folch and Krcmaric, 'Dictators in Exile', p. 561.
48. Ben Brumfield, 'Charles Taylor Sentenced to 50 Years for War Crimes', CNN, 31 May 2012, https://edition.cnn.com/2012/05/30/world/africa/netherlands-taylor-sentencing/index.html
49. Escribà-Folch and Krcmaric, 'Dictators in Exile', p. 564.
50. Ibid.
51. 'Q&A: The Case of Hissène Habré Before the Extraordinary African Chambers in Senegal', Human Rights Watch, 3 May 2016, https://www.hrw.org/news/2016/05/03/qa-case-hissene-habre-extraordinary-african-chambers-senegal#3
52. Diego Lopes da Silva et al., 'Trends in World Military Expenditure, 2021', Stockholm International Peace Research Institute, https://www.sipri.org/sites/default/files/2022-04/fs_2204_milex_2021_0.pdf
53. 'Taliban Says Doha Office Flag, Banner Raised with "Agreement of Qatar"', Reuters, 23 June 2013, https://www.

reuters.com / article / afghanistan - peace - taliban - qatar-idINDEE95M05120130623/

54. 'Full Text of Ferdinand "Bongbong" Marcos Jr's Inaugural Address', *Philippine Star*, 30 June 2022.
55. Bernard Gwertzman, 'For Marcos, A Restless Night of Calls to US', *New York Times*, 26 February 1986.
56. Francis X. Clines, 'The Fall of Marcos: Slipping Out of Manila; The Final Hours of Marcos: Pleading to Save Face, Then Escape in the Dark', *New York Times*, 26 February 1986.
57. Daniel Southerl, 'A Fatigued Marcos Arrives in Hawaii', *Washington Post*, 27 February 1986.
58. Nick Davies, 'The $10bn Question: What Happened to the Marcos Millions?', *Guardian*, 7 May 2016.
59. David Smith, 'Thomas Lubanga Sentenced to 14 Years for Congo War Crimes', *Guardian*, 10 July 2012.
60. Krcmaric, 'Should I Stay or Should I Go?' at p. 496.
61. 'How the Mighty Are Falling', *The Economist*, 5 July 2007.
62. Christina Lamb, 'Trapped in the Palace', *The Spectator*, 28 May 2011.

Chapter 2: The Enemy Within

1. 'Chad Habre Accuses Sudan of Complicity in April Coup Plot', BBC, Summary of World Broadcasts, 12 May 1989, cited in Philip Roessler, 'The Enemy Within', *World Politics* 63, no. 2 (2011), 300–46 at pp. 312–13.
2. Robert K. Massie, *Catherine the Great*, Head of Zeus, 2019, p. 312.
3. Ibid.
4. E. R. Dashkova (ed. and trans. Kyril Fitzlyon), *The Memoirs of Princess Dashkov*, 1958, pp. 78–80, cited in Simon Sebag Montefiore, *Catherine the Great & Potemkin*, Weidenfeld & Nicolson, 2001, p. 50.
5. Massie, *Catherine the Great*, pp. 305–21.

6. Ibid., p. 297.
7. Sebag Montefiore, *Catherine the Great*, p. 44.
8. Ibid., p. 36.
9. *Arkhiv kniaz'ia Vorontsova*, XXI, 49 (ed. P.I. Bartenev), cited in Simon Dixon, *Catherine the Great*, Ecco, 2010, p. 122.
10. Sebag Montefiore, *Catherine the Great*, p. 51.
11. Massie, *Catherine the Great*, p. 315.
12. Dixon, *Catherine the Great*, p. 123.
13. Massie, *Catherine the Great*, p. 316.
14. Erica Frantz, *Authoritarianism*, Oxford University Press, 2018, p. 56.
15. The following section is based on Bruce Bueno de Mesquita and Alastair Smith's *The Dictator's Handbook*, Public Affairs, 2012.
16. 'Population', Our World in Data, https://ourworldindata.org/grapher/population
17. The depiction of North Korea's famine is mostly based on Stephan Haggard and Marcus Noland's *Famine in North Korea: Markets, Aid, and Reform*, Columbia University Press, 2007.
18. The story recounted here is based on Ju Hyun-ah's 'The Arduous March', *Words Without Borders*, 1 May 2013, https://wordswithoutborders.org/read/article/2013-05/the-arduous-march/
19. Ibid.
20. Min Yoon, 'The Arduous March: Growing Up in North Korea During Famine', *Guardian*, 13 June 2014.
21. Ju Hyun-ah, 'The Arduous March'.
22. Haggard and Noland, *Famine in North Korea*, p. 68.
23. Daniel Byman and Jennifer Lind, 'Pyongyang's Survival Strategy: Tools of Authoritarian Control in North Korea', *International Security* 35, no. 1 (2010), 44–74 at p. 62.
24. Haggard and Noland, *Famine in North Korea*, p. 11.
25. See Ronald Wintrobe, *The Political Economy of Dictatorship*, Cambridge University Press, 1998, pp. 20–40.
26. de Mesquita and Smith, *The Dictator's Handbook*, p. 16.

27. Niccolò Machiavelli (trans. Tim Parks), *The Prince*, Penguin, 2009, p. 12.
28. Edward Goldring and Austin S. Matthews, 'To Purge or Not to Purge? An Individual-Level Quantitative Analysis of Elite Purges in Dictatorships', *British Journal of Political Science* 53, no. 2 (2023), 575–93 at p. 575.
29. Milan W. Svolik, *The Politics of Authoritarian Rule*, Cambridge University Press, 2012.
30. For an analysis of the immediate aftermath of coup attempts see Laure Bokobza et al., 'The Morning After: Cabinet Instability and the Purging of Ministers after Failed Coup Attempts in Autocracies', *Journal of Politics* 84, no. 3 (2020), 1437–52.
31. Arianne Chernock, 'Queen Victoria and the "Bloody Mary of Madagascar"', *Victorian Studies* 55, no. 3 (2013), 425–49 at p. 433.
32. Stephen Ellis, 'Witch-Hunting in Central Madagascar 1828–1861', *Past & Present* 175 (2002), 90–123 at p. 99.
33. Samuel Pasfield Oliver, *Madagascar: An Historical and Descriptive Account of the Island and its Former Dependencies*, Macmillan, 1886, p. 85.
34. Ibid., p. 80.
35. Ida Pfeiffer, *The Last Travels of Ida Pfeiffer: Inclusive of a Visit to Madagascar*, Harper & Brothers, 1861, p. 240.
36. Oliver, *Madagascar*, p. 86.
37. Brian Klaas, 'Vladimir Putin Has Fallen Into the Dictator Trap', *Atlantic*, 16 March 2022.
38. Adam E. Casey and Seva Gunitsky, 'The Bully in the Bubble', *Foreign Affairs*, 4 February 2022.
39. Andrew Roth, 'Putin's Security Men: The Elite Group Who "Fuel His Anxieties"', *Guardian*, 4 February 2022.
40. Ibid.
41. Casey and Gunitsky, 'The Bully in the Bubble'.
42. Yi Han-yong, *Taedong River Royal Family: My 14 Years Incognito in Seoul*, Dong-a Ilbo, 1996, cited in Anna Fifield, *The Great Successor*, John Murray, 2019, p. 14.

43. Fifield, *The Great Successor*, p. 43.
44. Ibid.
45. Jung H. Pak, 'The Education of Kim Jong-un', Brookings, February 2018, https://www.brookings.edu/articles/the-education-of-kim-jong-un/
46. Mark Bowden, 'Understanding Kim Jong Un, the World's Most Enigmatic and Unpredictable Dictator', *Vanity Fair*, 12 February 2015.
47. Jerrold M. Post, 'Saddam Hussein of Iraq: A Political Psychology Profile', *Political Psychology* 12, no. 2 (1991), 279–89 at p. 284.
48. Erica Goode, 'The World; Stalin to Saddam: So Much for the Madman Theory', *New York Times*, 4 May 2003.
49. Cited in Dave Gilson, 'The CIA's Secret Psychological Profiles of Dictators and World Leaders Are Amazing', *Mother Jones*, 11 February 2015.
50. Jerrold M. Post and Robert S. Robins, *When Illness Strikes the Leader*, Yale University Press, 1993, p. 55.
51. Ibid.
52. Alejandro Artucio, 'The Trial of Macias', *International Commission of Jurists*, November 1979, p. 16.
53. Ibid., p. 8.
54. Post and Robins, *When Illness Strikes the Leader*, pp. 55–6.
55. Associated Press, 'Killings Reported in Equatorial Guinea', *New York Times*, 25 January 1978.
56. Ibid.
57. Artucio, 'The Trial of Macias', p. 11.
58. Paul Kenyon, *Dictatorland*, Head of Zeus, 2018, pp. 260 and 262.
59. Randall Fegley, 'Equatorial Guinea, An African Tragedy', *Anthropology and Sociology*, Series II, vol. 39, p. 52 cited in Kenyon, *Dictatorland*, p. 262.
60. Bruce Bueno de Mesquita and Alastair Smith, 'Political Succession: A Model of Coups, Revolution, Purges and Everyday Politics', *Journal of Conflict Resolution* 61, no. 4 (2015), 707–43 at p. 708.

61. Artucio, 'The Trial of Macias', p. 16.
62. Kenyon, *Dictatorland*, p. 262.
63. Cited in Simon Baynham, 'Equatorial Guinea: The Terror and the Coup', *World Today* 36, no. 2 (1980), 65–71 at p. 65.
64. Kenyon, *Dictatorland*, p. 263.
65. Ibid.
66. Ibid.
67. Associated Press, 'Equatorial Guinea Reports Coup', *New York Times*, 6 August 1979.

Chapter 3: Weakening the Warriors

1. Cited in Paul Kenyon, *Dictatorland*, Head of Zeus, 2018, p. 162.
2. Nicholas Marshall, 'United States of America v. Cherno Njie (01) and Papa Faal (02)', United States District Court for the District of Minnesota, 3 January 2015, https://www.justice.gov/file/189936/download
3. Much of the depiction of the attempted Gambian coup is based on Stuart A. Reid's 'Let's Go Take Back Our Country', *Atlantic*, March 2016.
4. 'State of Fear', Human Rights Watch, 16 September 2015, https://www.hrw.org/report/2015/09/17/state-fear/arbitrary-arrests-torture-and-killings
5. Reid, 'Let's Go Take Back Our Country'.
6. Banka Manneh, interview with author, 24 February 2023.
7. Ibid.
8. Andrew Rice, 'The Reckless Plot to Overthrow Africa's Most Absurd Dictator', *Guardian*, 21 July 2015.
9. 'Amnesty International Report 2014/2015', Amnesty International, 25 February 2015, https://www.amnesty.org/en/pol10-0001-2015-en-2/
10. Rice, 'The Reckless Plot'.
11. Banka Manneh interview.
12. Ibid.

13. Reid, 'Let's Go Take Back Our Country'.
14. Rice, 'The Reckless Plot'.
15. Marshall, 'United States of America v. Cherno Njie (01) and Papa Faal (02)'.
16. Ibid.
17. Rice, 'The Reckless Plot'.
18. Marshall, 'United States of America v. Cherno Njie (01) and Papa Faal (02)'.
19. Reid, 'Let's Go Take Back Our Country'.
20. Ibid.
21. Marshall, 'United States of America v. Cherno Njie (01) and Papa Faal (02)'.
22. Reid, 'Let's Go Take Back Our Country'.
23. Ibid.
24. Ibid.
25. Banka Manneh interview.
26. Armin Rosen, 'A Prominent Dissident Was Just Charged in the US with Plotting to Overthrow One of Africa's Most Oppressive Governments', *Business Insider*, 22 March 2015.
27. Banka Manneh interview.
28. Rosen, 'A Prominent Dissident'.
29. Jonathan M. Powell and Clayton L. Thyne, 'Global Instances of Coups from 1950 to 2010: A New Dataset', *Journal of Peace Research* 48, no. 2 (2011), 249–59 at p. 252.
30. King James Bible, 1 Kings xvi, 11.
31. Edward F. Campbell, 'A Land Divided: Judah and Israel from the Death of Solomon to the Fall of Samaria', pp. 206–41, in Michael D. Coogan (ed.), *The Oxford History of the Biblical World*, Oxford University Press, 2001.
32. King James Bible, 1 Kings xvi, 18.
33. Powell and Thyne, 'Global Instances of Coups from 1950 to 2010'.
34. Ibid.
35. 'Britain's Simon Mann Sentenced to 34 Years for Coup Plot', France 24, 7 July 2008, https://www.france24.com/en/20080707-

britains-simon-mann-sentenced-34-years-coup-plot-equato-rial-guinea

36. Cecilia Macaulay, 'Equatorial Guinea's Obiang: World's Longest-serving President Eyes Re-election', BBC, 20 November 2022, https://www.bbc.com/news/world-africa-63674539

37. 'Equatorial Guinea', OPEC, https://www.opec.org/opec_web/en/about_us/4319.htm

38. 'GDP Per Capita', Our World in Data, 2023, https://ourworldindata.org/grapher/gdp-per-capita-worldbank?tab=chart&country=GNQ~TUR~MEX~KOR

39. Simon Mann, Cry Havoc, John Blake, 2012.

40. Ian Evans, 'We Were Betrayed, Claim Mercenaries Jailed After Ex-SAS Man's Failed Coup', Guardian, 25 April 2010.

41. Ibid.

42. Ibid.

43. Kim Sengupta, 'An African Adventure: Inside Story of the Wonga Coup', Independent, 12 March 2008.

44. David Pallister and James Sturcke, 'Simon Mann Gets 34 Years in Equatorial Guinea Jail', Guardian, 7 July 2008.

45. Jonathan Miller, 'Mann: I Was Not the Main Man', Channel 4, 11 March 2008, https://www.channel4.com/news/articles/politics/international_politics/mann+i+was+not+the+main+man/1761247.html

46. Antony Barnett and Martin Bright, 'Revealed: How Britain Was Told Full Coup Plan', Guardian, 28 November 2004.

47. Malcolm R. Easton and Randolph M. Siverson, 'Leader Survival and Purges After a Failed Coup d'Etat', Journal of Peace Research 55, no. 5 (2018), 596–608 at p. 599.

48. Brian Klaas, 'Why Coups Fail', Foreign Affairs, 17 July 2016.

49. Esme Kirk-Wade and Zoe Mansfield, 'UK Defence Personnel Statistics', House of Commons Library, 18 July 2023, https://researchbriefings.files.parliament.uk/documents/CBP-7930/CBP-7930.pdf

50. Paul Collier and Anke Hoeffler, 'Coup Traps: Why Does

Africa Have So Many Coups d'Etat?', working paper, Centre for the Study of African Economies, August 2005, https://ora. ox.ac.uk/objects/uuid:49097086-8505-4eb2-8174 -314ce1aa3ebb

51. Naunihal Singh, *Seizing Power*, Johns Hopkins University Press, 2014, p. 66.

52. James T. Quinlivan, 'Coup-Proofing: Its Practice and Consequences in the Middle East', *International Security* 24, no. 2 (1999), 131–65 at p. 141.

53. Williamson Murray and Kevin M. Woods, *The Iran–Iraq War: A Military and Strategic History*, Cambridge University Press, 2014, p. 287 cited in Caitlin Talmadge, *The Dictator's Army*, Cornell University Press, 2015, p. 154.

54. Hanna Batatu, *The Old Social Classes and the Revolutionary Movements of Iraq: A Study of Iraq's Old Landed and Commercial Classes and of Its Communists, Ba'athists, and Free Officers*, Princeton University Press, 1978, p. 1095 cited in Quinlivan, 'Coup-Proofing', p. 144.

55. Quinlivan, 'Coup-Proofing', p. 144.

56. Ibid., p. 150.

57. Cameron S. Brown, Christopher J. Fariss and R. Blake McMahon, 'Recouping After Coup-Proofing: Compromised Military Effectiveness and Strategic Substitution', *International Interactions* 41, no. 1 (2016), 1–30 at p. 4.

58. Cited in ibid., pp. 4–5.

59. Quinlivan, 'Coup-Proofing', pp. 143–4.

60. For a detailed discussion of the consequences of violence during coups, see Erica de Bruin's 'Will There Be Blood? Explaining Violence During Coups d'Etat', *Journal of Peace Research* 56, no. 6 (2019), 797–811.

61. Kristen A. Harkness, *When Soldiers Rebel*, Cambridge University Press, 2018, p. 57.

62. Ibid., p. 39

63. Ibid., p. 36.

64. J. 'Bayo Adekson, 'Ethnicity and Army Recruitment in

Colonial Plural Societies', *Ethnic and Racial Studies* 2, no. 2 (1979), 151–65 at p. 161 cited in Harkness, *When Soldiers Rebel*, p. 37.

65. Anthony Clayton, *Khaki and Blue: Military and Police in British Colonial Africa*, Ohio University, 1989, p. 160 cited in Harkness, *When Soldiers Rebel*, p. 37.

66. Kristen A. Harkness, 'The Ethnic Stacking in Africa Dataset: When Leaders Use Ascriptive Identity to Build Military Loyalty', *Conflict Management and Peace Science* 39, no. 5 (2022), 609–32 at pp. 619–20.

67. Chris Hedges, 'Kurds Unearthing New Evidence of Iraqi Killings', *New York Times*, 7 December 1991.

68. Ibid.

69. Quinlivan, 'Coup-Proofing', p. 151.

70. Erica de Bruin, *How to Prevent Coups d'Etat*, Cornell University Press, 2020.

71. Ibid., p. 97.

72. Cited in Harkness, *When Soldiers Rebel*, p. 146.

73. de Bruin, *How to Prevent Coups d'Etat*, pp. 97 and 98.

74. See 'Ghana Voters Back Nkrumah Proposal For One-Party Rule', *New York Times*, 26 January 1964.

75. de Bruin, *How to Prevent Coups d'Etat*, p. 96.

76. Lloyd Garrison, 'Coup in Ghana: Elaborately Organized Upheaval', *New York Times*, 5 March 1966.

77. Ibid.

78. Cited in de Bruin, *How to Prevent Coups d'Etat*, p. 99.

79. John J. Chin, Joseph Wright and David B. Carter, *Historical Dictionary of Modern Coups d'Etat*, Rowman & Littlefield, 2022, p. 438.

80. Harkness, *When Soldiers Rebel*, p. 73.

81. Chin, Wright and Carter, *Historical Dictionary*, p. 438.

Chapter 4: Rebels, Guns and Money

1. Leon Trotsky, *The History of the Russian Revolution*, Victor Gollancz, 1984, p. 511.
2. United Press International, 'Thousands Dead as Quakes Strike Nicaraguan City', *New York Times*, 24 December 1972.
3. 'Case Report Nicaragua-Earthquake', United States Agency for International Development, December 1972, https://pdf. usaid.gov/pdf_docs/pnadq757.pdf
4. 'Earthquakes of Past Bigger Than Managua's', *New York Times*, 26 December 1972.
5. 'Case Report Nicaragua-Earthquake'.
6. David Johnson Lee, 'De-centring Managua: Post-earthquake Reconstruction and Revolution in Nicaragua', *Urban History* 42, no. 4 (2015), 663–85 at pp. 668–9.
7. United Press International, 'Major Section of Managua to Serve as Mass Grave', *New York Times*, 27 December 1972.
8. Reuters, 'Managua Has Disappeared', *New York Times*, 24 December 1972.
9. Robin Navarro Montgomery, 'The Fall of Somoza: Anatomy of a Revolution', *Parameters* 10, no. 1 (1980), 47–57 at p. 51.
10. Rose Spalding, *Capitalists and Revolution in Nicaragua: Opposition and Accommodation, 1979–1993*, University of North Carolina Press, 1994, cited in Lee, 'De-centring Managua', p. 680.
11. Idean Salehyan, *Rebels Without Borders*, Cornell University Press, 2011, p. 126.
12. Alan Riding, 'Bishops in Nicaragua Say Troops Kill Civilians in Fighting Leftists', *New York Times*, 2 March 1977.
13. Montgomery, 'The Fall of Somoza'.
14. Laurie Johnston, 'Prize-Winning Editor Is Shot Dead in Nicaragua', *New York Times*, 11 January 1978.
15. Mateo Cayetano Jarquin, 'A Latin American Revolution: The Sandinistas, the Cold War, and Political Change in the Region,

1977–1990', doctoral dissertation (2019), Harvard University, Graduate School of Arts & Sciences, pp. 47–8.

16. Christopher Paul, Colin P. Clarke and Beth Grill, *Victory Has a Thousand Fathers: Detailed Counterinsurgency Case Studies*, RAND Corporation, 2010.

17. Cayetano Jarquin, 'A Latin American Revolution', p. 70.

18. Cynthia Gorney, 'Somoza is Assassinated in Ambush in Paraguay', *Washington Post*, 18 September 1980.

19. Max Boot, 'The Evolution of Irregular War: Insurgents and Guerillas from Akkadia to Afghanistan', *Foreign Affairs* 92, no. 2 (2013), 100–14.

20. Eric Dorn Brose, *German History 1789–1871*, Berghahn, 1997, p. 4.

21. Henry Louis Gates, Emmanuel Akyeampong and Steven J. Niven (eds.), *Dictionary of African Biography*, Oxford University Press, 2011, p. 172.

22. Ibid.

23. 'Chad Habre Accuses Sudan of Complicity in April Coup Plot', BBC, Summary of World Broadcasts, 12 May 1989, cited in Philip Roessler, 'The Enemy Within', *World Politics* 63, no. 2 (2011), 300–46 at pp. 312–13.

24. Associated Press, 'Chad President Reportedly Flees and Rebels March In', *New York Times*, 2 December 1990.

25. 'Chad's President Idriss Déby Dies After Clashes with Rebels', BBC, 20 April 2021, https://www.bbc.com/news/world-africa-56815708

26. Roessler, 'The Enemy Within', pp. 314–15.

27. Paul Collier et al., 'Breaking the Conflict Trap', World Bank, 2003, p. 68, https://openknowledge.worldbank.org/server/api/core/bitstreams/ce680d98-c240-5747-a573-b4896762e5f5/content

28. Ibid.

29. Ibid.

30. F. Ngaruko and J. D. Nkurunziza, 'Civil War and Its Duration in Burundi', Paper prepared for the World Bank and Yale

University case study project The Political Economy of Civil Wars, 2002, cited in ibid., pp. 68–9.

31. Ibid., p. 72.
32. Ibid., p. 75.
33. Blaine Harden, 'Diamond Wars: A Special Report', *New York Times*, 6 April 2000.
34. Mark Shaw, '"The Middlemen": War Supply Networks in Sierra Leone and Angola', Netherlands Institute of International Relations, working paper 10, March 2003, pp. 19–20, https://www.clingendael.org/sites/default/files/2016-02/20030300_cru_working_paper_10.pdf
35. Collier et al., 'Breaking the Conflict Trap'.
36. Marianne Moor and Liduine Zumpolle, 'The Kidnap Industry in Colombia', Pax Christi Netherlands, November 2001, https://paxforpeace.nl/wp-content/uploads/sites/2/2020/11/the-kidnap-industry-in-colombia-our-business-112001_0.pdf
37. Ibid.
38. Anja Shortland, *Kidnap*, Oxford University Press, 2019, p. 100.
39. Moor and Zumpolle, 'The Kidnap Industry in Colombia'.
40. Michael L. Ross, 'Booty Futures', working paper, 6 May 2005, p. 11, https://www.sscnet.ucla.edu/polisci/faculty/ross/papers/working/bootyfutures.pdf
41. Ibid., pp. 11–12.
42. See Stathis N. Kalyvas, *The Logic of Violence in Civil War*, Cambridge University Press, 2012.
43. Adam Lockyer, 'Foreign Intervention and Warfare in Civil Wars: The Effect of Exogenous Resources on the Course and Nature of the Angolan and Afghan Conflicts', doctoral dissertation, University of Sydney, Department of Government and International Relations, December 2008, pp. 109–10.
44. Nathan Leites and Charles Wolf, Jr, *Rebellion and Authority*, Markham, 1970, pp. 128–9.
45. Jeremy M. Weinstein, *Inside Rebellion*, Cambridge University Press, 2007, pp. 203–4.
46. Jürgen Brandsch, interview with author, 3 February 2023.

47. This is an argument advanced by Alex de Waal in *The Real Politics of the Horn of Africa*, Polity, 2015, p. 53.

48. Ibid.

49. 'Syria Refugee Crisis Explained', United Nations High Commissioner for Refugees, 14 March 2023, https://www.unrefugees.org/news/syria-refugee-crisis-explained/

50. Henry A. Kissinger, 'The Viet Nam Negotiations', *Foreign Affairs*, 1 January 1969.

51. Cited in Associated Press, 'Colombia's Guerilla War killed 260,000, Report Says', CBC, 2 August 2018, https://www.cbc.ca/news/world/colombia-guerrilla-farc-death-toll-1.4771858

52. Roland Dumas, cited in Alan Riding, 'Rebels in Control of Chad's Capital', *New York Times*, 3 December 1990.

53. 'Supported by France, Convicted by Africa', Human Rights Watch, 30 May 2016, https://www.hrw.org/sites/default/files/report_pdf/francehabre0616en_summaryweb_0.pdf

54. 'France Bombed Chadian Rebels to Stop *Coup d'Etat*: Foreign Minister', Reuters, 12 February 2019, https://www.reuters.com/article/us-france-chad-idUSKCN1Q11XB/

55. Ibid.

56. Lockyer, 'Foreign Intervention and Warfare in Civil Wars', pp. 203 and 205.

57. Vincent Schneiter, 'La Guerre de Libération au Nouristan', *Les Temps Modernes*, no. 408–9, July–August 1980, p. 240 cited in ibid., pp. 205–6.

58. Thomas A. Marks, 'Mao Tse-tung and the Search for 21st Century Counterinsurgency', *CTC Sentinel*, 2, no. 10 (2009), 17–20 at p. 18.

59. Lockyer, 'Foreign Intervention and Warfare in Civil Wars', p. 98.

Chapter 5: Enemies, Foreign and Domestic

1. Cited in Ulrich Pilster and Tobias Böhmelt, 'Coup-Proofing and Military Effectiveness in Interstate Wars, 1967–99', *Conflict Management and Peace Science* 28, no. 4 (2011), 331–50 at p. 331.
2. Ibid., pp. 331–50.
3. Cigdem V. Sirin and Michael T. Koch, 'Dictators and Death: Casualty Sensitivity of Autocracies in Militarized Interstate Disputes', *International Studies Quarterly* 59, no. 4 (2015), 802–14.
4. Ben Doherty, 'Former SAS Soldier Arrested and Charged in NSW for Alleged War Crime Over Killing of Afghan Civilian', *Guardian*, 20 March 2023.
5. Simon Sebag Montefiore, *Stalin: The Court of the Red Tsar*, Phoenix, 2004, p. 229.
6. Ibid., pp. 226–7.
7. Robert Service, *Stalin*, Pan, 2010, p. 343.
8. Ibid., pp. 351–2.
9. Sebag Montefiore, *Stalin*, p. 252.
10. Ibid., p. 237.
11. Ibid., p. 229.
12. Service, *Stalin*, p. 356.
13. Peter Whitewood et al., *The Red Army and the Great Terror: Stalin's Purge of the Soviet Military*, University Press of Kansas, 2015.
14. Sebag Montefiore, *Stalin*, p. 230.
15. Robert Service, *The Penguin History of Modern Russia: From Tsarism to the Twenty-first Century* (3rd edition), 2009, p. 225.
16. 'Great Purge', *Encyclopedia Britannica*, 2023, https://www.britannica.com/event/Great-Purge
17. Kenneth Pollack, *Armies of Sand*, Oxford University Press, 2019, p. 115.
18. Ibid., pp. 115–16.
19. Kenneth Pollack, *Arabs at War: Military Effectiveness, 1948–1991*, University of Nebraska Press, 2002, cited in Pilster and

Böhmelt, 'Coup-Proofing and Military Effectiveness in Interstate Wars, 1967-99', at p. 336.

20. The following section is based on Lindsey O'Rourke, *Covert Regime Change*, Cornell University Press, 2018.

21. Ibid., p. 2.

22. Ibid., p. 49.

23. Ibid., p. 53.

24. Evans Thomas, *The Very Best Men: Four Men Who Dared; The Early Years of the CIA*, Touchstone, 1995, p. 120 cited in ibid., p. 57.

25. 'The Bay of Pigs', John F. Kennedy Presidential Library and Museum, https://www.jfklibrary.org/learn/about-jfk/jfk-in-history/the-bay-of-pigs

26. 'Memorandum From the President's Special Assistant for National Security Affairs (Bundy) to President Kennedy', United States Department of State, Office of the Historian, 8 February 1961, https://history.state.gov/historicaldocuments/frus1961-63v10/d39

27. Bill Newcott, 'After 60 Years, Bay of Pigs Disaster Still Haunts Veterans Who Fought', *National Geographic*, 16 April 2021.

28. 'The Bay of Pigs', John F. Kennedy Presidential Library and Museum, https://www.jfklibrary.org/learn/about-jfk/jfk-in-history/the-bay-of-pigs

29. Newcott, 'After 60 Years, Bay of Pigs Disaster Still Haunts Veterans Who Fought'.

30. 'The Bay of Pigs Invasion', CIA, 18 April 2016, https://www.cia.gov/stories/story/the-bay-of-pigs-invasion/

31. 'Memorandum From the Chief of Operations in the Deputy Directorate for Plans (Helms) to Director of Central Intelligence McCone', United States Department of State, Office of the Historian, 19 January 1962, https://history.state.gov/historicaldocuments/frus1961-63v10/d292

32. Alexander Smith, 'Fidel Castro: The CIA's 7 Most Bizarre Assassination Attempts', NBC News, 28 November 2016,

https://www.nbcnews.com/storyline/fidel-castros-death/fidel-castro-cia-s-7-most-bizarre-assassination-attempts-n688951

33. Max Boot, 'Operation Mongoose: The Story of America's Efforts to Overthrow Castro', *Atlantic*, 5 January 2018.

34. Bruce Bueno de Mesquita, Randolph M. Siverson and Gary Woller, 'War and the Fate of Regimes: A Comparative Analysis', *American Political Science Review* 86, no. 3 (1992), 638–49 at p. 642.

35. For the connection between protest and foreign policy, see for example Jessica Chen Weiss, *Powerful Patriots: Nationalist Protest in China's Foreign Relations*, Oxford University Press, 2014.

36. D. Sean Barnett et al., 'North Korean Conventional Artillery', RAND Corporation, 2020, p. 2, https://www.rand.org/pubs/research_reports/RRA619-1.html

37. Ibid.

38. Julian Ryall, 'South Korea: Why is Seoul's Population Declining?,' Deutsche Welle, 19 June 2022, https://www.dw.com/en/south-korea-why-is-seouls-population-declining/a-62138302

39. Barnett et al., 'North Korean Conventional Artillery', p. 17.

40. Cameron S. Brown, Christopher J. Fariss and R. Blake McMahon, 'Recouping After Coup-Proofing: Compromised Military Effectiveness and Strategic Substitution', *International Interactions* 42, no. 1 (2016), 1–30 at pp. 2 and 8.

41. Ibid., p. 8.

42. Nicholas Miller, interview with author, 9 March 2023.

43. Malfrid Braut-Hegghammer, 'Why North Korea Succeeded at Getting Nuclear Weapons – When Iraq and Libya Failed', *Washington Post*, 2 January 2018.

44. John Wright, *Libya*, Ernest Benn, 1969, p. 199 cited in Malfrid Brautt-Hegghammer, *Unclear Physics*, Cornell University Press, 2016, p. 128.

45. Ibid.

46. Ibid., p. 143.

47. John K. Cooley, *Libyan Sandstorm*, Holt, Rinehart and Winston, 1982, p. 230 cited in Thomas Müller-Färber, 'How the Qaddafi Regime Was Driven into Nuclear Disarmament', doctoral dissertation, Hertie School of Governance, Berlin Graduate School for Transnational Studies, June 2016, p. 162.
48. Müller-Färber, 'How the Qaddafi Regime Was Driven into Nuclear Disarmament', p. 162.
49. Brautt-Hegghammer, *Unclear Physics*, pp. 157–8.
50. Akar Bharadvaj and Kevin Woods, 'When Strongmen Invade, They Bring Their Pathologies With Them', War on the Rocks, 18 May 2022, https://warontherocks.com/2022/05/when-strongmen-invade-they-bring-their-pathologies-with-them/
51. Caitlin Talmadge, *The Dictator's Army*, Cornell University Press, 2015, p. 162.
52. Kevin M. Woods et al., 'Saddam's Generals', Institute for Defense Analyses, 2011, p. 20.
53. Ibid., p. 14.
54. Ibid., p. 20.
55. 'Uzbekistan: Two Brutal Deaths in Custody', Human Rights Watch, 9 August 2002, https://www.hrw.org/news/2002/08/09/uzbekistan-two-brutal-deaths-custody
56. Nick Paton Walsh, 'Uzbek Mother Who Publicised "Boiling" Torture of Son Gets Hard Labour', *Guardian*, 13 February 2004.
57. Andrea Koppell and Elise Labott, 'US-Uzbek Ties Grow Despite Rights Concerns', CNN, 12 March 2002, https://edition.cnn.com/2002/US/03/12/ret.uzbek.us/
58. 'Joint Press Conference with President Islam Karimov', Tashkent, Uzbekistan, 8 December 2001, US Department of State Archive, https://2001-2009.state.gov/secretary/former/powell/remarks/2001/dec/6749.htm
59. Daniel J. O'Connor, 'Rethinking Uzbekistan: A Military View', *Military Review*, March–April 2020, https://www.armyupress.army.mil/Journals/Military-Review/English-Edition-Archives/March-April-2020/OConnor-Rethinking-Uzbekistan/

Chapter 6: You Shoot, You Lose

1. Cited in Héctor Tobar, 'Hugo Banzer, 75: Bolivian Dictator Turned President', *Los Angeles Times*, 6 May 2002.
2. Susan Ratcliffe (ed.), *Oxford Essential Quotations*, Oxford University Press, 2017, https://www.oxfordreference.com/display /10.1093/acref/9780191843730.001.0001/q-oro-ed5-00007069
3. Barbara Geddes, Joseph Wright and Erica Frantz, *How Dictatorships Work*, Cambridge University Press, p. 179.
4. Gene Sharp, *From Dictatorship to Democracy*, Serpent's Tail, 2012.
5. Kristian S. Gleditsch and Mauricio Rivera, 'The Diffusion of Nonviolent Campaigns', *Journal of Conflict Resolution* 61, no. 5 (2017), pp. 1120–45 at p. 1123.
6. A Serbian activist in conversation with the author, 16 February 2023.
7. Erica Chenoweth, *Civil Resistance*, Oxford University Press, 2021, p. 95.
8. Ibid., p. 114.
9. Ibid., p. 115.
10. Ibid.
11. See Christian Davenport, 'State Repression and Political Order', *Annual Review of Political Science* 10, no. 1 (2007), 1–23 at p. 7.
12. Erica Chenoweth and Maria J. Stephan, *Why Civil Resistance Works*, Columbia University Press, 2013.
13. 'Ukraine: Excessive Force Against Protestors', Human Rights Watch, 3 December 2013, https://www.hrw.org/news/2013/ 12/03/ukraine-excessive-force-against-protesters
14. Oksana Grytsenko and Shaun Walker, 'Ukrainians Call for Yanukovych to Resign in Protests Sparked by EU U-turn', *Guardian*, 2 December 2013.
15. Hanna Arhirova, '10 years Later, a War-weary Ukraine Reflects on Events That Began Its Collision Course with Russia', Associated Press News, 21 November 2023, https://apnews.

com/article/ukraine-uprising-anniversary-russia-war-maidan
-2f73f31a5aec45bd7dbcddae8f72edac

16. Susan Ormiston, 'Remembering the 2014 Ukraine Revolution, Which Set the Stage for the 2022 Russian Invasion', CBC News, 23 February 2023, https://www.cbc.ca/news/ukraine-2014-euromaidan-1.6756384

17. See Daniel Byman and Jennifer Lind, 'Pyongyang's Survival Strategy: Tools of Authoritarian Control in North Korea', *International Security* 35, no. 1 (2010), 44–74.

18. 'Amnesty International Report 2022/23: The State of the World's Human Rights', Amnesty International, 27 March 2023, https://www.amnesty.org/en/documents/pol10/5670/2023/en/

19. 'Russia: Police Raid Prominent Rights Group', Human Rights Watch, 4 December 2008, https://www.hrw.org/news/2008/12/04/russia-police-raid-prominent-rights-group

20. Katherin Machalek, 'Factsheet: Russia's NGO Laws', in 'Contending with Putin's Russia: A Call for American Leadership', Freedom House, 6 February 2013, p. 11, https://freedomhouse.org/sites/default/files/2020-02/SR_Contending_with_Putins_Russia_PDF.pdf

21. Ibid., p. 12.

22. Andrew Roth, 'Russian Court Orders Closure of Country's Oldest Human Rights Group', *Guardian*, 28 December 2021.

23. Mary Elise Sarotte, *The Collapse*, Basic Books, 2014, p. 9.

24. Matt Ford, 'A Dictator's Guide to Urban Design', *Atlantic*, 21 February 2014.

25. Siddharth Varadarajan, 'Dictatorship by Cartography', *Himal Southasian*, February 2007.

26. Matt Ford, 'A Dictator's Guide to Urban Design', *Atlantic*, 21 February 2014.

27. Yana Gorokhovaskaia and Isabel Linzer, 'Defending Democracy in Exile', Freedom House, June 2022, p. 4, https://freedomhouse.org/sites/default/files/2022-05/Complete_TransnationalRepressionReport2022_NEW_0.pdf

28. Ibid.
29. The depiction of Jia's experience is based on Jia Zu, 'I Will Never Forget the Tiannanmen Massacre', *Washington Post*, 4 June 1999.
30. Ibid.
31. Peter Ellingsen, 'Remembering Tiananmen', *Sydney Morning Herald*, 3 June 2014.
32. 'Tiananmen 30 Years On: China's Indelible Stain', Amnesty International, 1 June 2019, https://www.amnesty.org/en/latest/news/2019/06/china-tiananmen-crackdown-30-years-on/
33. Nicholas D. Kristof, 'Crackdown in Beijing; Troops Attack and Crush Beijing Protest; Thousands Fight Back, Scores Are Killed', *New York Times*, 4 June 1989.
34. Louisa Lim, *People's Republic of Amnesia*, Oxford University Press, 2014, p. 7.
35. Sheryl Wudunn, 'In Beijing, Rage and Despair Over the Soldiers' Brutality', *New York Times*, 5 June 1989.
36. Lily Kuo, 'China's Other Tiananmens: 30 Years On', *Guardian*, 2 June 2019, https://www.theguardian.com/world/2019/jun/02/chinas-other-tiananmens-30th-anniversary-1989-protests
37. Lim, *People's Republic of Amnesia*, p. 189.
38. Deng Xiaoping, 'Deng's June 9 Speech: "We Faced a Rebellious Clique" and "Dregs of Society"', *New York Times*, 30 June 1989.
39. Siegbert Schefke, *Als die Angst die Seiten wechselte*, Transit, 2019, pp. 61 and 62.
40. Ibid., p. 97.
41. Sarotte, *The Collapse*, p. 53.
42. Hartmut Zwahr, *Ende einer Selbstzerstörung*, Sax, 2014, p. 90.
43. Bernd-Lutz Lange and Sascha Lange, *David gegen Goliath*, Aufbau, 2019, pp. 82–4.
44. Zwahr, *Das Ende einer Selbstzerstörung*, p. 89.
45. See, for example, ibid., p. 90.
46. Ibid.
47. Sarotte, *The Collapse*, p. 71.
48. Ibid., p. 72.

49. Ibid., pp. 73–4.
50. Steven Levitsky and Lucan A. Way, 'Linkage Versus Leverage: Rethinking the International Dimension of Regime Change', *Comparative Politics* 38, no. 4 (2006), 379–400.
51. This manoeuvre is inspired by the real response of monarchies during the Arab Spring, as outlined in Yasmina Abouzzohour, 'Heavy Lies the Crown: The Survival of Arab Monarchies, 10 Years after the Arab Spring', Brookings, 8 March 2021, https://www.brookings.edu/articles/heavy-lies-the-crown-the-survival-of-arab-monarchies-10-years-after-the-arab-spring/

Chapter 7: No Other Option

1. Efraim Karsh, 'Conflict of Necessity', *Los Angeles Times*, 30 March 2003.
2. 'Assassination', *Encyclopaedia Britannica*, 5 December 2023, https://www.britannica.com/topic/assassination
3. Barbara Schmitz, 'War, Violence and Tyrannicide in the Book of Judith', pp. 103–19 in Jan Liesen and Pancratius Beentjes (ed), *Visions of Peace and Tales of War*, De Gruyter, 2010, p. 112.
4. Moses I. Finley, *The Ancient Greeks*, Penguin, 1977, p. 58 cited in Shannon K. Brincat, ' "Death to Tyrants": The Political Philosophy of Tyrannicide – Part 1', *Journal of International Political Theory* 4, no. 2 (2008), 212–40 at p. 215.
5. Aristotle (trans. Terence Irwin), *Nicomachean Ethics*, Hackett Press, 2000, p. 36 cited in ibid., p. 217.
6. Ibid., pp. 216 and 218.
7. Augustine (trans. R.S. Pine-Coffin), *Confessions*, Penguin, 1961, p. 207 cited in ibid., p. 220.
8. 'John of Salisbury', *Stanford Encyclopaedia of Philosophy*, 27 April 2022, https://plato.stanford.edu/entries/john-salisbury/
9. Cary Nederman, 'Three Concepts of Tyranny in Western Medieval Political Thought', *Contributions to the History of Concepts* 14, no. 2 (2019), p. 9.

10. John of Salisbury (ed. Cary J. Nederman), *Policraticus: Of the Frivolities of Courtiers and the Footprints of Philosophers*, Cambridge University Press, 1990, p. 210.

11. Nederman, 'Three Concepts of Tyranny in Western Medieval Political Thought', p. 9.

12. See Cary J. Nederman, 'A Duty to Kill: John of Salisbury's Theory of Tyrannicide', *Review of Politics* 50, no. 3 (1988), 365–89.

13. Robert S. Miola, 'Julius Caesar and the Tyrannicide Debate', *Renaissance Quarterly* 38, no. 2 (1985), 271–89 at p. 274.

14. Benjamin F. Jones and Benjamin A. Olken, 'Hit or Miss? The Effect of Assassinations on Institutions and War', *American Economic Journal: Macroeconomics* 1, no. 2 (2009), 55–87 at p. 56.

15. John Chin et al., 'Reshaping the Threat Environment: Personalism, Coups, and Assassinations', *Comparative Political Studies* 55, no. 4 (2022), 657–87.

16. The depiction of the assassination is in large part based on Frances Robles, '"They Thought I Was Dead": Haitian President's Widow Recounts Assassination', *New York Times*, 30 July 2021.

17. Ibid.

18. John Pacenti and Chris Cameron, 'US Prosecutors Detail Plot to Kill Haitian President', *New York Times*, 1 February 2023.

19. Ibid.

20. 'Haiti President's Assassination: What We Know So Far', BBC, 1 February 2023, https://www.bbc.com/news/world-latin-america-57762246

21. Jones and Olken, 'Hit or Miss?', p. 62.

22. Chin et al., 'Reshaping the Threat Environment'.

23. Ibid.

24. Elian Peltier and Raja Abdulrahim, 'Can Russia Tame Wagner in Africa Without Destroying It?', *New York Times*, 29 June 2023.

25. Ibid.

26. See Jason K. Stearns, *Dancing in the Glory of Monsters*, Public Affairs, 2012, p. 279.

27. Stuart Jeffries, 'Revealed: How Africa's Dictator Died at the Hands of his Boy Soldiers', *Guardian*, 11 February 2001.

28. Chin et al., 'Reshaping the Threat Environment'.

29. John Hoyt Williams, 'Paraguayan Isolation under Dr. Francia: A Re-Evaluation', *Hispanic American Historical Review* 52, no. 1 (1972), 102–22 at p. 102.

30. Dalia Ventura, 'Aimé Bonpland, el brillante botánico opacado por Alexander von Humboldt que se enamoró de Latinoamérica', BBC, 8 January 2022, https://www.bbc.com/mundo/noticias-59593096

31. Stephen Bell, *A Life in Shadow*, Stanford University Press, 2010, p. 62.

32. Ventura, 'Aimé Bonpland'.

33. Johann Rudolf Rengger, *Historischer Versuch über die Revolution von Paraguay und die Dictatorial-Regierung von Dr. Francia*, J. G. Cotta, 1827, p. 162.

34. Pjotr Sauer, 'Russian Soldiers Say Commanders Used "Barrier Troops" to Stop Them from Retreating', *Guardian*, 27 March 2023.

35. Ivan Nechepurenko, 'Putin Holds Highly Choreographed Meeting with Mothers of Russian Servicemen', *New York Times*, 25 November 2022.

36. Ibid.

37. Andrew Roth and Pjotr Sauer, 'Putin Talks to Mothers of Soldiers Fighting in Ukraine in Staged Meeting', *Guardian*, 25 November 2022.

38. Ibid.

39. Zaryab Iqbal and Christopher Zorn, 'Sic Semper Tyrannis? Power, Repression and Assassination Since the Second World War', *Journal of Politics* 68:3 (2006), pp. 489–501 at p. 492.

40. Dan Williams, 'After Duvalier: Haiti – A Scary Time for Voodoo', *Los Angeles Times*, 7 March 1986.

41. 'The Death. and Legacy of Papa Doc Duvalier', *Time*, 17 January 2011.
42. Albin Krebs, 'Papa Doc, a Ruthless Dictator, Kept the Haitians in Illiteracy and Dire Poverty', *New York Times*, 23 April 1971.
43. Williams, 'After Duvalier'.
44. Homer Bigart, 'Duvalier, 64, Dies in Haiti; Son, 19, Is New President', *New York Times*, 23 April 1971.
45. Rick Atkinson, 'US to Rely on Air Strikes if War Erupts', *Washington Post*, 16 September 1990.
46. 'Executive Order 12333 – United States intelligence activities', part 2, section 11, US National Archives and Records Administration, 1981, https://www.archives.gov/federal-register/codification/executive-order/12333.html
47. Frank Church et al., 'Alleged Assassination Plots Involving Foreign Leaders – An Interim Report', United States Senate, Report No. 94-465, 20 November 1975, p. 255, https://www.intelligence.senate.gov/sites/default/files/94465.pdf
48. Ibid., p. 1.
49. Most of the details on the Blue House Raid are taken from Mark McDonald, 'Failed North Korean Assassin Assimilates in the South', *New York Times*, 17 December 2010.
50. Norimutsu Onishi, 'South Korean Movie Unlocks Door on a Once-Secret Past', *New York Times*, 15 February 2004.
51. Ivan Watson and Jake Kwon, 'How a Plot to Kill Kim Il Sung Ended in Mutiny and Murder', CNN, 19 February 2018, https://edition.cnn.com/2018/02/18/asia/south-korea-failed-assassination-squad-unit-684-intl/index.html
52. Onishi, 'South Korean Movie Unlocks Door'.
53. Watson and Kwon, 'How a Plot to Kill Kim Il Sung Ended in Mutiny and Murder'.
54. Ibid.
55. '34 Die as Korean Prisoners "Invade" Seoul', *New York Times*, 24 August 1971.
56. Andrei Lankov, 'How a Secret Plot to Assassinate North Korea's Leader Spiraled Out of Control', NK News, 7 August 2023,

https://www.nknews.org/2023/08/how-a-secret-plot-to-assassinate-north-koreas-leader-spiraled-out-of-control/

57. Ibid.
58. Onishi, 'South Korean Movie Unlocks Door'.
59. Ibid.
60. Ibid.
61. Lankov, 'How a Secret Plot to Assassinate North Korea's Leader Spiraled Out of Control'.
62. Choe Sang-Hun, 'South Korea Plans "Decapitation Unit" to Try to Scare North's Leaders', *New York Times*, 12 September 2017.
63. Ankit Panda, 'South Korea's "Decapitation" Strategy Against North Korea Has More Risks Than Benefits', Carnegie Endowment for International Peace, 15 August 2022, https://carnegieendowment.org/2022/08/15/south-korea-s-decapitation-strategy-against-north-korea-has-more-risks-than-benefits-pub-87672
64. Ibid.
65. Ibid.
66. Megan DuBois, 'North Korea's Nuclear Fail-Safe', *Foreign Policy*, 16 September 2022.
67. Shane Smith and Paul Bernstein, 'North Korean Nuclear Command and Control: Alternatives and Implications', Defense Threat Reduction Agency, August 2022, https://wmdcenter.ndu.edu/Portals/97/Documents/Publications/NK-Nuclear-Command-and-Control_Report.pdf
68. DuBois, 'North Korea's Nuclear Fail-Safe'.
69. Ibid.
70. This portrayal of the Venezuelan assassination attempt is based on Christoph Koettl and Barbara Marcolini, 'A Closer Look at the Drone Attack on Maduro in Venezuela', *New York Times*, 10 August 2018.
71. See Chin et al., 'Reshaping the Threat Environment'.

Chapter 8: Be Careful What You Wish For

1. Ryan Chilcote and Aliaksandr Kudrytski, 'Belarus Strongman Balances Between Ukraine War, Putin, EU', Bloomberg, 2 April 2015.
2. Andrea Kendall-Taylor and Erica Frantz, 'How Autocracies Fall', *Washington Quarterly* 37, no. 1 (2014), 35–47 at p. 36.
3. Cited in Sarah J. Hummel, 'Leader Age, Death, and Political Reform in Dictatorships', University of Illinois at Urbana-Champaign, working paper, 12 December 2017, https://publish.illinois.edu/shummel/files/2017/12/LeaderDeath171106.pdf
4. Seva Gunitsky, interview with author, 12 January 2023.
5. Rob Matheson, 'Sudanese Celebrate End of Omar al-Bashir's 30-year Rule', Al Jazeera, 11 April 2019, https://www.aljazeera.com/videos/2019/4/11/sudanese-celebrate-end-of-omar-al-bashirs-30-year-rule
6. The depiction of this story is largely based on the BBC video made by witnesses filming with their telephones, 'Sudan's Livestream Massacre', BBC, 12 July 2019, https://www.bbc.com/news/av/world-africa-48956133
7. 'They Were Shouting "Kill Them"', Human Rights Watch, 17 November 2019, https://www.hrw.org/report/2019/11/18/they-were-shouting-kill-them/sudans-violent-crackdown-protesters-khartoum
8. Ibid.
9. 'Sudan's Livestream Massacre'.
10. Ibid.
11. Michelle Gavin, 'Sudan's Coup: One Year Later', Council on Foreign Relations, 24 October 2022, https://www.cfr.org/blog/sudans-coup-one-year-later
12. Aidan Lewis, 'What is Happening in Sudan? Fighting in Khartoum Explained', Reuters, 13 July 2023, https://www.reuters.com/world/africa/whats-behind-sudans-crisis-2023-04-17/

13. Declan Walsh and Abdi Latif Dahir, 'War in Sudan: Who is Battling for Power, and Why It Hasn't Stopped', *New York Times*, 26 October 2023.

14. Bruce Bueno de Mesquita and Alastair Smith, *The Dictator's Handbook,* Public Affairs, 2012.

15. See Barbara Geddes, Joseph Wright and Erica Frantz, *How Dictatorships Work*, Cambridge University Press, 2018, p. 230.

16. Andrej Kokkonen and Anders Sundell, 'Leader Succession and Civil War', *Comparative Political Studies* 53, nos 3–4 (2019), 434–68 at p. 434.

17. Andrej Kokkonen and Anders Sundell, 'Delivering Stability: Primogeniture and Autocratic Survival in European Monarchies 1000–1800', Quality of Government Institute, Working Paper Series (3 April 2012), p. 4.

18. 'Primogeniture and Ultimogeniture', *Encyclopaedia Britannica*, 27 October 2023, https://www.britannica.com/topic/primogeniture

19. Kokkonen and Sundell, 'Delivering Stability', p. 6.

20. Xin Nong, 'Informal Succession Institutions and Autocratic Survival: Evidence from Ancient China', working paper, 3 March 2022, https://xin-nong.com/files/Informal_Succession_Xin_EHA.pdf

21. Kokkonen and Sundell, 'Delivering Stability', p. 4.

22. Anne Meng, 'Winning the Game of Thrones: Leadership Succession in Modern Autocracies', *Journal of Conflict Resolution* 65, no. 5 (2021), 950–81.

23. Erica Frantz and Elizabeth A. Stein, 'Countering Coups: Leadership Succession Rules in Dictatorships', *Comparative Political Studies* 50, no. 7 (2017), 935–62.

24. Chris Hodges, 'Damascus Journal: Fist May Be of Iron, but is Assad's Hand Weak?', *New York Times*, 17 December 1991.

25. Jason Brownlee, 'Hereditary Succession in Modern Autocracies', *World Politics* 59, no. 4 (2007), 595–628 at p. 618.

26. Eyal Zisser, 'Does Bashar al-Assad Rule Syria?', *Middle East Quarterly* 10, no. 1 (2003), 15–23 at p. 17.

27. Amos Chapple, 'What's Changed? Armenia One Year After Revolution', *Radio Free Europe/Radio Liberty*, 23 April 2019.

28. Ibid.

29. Erica Chenoweth and Maria J. Stephan, *Why Civil Resistance Works*, Columbia University Press, pp. 213–15.

30. See Markus Bayer, Felix S. Bethke and Daniel Lambach, 'The Democratic Dividend of Nonviolent Resistance', *Journal of Peace Research* 53, no. 6 (2016), 758–71.

31. Erica Frantz, *Authoritarianism*, Oxford University Press, p. 126.

32. George Derpanopoulos et al., 'Are Coups Good for Democracy?', *Research and Politics* 3, no. 1 (2016), 1–7 at p. 2.

33. John J. Chin, David B. Carter and Joseph G. Wright, 'The Varieties of Coups d'Etat: Introducing the Colpus Dataset', *International Studies Quarterly* 65, no. 4 (2021), 1040–51.

34. Paul Collier and Anke Hoeffler, 'Coup Traps: Why Does Africa have so many Coups d'Etat?', working paper, Centre for the Study of African Economies, August 2005, https://ora. ox.ac.uk/objects/uuid:49097086-8505-4eb2-8174 -314ce1aa3ebb

35. Ibid.

36. See, for example, Clayton L. Thyne and Jonathan M. Powell, '*Coup d'Etat* or Coup d'Autocracy? How Coups Impact Democratization, 1950–2008', *Foreign Policy Analysis* 12, no. 2 (2016), pp. 192–213.

37. Cited in Benjamin F. Jones and Benjamin A. Olken, 'Do Assassins Really Change History?', *New York Times*, 10 April 2015.

38. Benjamin F. Jones and Benjamin A. Olken, 'Hit or Miss? The Effect of Assassinations on Institutions and War', *American Economic Journal: Macroeconomics* 1, no. 2 (2009), pp. 55–87 at p. 70.

39. Giuditta Fontana, Markus B. Siewert and Christalla Yakinthou, 'Managing War-to-Peace Transitions after Intra-State Conflicts: Configurations of Successful Peace Processes', *Journal of Intervention and Statebuilding* 15, no. 1 (2023), 25–47 at p. 25.

40. For a discussion of the risks of losing wars, see Andrea Kendall-Taylor and Erica Frantz, 'Putin's Forever War', *Foreign Affairs*, 23 March 2023, and Sarah E. Croco, 'The Decider's Dilemma: Leader Culpability, War Outcomes, and Domestic Punishment', *American Political Science Review* 105, no. 3 (2011), 457–77.

41. See Barbara F. Walter, 'Conflict Relapse and the Sustainability of Post-Conflict Peace', World Bank, World Development Report 2011 Background Paper, 13 September 2010, https://openknowledge.worldbank.org/server/api/core/bitstreams/3633592d-58d0-5ed5-9394-aea81448f25c/content

42. The depiction of the attack is mostly based on 'Burundi: The Gatumba Massacre', Human Rights Watch, September 2004, https://www.hrw.org/sites/default/files/reports/burundi0904.pdf

43. Ibid.

44. Ibid.

45. Zoeann Murphy, '"He was Alive. They Burned Him": Congolese Refugees Call for Long-overdue Justice', *Washington Post*, 19 September 2014.

46. 'UN Demands Justice After Massacre of 150 Refugees in Burundi', *New York Times*, 16 August 2004.

47. Agathon Rwasa, interview with author, 14 March 2023.

48. 'Burundi: 15 Years On, No Justice for Gatumba Massacre', Human Rights Watch, 13 August 2019, https://www.hrw.org/news/2019/08/13/burundi-15-years-no-justice-gatumba-massacre

49. Georges Ibrahim Tounkara, 'Burundi: Ex-rebel Agathon Rwasa to Run for President', Deutsche Welle, 17 February 2020, https://www.dw.com/en/burundi-ex-rebel-agathon-rwasa-to-run-for-president/a-52404700

50. Marielle Debos, *Living by the Gun in Chad*, Zed Books, 2016, p. 103.

51. '2003-2011: The Iraq War', Council on Foreign Relations, https://www.cfr.org/timeline/iraq-war

52. 'L. Paul Bremer III', *Encyclopaedia Britannica*, 26 September 2023, https://www.britannica.com/biography/L-Paul-Bremer-III

53. L. Paul Bremer, 'Coalition Provisional Authority Order Number 1', Coalition Provisional Authority, 16 May 2003.

54. L. Paul Bremer, 'Coalition Provisional Authority Order Number 2', Coalition Provisional Authority, 23 May 2003.

55. James P. Pfiffner, 'US Blunders in Iraq: De-Baathification and Disbanding the Army', *Intelligence and National Security* 25, no. 1 (2010), 76–85 at p. 79.

56. Cited in ibid., p. 79.

57. Pfiffner, 'US Blunders in Iraq', at p. 76.

58. Bruce R. Pirnie and Edward O'Connell, *Counterinsurgency in Iraq (2003–2006)*, RAND Corporation, 2008.

59. 'The Gamble: Key Documents', *Washington Post*, 7 February 2009.

60. Tom Bowman, 'As the Iraq War Ends, Reassessing the US Surge', National Public Radio, 16 December 2011, https://www.npr.org/2011/12/16/143832121/as-the-iraq-war-ends-reassessing-the-u-s-surge

61. Alexander B. Downes and Jonathan Monten, 'Forced to be Free? Why Foreign-Imposed Regime Change Rarely Leads to Democratization', *International Security* 37, no. 4 (2013), 90–131 at p. 129.

62. For a discussion of intervening states' motivations, see Jeffrey Pickering and Mark Peceny, 'Forging Democracy at Gunpoint', *International Studies Quarterly* 50, no. 3 (2006), 539–59.

63. Cited in Arthur M. Schlesinger, *A Thousand Days: John F. Kennedy in the White House*, Houghton Mifflin, 1965, p. 769.

64. See Bruce Bueno de Mesquita and George W. Downs, 'Intervention and Democracy', *International Organization* 60, no. 3 (2006), 627–49 at p. 632.

65. Downes and Monten, 'Forced to Be Free?', p. 94.

66. Ibid.

67. Andrea Kendall-Taylor and Erica Frantz, 'When Dictators Die', *Foreign Policy*, 10 September 2015.

68. Sarah J. Hummel, 'Leader Age, Death and Political Reform in Dictatorships', working paper, University of Illinois at Urbana -Champaign, 12 December 2017, https://publish.illinois.edu/shummel/files/2017/12/LeaderDeath171106.pdf

69. For a discussion of the way tyrants can concentrate power in their hands, see Milan W. Svolik, *The Politics of Authoritarian Rule*, Cambridge University Press, 2012.

70. Jun Koga Sudduth and Curtis Bell, 'The Rise Predicts the Fall: How the Method of Leader Entry Affects the Method of Leader Removal in Dictatorships', *International Studies Quarterly* 62, no. 1 (2018), 145–59.

Chapter 9: How to Topple a Tyrant

1. Cited in David Hoffman, 'Putin Faces a State of Disorder', *Washington Post*, 3 January 2000.

2. 'Guaido Versus Maduro: Who Backs Venezuela's Two Presidents?', Reuters, 24 January 2019.

3. Alan Riding, 'US Leads Efforts to Oust Somoza and Lead Nicaragua to Democracy', *New York Times*, 16 November 1978.

4. Mateo Cayetano Jarquin, 'A Latin American Revolution: The Sandinistas, the Cold War, and Political Change in the Region, 1977–1990', doctoral dissertation, 2019, Harvard University, Graduate School of Arts & Sciences, p. 74.

5. Jason Brownlee, 'Hereditary Succession in Modern Autocracies', *World Politics* 59, no. 4 (2007), 595–628 at p. 613.

6. The depiction of the NSO Group in Mexico is largely based on Natalie Kitroeff and Ronen Bergman, 'How Mexico Became the Biggest User of the World's Most Notorious Spy Tool', *New York Times*, 18 April 2023.

7. Ronen Bergman and Mark Mazzetti, 'The Battle for the World's Most Powerful Cyberweapon', *New York Times Magazine*, 28 January 2022.

8. Ibid.

9. 'The Persecution of Ahmed Mansoor', Human Rights Watch, 27 January 2021, https://www.hrw.org/report/2021/01/27/persecution-ahmed-mansoor/how-united-arab-emirates-silenced-its-most-famous-human

10. Bergman and Mazzetti, 'The Battle for the World's Most Powerful Cyberweapon'.

11. Marcel Dirsus and David Landry, 'Interview [with Agathe Demarais]: Sanctions', *Hundred*, 21 November 2022, https://thehundred.substack.com/p/interview-sanctions

12. Ibid.

13. Ibid.

14. Agathe Demarais, interview with author, 13 April 2023.

15. Abel Escribà-Folch and Joseph Wright, 'Dealing with Tyranny: International Sanctions and the Survival of Authoritarian Rulers', *International Studies Quarterly* 54, no. 2 (2010), 335–59 at p. 335.

16. Ibid., p. 341.

17. Ibid., p. 355.

18. Janis Kluge cited in Jeanne Wahlen and Catherine Belton, 'Sanctions Haven't Stopped Russia, But a New Oil Ban Could Cut Deeper', *Washington Post*, 15 February 2023.

19. The depiction of Bobi Wine's arrest is mostly based on Abdi Latif Dahir, 'Uganda's Top Opposition Leader Says He is Under House Arrest', *New York Times*, 5 October 2023.

20. Ibid.

21. For more information on the Gambian opposition, see Jeffrey Smith, 'Gambia's Opposition Unites', *Foreign Affairs*, 25 November 2016.

22. See Yana Gorokhovaskaia and Isabel Linzer, 'Defending Democracy in Exile', Freedom House, June 2022, p. 4, https://freedomhouse.org/sites/default/files/2022-05/Complete_TransnationalRepressionReport2022_NEW_0.pdf

23. Rory Cormac, 'So you could argue that . . .', Twitter (renamed 'X'), 7 March 2023, https://x.com/RoryCormac/status/1633147729114193923?s=20

24. See Milan W. Svolik, *The Politics of Authoritarian Rule*, Cambridge University Press, 2012.

25. 'Shareholder Structure', Volkswagen Group, 31 December 2022, https://www.volkswagen-group.com/en/shareholder-structure-15951

26. Roshan Goswami, 'Lucid, Activision, EA, Uber: Here's Where Saudi Arabia's Sovereign Wealth Fund Has Invested', CNBC, 11 July 2023, https://www.cnbc.com/2023/07/11/activision-ea-uber-heres-where-saudi-arabias-pif-has-invested.html

27. The portrayal of ZunZuneo here is mostly based on an Associated Press article, 'US Secretly Created "Cuban Twitter" to Stir Unrest and Undermine Government', *Guardian*, 3 April 2014.

28. Ibid.

29. Ibid.

30. Associated Press, 'US Aid Chief Faces Questions Over "Cuban Twitter"', *Guardian*, 8 April 2014.

31. 'Sputnik and the Space Race', National Archives, Dwight D. Eisenhower Library, https://www.eisenhowerlibrary.gov/research/online-documents/sputnik-and-space-race

32. Amy Ryan and Gary Keeley, 'Intelligence Success or Failure?', *Studies in Intelligence* 61, no. 3 (2017), extracts.

33. See, for example, Christopher Ingraham, 'Satellite Data Strongly Suggests that China, Russia and Other Authoritarian Countries Are Fudging Their GDP Reports', *Washington Post*, 15 May 2018.

34. Andrew Natsios, 'Don't Play Politics with Hunger', *Washington Post*, 9 February 1997, cited in Emma Campbell, 'Famine in North Korea: humanitarian policy in the late 1990s', Overseas Development Institute, *HPG Working Paper*, December 2015, p. 6, https://cdn.odi.org/media/documents/10213.pdf

35. Campbell, 'Famine in North Korea', p. 6.

36. Ibid., p. 8.

37. Ibid., p. 5.

38. Susan Ratcliffe (ed.), *Oxford Essential Quotations*, Oxford University Press, 2016, https://www.oxfordreference.com/display/10.1093/acref/9780191826719.001.0001/q-oro-ed4-00018657

39. Cited in David Rothkopf, 'Why It's Too Early to Tell How History Will Judge the Iran and Greece Deals', *Foreign Policy*, 14 July 2015.

40. Ratcliffe, *Oxford Essential Quotations*.

Index